PETER LINDENBAUM is a professor of English at Indiana University.

CHANGING LANDSCAPES

Changing Landscapes

ANTI-PASTORAL SENTIMENT IN THE

ENGLISH RENAISSANCE

PETER LINDENBAUM

THE UNIVERSITY OF GEORGIA PRESS

ATHENS AND LONDON

© 1986 by the University of Georgia Press
Athens, Georgia 30602
All rights reserved
Set in 10 on 12 Linotron 202 Merganthaler Bembo
The paper in this book meets the guidelines for permanence and durability of the
Committee on Production Guidelines for Book Longevity of the Council on Library
Resources.

Printed in the United States of America
90 89 88 87 86   5 4 3 2 1

Library of Congress Cataloging in Publication Data

Lindenbaum, Peter.
Changing landscapes.
Includes index.
1. English literature—Early modern, 1500–1700—
History and criticism. 2. Paradise in literature.
3. Shepherds in literature. I. Title.
PR419.P33L5 1986   820'.9'321734   85-24546
ISBN 0-8203-0835-8

To the Memory of My Parents

CONTENTS

Preface   ix

Chapter I · Pastoral and Anti-Pastoral   1

Chapter II · Sidney's Old Arcadia   22
   "Very Born Arcadians" and Foreign Shepherds   24
   Defining Arcadia   34

Chapter III · Sidney's New Arcadia   53
   The Process of Revision   53
   Heroic Action   57
   Arcadian Sojourn   69
   Doing and Suffering   82

Chapter IV · Shakespeare's "Golden Worlds"   91
   The Forest of Arden   96
   Eden and Bohemia   111
   Returning Home   127

Chapter V · Milton's Paradise   136
   Counseling Ignoble Ease   143
   Edenic Work in a Wilderness of Sweets   151
   "The Crown of All Our Bliss"   158
   Justifying God's and Milton's Ways   177

Chapter VI · English Anti-Pastoralism: Sources and
    Analogues   180

        Notes   191

        Index   229

PREFACE

ONE OF THE MANY critics to whom the present study is indebted has remarked that the most valuable and alert writings on pastoral in the past few decades have been footnotes to Empson. I do not wish to assert the value of my own work, but a footnote to Empson's *Some Versions of Pastoral* this study certainly is. Its title might well have been "Some Versions of Anti-Pastoral." I have refrained from using that title, though, partly from a hesitancy to encroach on someone else's critical land, but mainly because I am using the terms "pastoral" and "anti-pastoral" in the chapters that follow in a rather un-Empsonian way and wish to avoid confusion. Pastoral, as Empson and most others today use the term, is a comparative mode: two types of life, the simple and the complex, are juxtaposed as a means of commenting upon human life as a whole through concentration on a comprehensible, simplified version of it. Pastoral writing need not, often does not, take any stand on the simplified life it pictures; it does not necessarily exhort us to leave our centrally heated homes to take up residence in thatched cottages. But in order to get its analysis started, it does posit as a preliminary working hypothesis what I am calling the "pastoral ideal": the idealized picture of man at ease in a country setting. Poets and readers of the pastoral convention understand that this ideal is put forward largely for purposes of further discussion. We might well expect, then, considerable criticism and questioning of that pastoral ideal in all pastoral writing. What I think distinguishes the English Renaissance writers I am calling "anti-pastoral" is the speed, strength, and persistence with which they announce their opposition to the kind of life it is necessary to picture if one is to write pastoral at all. Pastoral is for these writers not so much a mode of comparison, exploration, and subtle discrimination between rival claims as an occasion for asserting attitudes that are quite incompatible with pursuit of a simple, easy life anywhere, whether in the city or in the country.

As I endeavor to show in my first chapter, in their unwillingness to suspend judgment of the pastoral ideal even briefly, English anti-pastoralists were in part guilty of what Harold Bloom has called "poetic misprision," the misrepresentation by poets of one generation of their poetic predecessors and progenitors. The pastoral mode does *not* necessarily express nostalgic escapism, but the English Renaissance anti-pastoralists tended to picture it as though it did. I say "in part" guilty of poetic misprision, though, because (and this too is the burden of my first chapter) there were good grounds for this misprision in the changes the pastoral mode had undergone since classical times. Bloom's name, unlike Empson's, does not appear subsequently in these pages, both because the present study was begun long before I became aware of Bloom's version of literary history (no anxiety of influence here) and because I wish to distance myself from Bloom's reliance upon the Freudian paradigm of the family romance as an explanation for the appearance of this particular misprision. The writers I study were not Bloom's "strong poets" simply establishing their own poetic egos and identities at the expense of their pastoral fathers. Their art was more conscious than the Freudian paradigm suggests, and their primary concerns in writing were not so much personal and artistic as social and even religious. Pastoral writing and their arguments with its conventions and implied ideals presented them with an opportunity to put forward their own ethical, social, and political ideas. It is those ideas, finally, which I think make their works particularly distinctive within the pastoral tradition, and in my concluding pages I attempt to place those ideas in the context of the English Renaissance as a whole.

ONE OF THE FEW advantages of taking a very long time to write and rewrite a book is that one discovers a remarkably large number of fine and generous people out there who are willing to take time off from their own work to read someone else's and provide encouragement and advice. The following have read the whole or parts of the manuscript for me in its varied forms and I am very grateful to all of them: Jonas Barish (a figure of extraordinary patience and good will, who survived the manuscript twice, once in its earliest state and then again in its latest), Stephen Orgel, Donald Friedman, Norman Grabo, Laurence Jacobs, Stanley Fish, Thomas Kranidas, David Bevington, and numerous colleagues at Indiana University—Rudolf Gottfried, Georges Edelen, Kenneth R. R. Gros Louis, Merritt Lawlis, Charles Forker, Lewis H. Miller, Jr., Boyd Berry, and James Halporn. Several of these people may well have forgotten that they read parts of the manuscript, so long has been its gestation, but I have not. They are, of course, not responsible for whatever blemishes or even outright faults might remain in the book—although they may be guilty of not having shouted loudly enough at its author. My wife, Sheila, in a desperate attempt to keep me writing and moving forward, did her best not to listen to oral versions or to read unfinished chapters; she did not always succeed.

I wish to thank also that wonderful institution the National Endowment for the Humanities, which, further back than I care to remember, awarded me a Younger Humanist Fellowship after I brashly promised that I could polish off the project in a single year. Thanks too to Indiana University's Office of Research and Graduate Development for a Summer Faculty Fellowship and for honoring persistent requests for typing and xeroxing.

Portions of the chapters that follow have appeared earlier in slightly or considerably different form. Several paragraphs from the two chapters on Sidney appeared originally in "Sidney's *Arcadia:* The Endings of the Three Versions," *Huntington Library Quarterly,* 34 (1971), and "The Geography of Sidney's *Arcadia,*" *Philological Quarterly,* 63 (1984); and several pages of the opening to Chapter IV are taken from "Education in *The Two Gentlemen of Verona,*" *Studies in English Literature,* 15 (1975). The discussion of *The Winter's Tale* appeared originally as "Time, Sexual Love, and the Uses of Pastoral in *The Winter's Tale,*" *Modern Language Quarterly,* 33 (1972), and that of *The Tempest* as "Prospero's Anger," *Massachusetts Review,* 25 (1984). And finally, some of the introductory paragraphs and virtually all of the last two sections of the chapter on *Paradise Lost* are an amended version of "Lovemaking in Milton's Paradise," *Milton Studies,* 6 (1974). I am grateful to the editors of all these journals for permission to reprint these materials here.

CHANGING LANDSCAPES

CHAPTER I

Pastoral and Anti-Pastoral

AS OFTEN AS NOT in Renaissance England, when authors set out to write pastoral poetry or a pastoral episode in the midst of a longer work in a different genre, they treated the pastoral setting and the life pursued there with considerable hesitation, distrust, and occasionally even outright dislike. They thereby expressed what I shall be calling "anti-pastoral" sentiment. This sentiment is not merely another Renaissance expression of the need to distinguish appearance from reality: Arcadia, the specifically pastoral setting, is not usually presented in the manner of Armida's garden in the *Gerusalemme liberata* or Acrasia's Bower of Bliss in Book II of *The Faerie Queene,* as a false paradise in which a beholder is likely to be deceived into thinking that an inherently evil place is good. Suspicion or dislike of Arcadia is most often couched in a formula in which a figure entering a pastoral landscape is brought to realize that, contrary to his expectations, life in the country is essentially no different from life elsewhere, at court or in the city. Arcadia is only what it claims to be, and its disturbing quality, in the view of the anti-pastoralist, lies in what it honestly offers to man—a life of leisure and freedom from the cares and responsibilities of the normal world. Anti-pastoral sentiment expresses the view that in this world of ours man simply has no time for relaxation or even momentary escape from the pressing activity of day-to-day living.

Virtually every major and minor author in the English Renaissance tried his hand at pastoral writing. In claiming that there is such a thing as extensive anti-pastoral sentiment, even an anti-pastoral tradition, amidst that great outpouring of pastoral literature, I should make clear at once that I am not inventing a new genre or using "pastoral" and "anti-pastoral" as generic terms. Rather, when I speak of "pastoral" and opposition to it, I shall be referring to the picture of life traditionally presented in pastoral writing and to the ideals implied by that picture. I shall discuss both versions of Sidney's *Arcadia,* several of Shakespeare's green-world comedies, and Milton's *Paradise Lost,* and I cannot even claim that such texts are unequivocally within the pastoral mode: both the *New* and the *Old Arcadia* have at least as good a claim to be considered epic, and *Paradise Lost* can plainly be considered pastoral only in part. It can be argued that "pure" pastoral, because it centers on a type of life that is essentially inactive, can be found only in forms, like the lyric, which resist dramatic action or plot. The works I examine, even the least dramatic of Shakespeare's plays, have a considerable amount of dramatic complication or activity. Yet all these works relate firmly to and are fully part of the literary pastoral tradition, since all start explicitly or implicitly from a disagreement with attitudes their authors associated—fairly or unfairly—with earlier pastoral writing.[1] Thomas G. Rosenmeyer has remarked that "a pastoral poem, qua pastoral, exercises a symbolic effect that is logically and aesthetically prior to the particularities of the individual work";[2] I would extend such an observation to include not simply a pastoral poem but any specifically pastoral scene or episode, even an Eden, in a longer work. When a reader starts a lyric which he recognizes as pastoral or comes upon an obviously pastoral scene or sequence in a longer work of a different genre, he identifies that poem or episode with an established poetic tradition; when he makes that association, he has fairly definite expectations about the type of life to be pictured and a set of values and ideals to be put forward, at least temporarily. An anti-pastoral writer typically pictures that life and posits those ideals and then immediately starts raising objections to them.[3]

What makes the Elizabethan argument with pastoralism particularly lively is that those carrying it out were not, in fact, completely fair to what they were opposing. A sojourn in Arcadia had come to stand for many different things by Sidney's time, several of them quite honorable and morally legitimate. A decision to take up a shepherd's garb could, for instance, signify a perfectly acceptable withdrawal into the self so as to follow Virgil's example and write lyric poetry. "The central meaning of pastoral" for many Elizabethans, Hallett Smith tells us, was the "rejection of the aspiring mind," that type of mind they could see bodied forth in Marlowe's Tamburlaine, in Mary Queen of Scots, or even in the rebellious angels.[4] To see what claims could be made for the assumption of a shepherd's role, we might cite Francis Bacon's gloss on the story of Cain and Abel; in that story,

> we see . . . an image of the two estates, the contemplative state and the active state, figured in the two persons of Abel and Cain, and in the two simplest and most primitive trades of life; that of the shepherd, (who, by reason of his leisure, rest in a place, and living in view of heaven, is a lively image of a contemplative life,) and that of the husbandman: where we see again the favour and election of God went to the shepherd, and not to the tiller of the ground.[5]

Sidney was aware of the association between the pastoral and contemplative lives, as we know when we see him have Pyrocles defend staying in Arcadia by claiming a desire to devote himself to contemplation. Yet the structure of the *Old Arcadia* shows that Sidney himself disallows such an appeal and chooses instead to view Arcadia primarily as a place of retreat and escape. If one wishes to oppose a given stand, the task becomes a good deal easier when one limits or misrepresents the opponent's position, and Sidney, fond as he is of specious argument, is certainly capable of such rhetorical subterfuge. So, too, Shakespeare. But much besides the associations with poetic purpose and the contemplative life had been attached to, or confused with, pastoral writing by Sidney's and Shakespeare's time, and much of that added significance could well lead an Elizabethan to view pastoral writing as escapist in its appeal. So varied were the associations, in fact, that it becomes difficult to determine whether Sidney's and Shakespeare's misrepresentation of pastoral's central appeal as escapist was deviously and wittily intentional or simply a partial misapprehension of an elusive body of poetry. The misrepresentation needs to be examined, and as preparation for Sidney's, Shakespeare's, and Milton's anti-pastoral arguments I want to cite several earlier texts to suggest both the sources of possible confusion over the implications of pastoral writing and the grounds for opposing such writing. My aim is to sketch briefly what the term "pastoral" and its customary setting of "Arcadia" were likely to have meant to Sidney and his first readers when they in their respective ways embarked upon a work entitled *Arcadia* in the late 1570s. I shall begin with Virgil's First Eclogue. It is this poem which, despite proper lip service paid to Theocritus, represented the beginning of the pastoral tradition for most Renaissance poets and readers.

VIRGIL'S FIRST ECLOGUE presents two characters, Tityrus and Meliboeus: the former is secure, at his ease, and, because of the help of a Roman *deus*, master of his own land; the latter, grieving, has just been dispossessed of his farm, which is evidently to be handed over to a retired soldier. By means of these two characters the poem provides a picture both of the ideal pastoral existence and of its tenuousness. That double vision is presented to us from the poem's opening lines, in which the newly evicted Meliboeus describes the details of Tityrus's pastoral life and contrasts Tityrus's present life with his own:

> Tityre, tu patulae recubans sub tegmine fagi
> siluestrem tenui Musam meditaris auena;
> nos patriae finis et dulcia linquimus arua.
> nos patriam fugimus; tu, Tityre, lentus in umbra
> formonsam resonare doces Amaryllida siluas.
>
> [1–5][6]

[Tityrus, as you lie there under the cover of the spreading beech tree, you practice woodland music on your thin oaten pipe; we are leaving our native borders and sweet farmlands: we go in exile from our homeland; you, Tityrus, at ease in the shade teach the woods to resound with "fair Amaryllis."]

Tityrus tells us in his own first line that his life is one of pastoral *otium* or peace (6); Meliboeus's description of that life gives Tityrus no serious responsibilities and little to do but play upon his shepherd's pipe. Though bare rocks and marshland encroach upon his pastures (47–48), Tityrus has enough to serve his need and does not worry. He has gained the affections of his Amaryllis and is a blessed man indeed: as Meliboeus tells us, when Tityrus was recently in Rome not only did Amaryllis sigh for him, but the very pines, springs, and orchards called after him as well: "ipsae te, Tityre, pinus, / ipsi te fontes, ipsa haec arbusta uocabant" (38–39). Meliboeus is given to poetic overstatement, perhaps, especially now that he is being excluded from the pastoral landscape, but his use of the pathetic fallacy reveals a characteristic of pastoral life frequently assumed in idealizing pastoral poetry, that of a harmony between the shepherd and the natural world around him.

Tityrus is, however, clearly only one happy man picked out among many not nearly as fortunate, although not necessarily any the less deserving. Since Meliboeus uses the plural form *nos* and speaks of the disturbance in all the other fields in the area (11–12), his eviction seems to have been a more common occurrence than Tityrus's good fortune; it is only because Tityrus happens to have found a Roman benefactor that he can continue to enjoy his ideal pastoral existence. Not only Meliboeus's fate but Tityrus's attainment of pastoral peace and leisure depends upon events occurring in Rome. This may reassert the fragility of the pastoral ideal, but it does not alter Tityrus's enjoyment of his state or our impression of his happiness. No threat is leveled against Tityrus himself, and his *otium* remains an island of joy and happiness, perfect and set apart.

Rosenmeyer has noted a quality of relaxed discontinuity in Theocritus's verse, and in the First Eclogue at least, Virgil seems to have taken some of that quality over into his own version of pastoral.[7] Meliboeus asks who Tityrus's Roman "god" is and never gets a direct answer to his question. That evasion is only one of several discontinuities in the poem; taken all together, they create a stylistic complement to the detached *otium* of Tityrus's pastoral existence. The poem is decidedly undramatic: its two characters always seem to be speaking *at* rather than *to* one another. Meliboeus starts the poem speaking to Tityrus and ends speaking to himself and his flock (and it is only then that Tityrus offers him the relief of a night's lodging). In the course of the poem, Meliboeus contrasts his own plight with Tityrus's happy state and Tityrus himself speaks of his good fortune and of his "god," but neither figure reacts in a forceful or personal manner to what the other says. After Tityrus has expressed his delight in his present pastoral leisure, Meliboeus responds that he is not envious but only surprised at Tityrus's good fortune:

> Non equidem inuideo, miror magis; undique totis
> usque adeo turbatur agris.
> [11–12]

[In truth, I do not begrudge you; I marvel the more so great is the confusion on every farm all around us.]

While Meliboeus throughout laments his plight, he never does commit himself to the engagement that outright envy of another's good fortune entails. And Tityrus, for his part, pays little attention to Meliboeus's complaints. He does offer Meliboeus a single night's rest in the poem's final lines, but this offer is hardly seen as lasting relief for Meliboeus's troubles. Yet Virgil does not criticize the coolness and detachment of Tityrus. There is no suggestion—and this is in contrast with much English Renaissance pastoral—that Tityrus is morally obligated to leave his pastoral bower and, let us say, work for the amelioration of the social conditions that brought about Meliboeus's misery. Had Meliboeus been envious rather than surprised at Tityrus's good fortune, had Meliboeus been less detached, or had Tityrus been moved by Meliboeus's complaints, we might have had more of a sense of dramatic development in the eclogue. Instead, the initial distance or distinction between the two speakers, insisted upon in Meliboeus's repeated and heavily stressed use of *nos* and *tu* in the opening lines, establishes a pattern for the poem as a whole; the First Eclogue stands primarily as a statement of contrast between Tityrus's pastoral happiness and Meliboeus's distress, and the lack of dramatic interaction between the two figures is an implicit reinforcement and extension of the uncomplicated and disengaged life that Tityrus enjoys.

Some two or three pages do not do justice to a single Virgilian eclogue, much less the whole collection of ten pieces.[8] And we should not lose sight of the fact that it is Meliboeus, the exile, who possesses the more poetic sensibility in the poem. But the picture (provided mainly by Meliboeus) of Tityrus lying at his ease beneath the spreading beech tree and playing upon his shepherd's pipe does, I think, adequately represent the pastoral ideal which was to be the source of much of the pastoral mode's future appeal—and the bane of modern critics trying to define that appeal. Renato Poggioli has been perhaps boldest in attempting such a definition, and unfortunately, because of his explicitness, he is the easiest to fault. He begins his essay "The Oaten Flute" with the statement that "the psychological root of the pastoral is a double longing after innocence and happiness, to be recovered not through conversion or regeneration, but merely through retreat." The pastoral ideal "shifts on the quicksands of wishful thought" ("the weakest of all moral and religious resorts"), and the task of the pastoral imagination is "to exalt the pleasure principle at the expense of the reality principle." Such a view pushes him into expression that implies a moral disapproval of the pastoral impulse generally: "the pastoral longing is but a wishful dream of happiness to be gained without effort, of an erotic bliss made absolute by its own irresponsibility."[9] For Poggioli, as for Walter W. Greg, Bruno Snell, and others before him, pastoral from the very beginning of its history has been primarily escapist literature, and he is thus open to criticism—and indeed has been criticized—for oversimplifying pastoral's main appeal.[10] As those who have corrected Poggioli have brought us to see, pastoral is not necessarily escapist in appeal, and there is much of a positive nature to be said on behalf of its ideal of *otium*. That ideal seeks to eternalize a single moment, to take it out of time; it postulates a state of inner peace and calm, an indifference to, rather than a flight from, life in the more complex and civilized world. If there is a withdrawal from the complex city or court, it is not merely an escape from the normal world but rather a withdrawal into a better and different kind of life which puts forth claims of its own, a life of poetic song or of Epicurean freedom, the inner life of the mind or spirit. It was this prospect of inner freedom and devotion to the life of the mind that Renaissance Neoplatonists would fasten upon to express their own contemplative ideal.[11]

Poggioli's approach toward pastoral remains of interest and relevance, though, because in oversimplifying pastoral's central appeal he proceeded much as English anti-pastoralists did before him. It is that congruence which suggests that Poggioli's attempt at definition was not, in fact, a mere error on his part. Much of his own study was based on the English Renaissance literature which is the main focus of the present work, and to a great extent poets such as Sidney, Spenser, Shakespeare, and Marvell can be held accountable for misleading those who might wish to render their assumptions and implications in bald critical prose. The question we are driven back to is, Why did they in their turn so often present pastoral as a mode of escape? I have already suggested simple willfulness or rhetorical subterfuge as one possible reason. But they for their part might wish to offer excuses or explanations. Pastoral had undergone changes since Theocritus's and Virgil's time, and they could well claim that several intervening pastoral writers had in turn misled them. No one of these, perhaps, is more culpable or more important than Jacopo Sannazaro, whose *Arcadia*, first published in 1502, was one of the most popular and influential pastoral works of the sixteenth century and the likely source of Sidney's title.[12] Since the Italian *Arcadia* in many ways represents much of Renaissance pastoral before Sidney and clearly embodies the attitudes which Sidney associated with the pastoral mode and which he was opposing, it merits detailed consideration here.

Sannazaro's *Arcadia* is not an easy work to characterize. "Arcadia" has several different meanings within the work, and Sannazaro himself seems both to approve and to disapprove of pastoral life and its concomitant point of view: in the course of the narrative, the author's self-acknowledged pastoral persona states that "it is better to till a small field than to let a large one run miserably wild through ill government" but also comments, "hardly can the savage beasts, much less youths brought up in noble cities, dwell with delight among Arcadia's solitudes."[13] The work is more than a collection of pastoral poems with prose introductions but not yet a pastoral romance, although it contains the basic narrative unit or sequence of subsequent Renaissance pastoral romances: a love-stricken urban or court figure in flight from the city seeks relief among the humble shepherds in a sympathetic pastoral landscape, only to return eventually to the court he initially fled. There is a gesture toward developing that embryonic narrative into a full-fledged plot, but it remains only a gesture, introduced halfway through the work and never fully acted upon. In the Seventh Prose section the "I" of the piece, Sincero (Sannazaro's pastoral persona), tells us he has come to Arcadia in an attempt to leave behind thoughts of his Neapolitan mistress. Nothing gives him pleasure; no feast or sport can reduce his misery, much less increase his joy ("Niuna cosa m'aggrada, nulla festa nè gioco mi può, non dico accrescere di letizia, ma scemare de le miserie" [p. 113]); and yet this same figure has described himself participating in the happy pastoral gatherings, games, and festivals of the earlier prose sections, with no hint of dissatisfaction whatsoever.

Despite such rhetorical and narrative inconsistencies, the *Arcadia* does finally present a coherent impression of the uses and range of pastoral writing. Arcadia for Sannazaro is not only the landscape in which Sincero seeks relief from his suffering; it is also what might best be called the state of mind in which one devotes oneself to the writing of poetry. In the First Prose section, the scene is set for the initial eclogue with one of the work's many literary borrowings, a catalogue of trees heavily indebted to Ovid's description of the grove in which Orpheus sang his tales of boys loved by the gods and of maidens inflamed by unnatural lust.[14] In the Ovidian account, Orpheus's hill was initially devoid of shade; the trees came there in response to the sound of Orpheus's lyre, and the catalogue of trees is a tribute to the power of his song. Sannazaro's insistence upon the "lowness" of pastoral song (a reference to its Renaissance status as the most humble of poetic genres) deprives his shepherds of the power to create a landscape in Orpheus's manner; they must gather in a grove already physically present. Yet by relying upon that Ovidian passage early in his work, Sannazaro is announcing a major subject of his piece, poetry itself. That announcement is followed by extensive and pointed borrowing from both classical and Renaissance poets, borrowing so extensive that the work at times becomes a literary mosaic.[15]

What perhaps most reveals the *Arcadia* as a work concerned with literary art is Sannazaro's practice of having even the unhappiest of eclogues provide great pleasure to the shepherds hearing them. After Serrano's and Opico's lament over the decay of the world and its decline from the conditions of the Golden Age, we are told that their song was heard with great delight by the company gathered there ("non senza gran diletto da tutta la brigata ascoltato" [p. 107]). And after the Tenth Eclogue, which was requested to be a poem in praise of a recent generation of poets but which in its execution became another lament over the bad conditions of the present age, we encounter a similar response:

Se le lunghe rime di Fronimo e di Selvaggio porsono universalmente diletto a ciascuno de la nostra brigata, non è da dimandare. [P. 173]

[There is no need to ask if the lengthy verses of Fronimo and Selvaggio gave universal delight to everyone in our party.]

The praise of the singers and the delight acknowledged by the listeners in these two instances and after the more personal Second, Third, and Fourth eclogues are indications that the shepherds are viewing the poems more as artistic performances than as expressions of personal grief. These words of praise and pleasure amount to an open admission by Sannazaro that he is writing within a convention and a tradition: such praise tells the reader that he, like the shepherds present, is to look to the art in the songs and not to the biography of the singer; the eclogue is acknowledged as a set piece to be placed in a poetic tradition and compared with other similar poems in that tradition. Pastoral poetry thereby becomes in Sannazaro's *Arcadia* a type of artistic exercise, something that Sannazaro admits openly again in the concluding prose section of the work when he takes leave of his oaten flute with the words "Tu a la mia bocca et a le mie mani sei non molto tempo stata piacevole esercizio" [You have been for no short time a pleasing exercise for my mouth and hands (p. 216)].

If Sannazaro's Arcadia is a place or a state of mind in which one dedicates oneself to poetry, that poetry turns out to be of a particularly narrow and circumscribed scope. There is some joy in Sannazaro's pastoral world, especially in the pastoral games and festivals; but the record of that joy is confined primarily to the early prose sections, and even they are in marked and somewhat disturbing contrast to the individual eclogues they are designed to preface. Once the subject of death is introduced in the Fifth Prose section, however, the mood in the eclogues and the prose sections becomes more uniform, the somberness lightened only in those moments of pleasure acknowledged by the shepherds upon hearing eclogues well performed. As David Kalstone observes, the eclogues themselves are throughout virtually all laments: laments for the dead, laments over the loss of the Golden Age or over the evils of the present one, or simply lovers' laments.[16] The love laments predominate, and the uniform tone or mood of the latter half of the *Arcadia* is enforced by Sannazaro's imposition of Renaissance interests upon the earlier pastoral tradition—the conception of love as an all-consuming and usually unreciprocated passion. Achieved, reciprocated love was part of the ideal pastoral existence enjoyed by Virgil's Tityrus, although only a minor part of it: Tityrus himself referred to a change in his affections from Galatea to Amaryllis in relatively casual fashion—"Postquam nos Amaryllis habet,

Galatea reliquit" [After Amaryllis possessed and Galatea had left me (line 30)]—implying that such a change was a matter of course in normal pastoral experience.[17] When in the Seventh Prose section Sannazaro begins to focus more steadily upon Sincero's retreat into Arcadia and upon his encounter there with other lovers who to varying degrees reflect his plight, Arcadia becomes preeminently a landscape of love, a refuge for unhappy lovers of the Petrarchan sort. Hereafter love is to be what it was not in Theocritus and Virgil, a serious and full-time pastoral occupation.[18]

It is, though, the limits Sannazaro places upon pastoral song and upon the unhappy emotion he puts at the center of his pastoral world that tell us most about his conception of Arcadia and of the whole pastoral mode. Throughout, Sannazaro-Sincero is relatively content to record for us what, in full accord with pastoral convention, he refers to as "le rozze Ecloghe da naturale vena uscite" [rude eclogues issuing from a natural vein (p. 50)] when those eclogues are the laments of other shepherds or, if they are his own, when the emotion that gives rise to them can be controlled or borne. But when his personal grief becomes too strong, he either expresses dissatisfaction with Arcadia (and thus by extension with himself as a pastoral poet) or drops the pastoral pretense entirely and breaks off writing. The outburst, already cited, against Arcadia's solitudes as unfit for beasts, not to say youths of noble cities, comes when Sincero acknowledges that his self-imposed exile from his beloved's presence has offered him no relief but has only increased his pain. Despite all of Sannazaro's borrowing from Petrarch, Sincero is denied even Petrarch's solace of nourishing himself on the memory of his beloved. In his exile, while he cannot stop thinking of her, he is losing the ability to picture his mistress firmly in his mind (p. 111). And yet, later in the Twelfth Prose section's underworld journey back to Naples, when Sincero finally understands that his mistress has died, he curses the hour he left Arcadia (p. 202); plainly he would prefer even the exiled lover's imaginative and physical separation from his beloved to the knowledge that she is lost forever.

The Epilogue section, a farewell to his sampogna or shepherd's pipe, builds upon this feeling of dissatisfaction. In taking leave of his oaten flute, Sannazaro is also leaving Arcadia and pastoral poetry, but not simply for the traditional reason suggested earlier in the work, that he must follow Virgil's example and move on to higher poetic forms; rather, the death of his beloved has deprived him of both subject and desire to write:

io ora con sospiri e lacrime abondantissime ti consacro in memoria di quella, che di avere infin qui scritto mi è stata potente cagione; per la cui repentina morte, la materia or in tutto è mancata a me di scrivere, et a te di sonare. [P. 218]

[I now with sighs and most abundant tears consecrate you (his oaten flute) in memory of her who has been for me a powerful source of whatever I have written, and because of whose sudden death I now lack all matter for writing and you for sounding.]

Attempting to express the extent of his grief, Sannazaro-Sincero a sentence before has announced that any future shepherd taking up the abandoned sampogna must be made to understand that this particular pipe knows only how to weep and lament (p. 217). But that pipe has in fact already in the past, in the *Arcadia* we have just read, been devoted almost exclusively to lamenting music. Breaking off pastoral song for the reason now stated, the death of the poet's beloved, sets a limit upon just how much grief pastoral poetry, or at least Sannazaro's pastoral poetry, might encompass.

The pastoral poetry that Sannazaro-Sincero leaves behind him would seem to deal primarily, then, with lamenting and with unhappy emotion but with bearable or supportable unhappiness, with precisely the kind of emotion that most of the eclogues have been expressing, and not with the harsh and incontrovertible fact of death encountered close at hand. In reading Virgil's *Eclogues* we understand that the social conditions leading to Meliboeus's eviction or Gallus's all-consuming passion are threats to the pastoral ideal of ease and achieved happiness; but such suggestions of human suffering are presented and remain fully part of Virgil's fictive pastoral world. In Sannazaro's *Arcadia*, even as we are deprived of Tityrus's circumscribed pastoral joy, so are we insulated from the full force of human misery. Because Sannazaro-Sincero only tells us of the death of his mistress and then backs away from treating that subject in pastoral verse, he wants us to view human tragedy, to use terms which Erwin Panofsky applies to Virgil's work but which might best be reserved for Sannazaro's, not as a "stark reality" but only "through the soft, colored haze of sentiment."[19] Especially in the second half of his work, Sannazaro appears to be striving to keep to that mood of suffused melancholy which Panofsky has singled out as the distinguishing mark of the later pastoral tradition. By the limits Sannazaro places upon his pastoral verse and prose, by referring to death but refusing to treat it as a subject for poetry, he defines Arcadia as a soothing dwelling place for the troubled human spirit; Arcadia becomes a realm of fantasy in which the rough edges of human experience are rounded off and which ceases to exist or must be abandoned when reality impinges upon it too sharply. And the pastoral mode in Sannazaro's hands thereby threatens to become a vehicle for mere indulgence in sentimental feeling.

TO VIEW PASTORAL as escapist indulgence in sentimental feeling could be simply to assume Sannazaro rather than Virgil or Theocritus as one's pastoral model. But the matter is more complicated. More than strictly pastoral works could and in fact did encourage Elizabethans to look upon Arcadia as a place of escape from the cares and responsibilities of everyday life. By Sidney's and Shakespeare's time, Arcadia, the landscape of pastoral poetry, had long since merged with two other conceptions, that of the life envisioned in the pagan myth of the Golden Age and the parallel Christian account of life in Eden before the fall from grace. The differences among the three conceptions were usually overlooked or ignored, so that when one spoke of Arcadia or even of the ordinary English countryside, prelapsarian Eden or life in the Golden Age would quickly and even inevitably come to mind. These other two conceptions thus became part of Arcadia's meaning and implications.

The myth of the Golden Age has been closely related to pastoral writing since the time of Virgil. Strictly speaking, pastoral and Golden Age life are not the same, although the two were and still are easily confused.[20] The Fourth Eclogue of Virgil is a prophecy of a Golden Age which is to begin in the immediate future with the birth of an unnamed child during Pollio's consulship and which is to be a return to the kind of life led by men in the world's first age. Justice is to return, and the rule of Saturn is to begin anew. The Age of Iron will pass gradually from the earth, and a golden race of men will inherit it. The earth will produce fruit without man's toil, the ox will no longer be frightened by the lion, and goats will make their way home, unguided, with udders full of milk. In time there will be no more shipping, no more wars, and no wounding of the earth with ploughs. This vision plainly pictures the conditions Arthur O. Lovejoy and George Boas have labeled "soft primitivism," and just such an image of life also lies behind the ease and freedom of the pastoral ideal: neither the Golden Age myth nor pastoral writing generally is concerned with the real difficulties and hardships that life close to nature involves or with a realistic description of the actual conditions of country life.[21] But though men in the original Golden Age may have lived a life of pastoral *otium*, pastoral man does not necessarily enjoy all the blessings of Golden Age man. The type of life described in the visionary Fourth Eclogue is not the same as that of the pastoral present as seen in the other eclogues, and this poem is sung, as Virgil tells us in its first line, "paulo maiora," on a grander scale, than the other poems in the pastoral collection.

Theocritus included no reference to the Golden Age in his pastoral verse. What began in Virgil as an experiment, an enlargement of pastoral's sphere included in his praise of a ruler, soon lost that sense of experimentation in the Roman poets following him.[22] And Renaissance pastoral poetry ushered in a large number of panegyrics celebrating or prophesying a return to the Golden Age, under whichever ruler or new parent happened to be the patron of a poet receiving (or seeking) support.[23] Such praise looked to the present or immediate future, as did Virgil's Fourth Eclogue, to the new age being brought in; but equally common, no doubt because of Sannazaro's influence, were backward glances at the first irrecoverable Golden Age. The nostalgia for a lost better age, exhibited in Sannazaro's Sixth Eclogue and in Tasso's famous lament over the disappearance of a time of free love ("O bella età de l'oro"), would appear over and over again in Renaissance pastorals, since that feeling could fit the new use of pastoral for satirical attack upon the corrupt present.

But a shepherd who looks to a future Golden Age or laments the loss of a past one casts doubt on his own felicity.[24] Although the Golden Age was established by Sidney's time as a theme appropriate to (or at least familiar in) pastoral writing, the use of that myth to express a yearning for the past or a hope for the future still implies a recognition that pastoral life is not precisely the same thing as Golden Age life. There was, however, another way in which the pastoral mode had been associated with the myth of the Golden Age, and a way which tied pastoral life more firmly to Golden Age life. In the fourth century, the grammarian Aelius Donatus accounted for the order of Virgil's works by suggesting that the three genres in which Virgil chose to write were intended by the poet to correspond to the history of mankind as a whole: man's life was first pastoral, then agricultural, when the fields were tilled, and finally, when contention arose over possession of arable and fertile ground, martial; hence Virgil wrote bucolics first, then georgics, and last, an epic. Donatus previously concluded a brief review of various theories on the origin of pastoral verse with a statement that is notable for the explicit connection it makes between pastoral and Golden Age life. In the words of the Elizabethan translator of Donatus's life of Virgil,

> What ever they all say, this is most certen, that the *Bucolik* verse, tooke beginninge of great antiquitie, when men ledde only sheapheardes lives, and therefore the simplicitie of such personages doth represent a shew of the golden worlde.[25]

The Renaissance critic Julius Caesar Scaliger argued similarly that pastoral must be the oldest of poetic genres since it is that type of poetry which man in his original pastoral condition must have sung. Scaliger did not think very highly of pastoral, which he found the mildest, most naive, and most inept of verse forms, but his view of the pastoral mode's antiquity did enable him to explain, in a delightfully literalistic manner, why the subject of love figures so prominently in pastoral verse: love, he claimed, was pastoral's earliest theme, and understandably so, since that poetry was originally the creation of lightly clad young people of both sexes who were thrown together a great deal and who had ample opportunity to witness and be inflamed by the sexual activities of their sheep.[26]

Scaliger's view that pastoral was the oldest form of poetry may not have been universally accepted in the Renaissance—the English critic George Puttenham, for instance, insisted that the pastoral eclogue was a late and sophisticated form, although he did not doubt that mankind's first condition was pastoral[27]—and Scaliger's opinions, especially on the early introduction and propriety of love as a subject in pastoral poetry, were by no means necessarily correct. But with Scaliger's views current and respected, and with Donatus's observations newly and repeatedly available in the Preface to the several editions of Phaer's translation of the *Aeneid,* it is unlikely that even the most learned of Elizabethan viewers of *As You Like It* would have been surprised, much less moved to object, to hear it said that the exiled courtiers living a pastoral existence in the Forest of Arden "fleet the time carelessly, as they did in the golden world." Nor would it seem incongruous to Sidney's first readers to see Pyrocles justify stopping for a while in a place called Arcadia by imputing to the landscape there the perpetual spring ordinarily associated only with the mythical period at the beginning of human history.

It was easy enough, then, to confuse Arcadia and the Golden Age. More interesting, and especially for a Christian poet wishing to oppose any kind of sojourn in a pastoral landscape, is the substitution of Eden for the Golden Age in that equation. What made this substitution possible, of course, was the merging in the Middle Ages and after of the pagan myth of the Golden Age and the Judaeo-Christian myth of Eden. How these two accounts of a happier time in the distant past became not simply alternative or parallel versions of the same myth but virtually one and the same has been documented many times, and several late examples alone should suffice to show how easy and commonplace the substitution was.[28] We might note, for instance, the breezy assurance with which an anonymous commentator on the 1596 edition of Conti's *Mythologiae,* one of those handbooks which (as Douglas Bush remarks) enabled Renaissance readers and writers alike to appear more learned in classical texts than they actually were, could declare:

> Dubitare non potest quin Aureae aetatis aenigmate veteres Ethnici illam vitam designarint, quam homines ante peccatum vixerunt. Aetatis verò ferreae nomine eam, quam iam post offensum à primis hominibus Deum omnes experimur.[29]
>
> [By the allegory of the Golden Age, the ancient pagans certainly referred to the life which men lived before sin. By the name of Iron Age, they meant that time which we all now experience after the offence to God by the first men.]

The English Neoplatonic enthusiast Henry Reynolds reveals a similar assurance a generation later; here it is a "but" which suggests that there is simply no other way of viewing the Golden Age than as a version of Eden:

> What could they meane by their *Golden-Age,* when
> *Nulli subigebant arua coloni,*
> *Ipsaque tellus*
> *Omnia liberius nullo poscente ferebat,*
> But the state of Man before his Sin? and consequently, by their Iron age, but the worlds infelicity and miseries that succeeded his fall?[30]

Arthur Golding, perhaps Sidney's one-time literary collaborator (on the translation of DuPlessis Mornay's *De la verité de la religion chrestienne*), would appear to wish to approach such parallels with more caution. He appended to his translation of the *Metamorphoses* an introductory epistle in which he worried over how much use an orthodox Christian might make of classical literature and culture. He fully acknowledged that "nothing may in worthiness with holy writ compare."[31] Nevertheless, he proceeded in that epistle to go ahead and compare "Ovids scantlings" with "the whole true patterne" of Scripture (379) and found numerous parallels; one of them, as we might well expect, is that between Ovid's portrayal of the Golden Age and the Bible's picture of Eden:

> Moreover by the golden age what other thing is ment,
> Than Adams tyme in Paradyse, who beeing innocent

Did lead a blist and happy lyfe untill that thurrough sin
He fell from God?

[469–72]

There remain some differences between the two myths. Even if Ovid gave much greater emphasis to the Golden and Iron ages, there were still two other ages intervening, which fact inhibits any total identification with the Christian scheme of a pre- and postlapsarian existence. And the pagan version postulates many people enjoying the Golden Age; the Judaeo-Christian myth places only Adam and Eve in Eden. But Golding anticipates the objections of an overscrupulous reader: he admits that when the classical poets took their fables out of Scripture, they "shadowed" biblical truth with their glosses and "went about / Too turne the truth too toyes and lyes" (530–31). There may be some discrepancies between the pagan accounts and Holy Writ, but they simply put more responsibility on the reader, whose task it is to "plucke" the pagan "visers" from the truth and to look past the literal statement of the poetry to the real meaning to be found beneath (538–44).

THE EASY CONFLATION or confusion of Eden with the Golden Age and of both with Arcadia can help to explain the escapism that English Renaissance authors frequently saw as implicit in pastoral writing and in accounts of a sojourn in a pastoral setting. The pagan and Judaeo-Christian accounts of man's earliest history express dissatisfaction with the way things are now and nostalgic longing for a happier period at the beginning of human history. Both myths embody a yearning for the unattainable, since they look back to an irrecoverable past. The pastoral ideal, on the other hand, is still attainable in the present: pastoral detachment, freedom, and *otium* can be obtained, or at least sought, by leaving the city or court and taking up the simple life of the country or merely by assuming the attitudes and values of a humble country person. One is by no means obligated to make the full identification or association of Arcadia with prelapsarian Eden, just as one need not assume Sannazaro rather than Virgil as one's pastoral model or as the best representative of the pastoral tradition. But when pastoral becomes, in the words of the Elizabethan translator of Donatus, "a shewe of the golden worlde" or Eden, it too pictures an impossible ideal and reflects the nostalgia found in the two myths of man's earliest history. And when this nostalgia is in turn joined with the change that Arcadia or other specifically pastoral landscapes sustained in the hands of Sannazaro and a Renaissance follower like Montemayor, pastoral writing and its characteristic landscape become, in effect, escapist twice over.

Given the changes the pastoral mode has undergone since Virgil's time, then, reasonable readers and writers might well see grounds for objecting to it and its implications. Criticism of pastoral actually takes several different forms in the English Renaissance. Some of the opposition expresses that Elizabethan common sense which criticized Petrarchanism for its rhetorical excesses. Sidney in the *Old Arcadia* and Shakespeare in *As You Like It* initially set out, it would appear, by criticizing the pretense of an artificial literary mode that had rich and poor, sophisticated courtier and humble shepherd, converse unselfconsciously on equal terms. But criticism of or opposition to pastoral becomes more significant when authors not only offer a literary critique of the pastoral pretense or its highly artificial conventions but lodge an objection to the whole prospect of life in a pastoral setting while they proceed under the assumption that Arcadia is a realm of escape from normal cares and responsibilities. This assumption is, as I have suggested, fostered particularly by the association of pastoral Arcadia with Eden. Such an objection is not, we should note, simply to the idea of man's once having lived in a perfect state; we are not dealing here with writers whose belief in material progress precludes postulating a better time in the distant past. They object, rather, to a cast of mind that either seeks an easy, carefree existence anywhere in our present world or indulges overmuch in dreams of better times and better places, thereby avoiding full concentration upon the facts of man's present existence. An anti-pastoral attitude marks a commitment to talk about man as he is and not as he might be in some perfect moral state either in the past or in the future; and for an English Renaissance Christian this commitment leads to the insistence that man, while obligated to alleviate the burdens imposed upon him by original sin, cannot and should not ever lose sight of his fallen condition.

The specific form of Sidney's and Shakespeare's anti-pastoral argument proceeds along the lines suggested in my opening paragraph: life in Arcadia, when viewed correctly, is no different in its essentials from life elsewhere; anyone who expects to find a different life there or a setting in which he can relax and escape from normal responsibilities—anyone, in short, expecting to find Arcadia a version of Eden or the Golden Age—needs correction and enlightenment. In Arcadia such a figure learns the truth about his pastoral surroundings and his own fallen nature. But objections to Arcadia because it might be confused with an Eden no longer with us, and might thereby distract from full concentration upon the dangers and responsibilities of life in our fallen world, ought not to apply to Eden itself. That place is, after all, legitimately and qualitatively different from other pastoral landscapes. Yet Milton, in treating Paradise and man's life there, works out an equivalent in unfallen terms to the antipastoral argument put forward by Sidney and Shakespeare; it is an argument that puts him at odds with earlier portrayals of that purportedly quite special place, just as Sidney's Arcadia pits its author against earlier versions of a merely pastoral landscape. While never letting us lose sight of the fact that Adam and Eve remain unfallen before the fall, Milton gives them a life in Eden with enough complexity and difficulty to enable the reader to see his own present likeness in prelapsarian Adam and Eve; and as *Paradise Lost* progresses, both Adam and the reader receive an education similar to that of Sidney's and Shakespeare's characters who stop to linger for a while in a natural landscape or an Arcadia of the mind. Because Milton refuses to look upon Eden as significantly different from any other landscape or as a place one can envision as free from the cares of life in our complex world, he not only enters the ranks of the antipastoralists but can be said to express the most absolute form of their sentiment. Sidney is concerned to eliminate the Edenic overtones associated with Arcadia; in Milton's hands, not even Eden, finally, is exempt from the strictures against a life of uncomplicated ease and retirement which many in the English Renaissance found suspect.

WE KNOW FROM the Gloucester subplot of *King Lear* alone that Shakespeare read all or part of Sidney's *Arcadia* by 1605, if not before; and we know from explicit references and verbal echoes that Milton was very familiar both with Shakespeare's pastoral plays and with Sidney's heroical-pastoral romance, although, in print at least, he might wish to deny (and loudly so) the legitimacy of the latter as a major or serious work of literature.[32] But the tracing of anti-pastoral sentiment through these three writers points beyond mere literary influence: Shakespeare and Milton did not express opposition to pastoral assumptions simply because Sidney had done so before them. Anti-pastoral sentiment is, as I have already suggested, more than an exclusively literary phenomenon; it is an expression of what I take to be major social, ethical, and religious impulses of the English Renaissance. It is this premise which has in large part dictated the choice of the authors studied in the chapters that follow. Anti-pastoral writers, I would argue, undertook pastoral but found themselves opposed, on extraliterary grounds, to assumptions they associated with prior pastoral writing. Their own previously held beliefs and attitudes prevented them from endorsing the pastoral ideal they saw embraced rather wholeheartedly in their immediate pastoral (and usually Continental) predecessors. Sidney and Milton are included in the present study because of the relative assurance with which we can identify the primary impulses behind their opposition to what they understood to be pastoral assumptions. We are coming more and more to see Sidney's Protestantism as genuine religious belief and not just the badge of his adherence to the political party or group in Elizabethan England favoring an aggressive foreign policy against Spain; yet, to judge from the *Arcadia* itself (in either version), the main impetus for his opposition to pastoralism probably remains the particular kind of English Humanist training he had received, a training designed to prepare him for active service to his state and disposing him against any kind of life that might resemble inactivity. On the other hand, the prime impetus behind Milton's objection to an easy Eden, to the vision of a life of uncomplicated and meaningless relaxation, is more easily identifiable as an outgrowth of specifically Protestant beliefs. For, as we shall see, at those points where Milton was being most distinctive and original in his treatment of Eden, he was also expressing what was most Protestant in him.

There were other candidates for study as well, most notably Spenser and Marvell, both of whom carried on extended examination of the pastoral convention and its concomitant assumptions. Sidney's and Milton's anti-pastoralism is, by comparison with these other two writers', more consistent and distinct. For a Meliboe in Spenser killed off without our much regretting it, there is also a Colin Clout whose poetic and contemplative vision we would prefer to have remained intact, without intrusion from the heroic world of more mundane fact. Marvell writes poems of both what one critic has called "pastoral success" and "pastoral failure": the former include poems in which the pastoral sojourner or the poet himself "consolidates gains" in the pastoral landscape and becomes "reoriented towards the world"; the latter, anti-pastoral poems, "describe an inability to stay inside the protected world where 'letting things be' is possible."[33] To include Spenser and Marvell here would both enlarge my study inordinately and also complicate and blur its central argument. There is more of a legitimate debate over the claims of pastoral in these other writers' works, or at least an appearance of a legitimate debate, in which both parties are given appropriate time. What Sidney and Milton reveal is the extremes toward which these other two poets tend or lean but do not consistently commit themselves, because, I would argue, for better or worse Spenser and Marvell did not feel the influence of English Christian Humanism or Protestantism as strongly or directly. In Sidney and Milton we simply see those influences, and the anti-pastoralism arising from them, in clearer, more uncomplicated, and more overt form.

There are several other reasons as well for the particular inclusion of Sidney. The *Old Arcadia,* probably begun in 1577 (though individual eclogues incorporated into it were written earlier), in conception at least has claim to temporal priority over *The Shepheardes Calendar* as the first major pastoral (or anti-pastoral) work of the English Renaissance. The *Old Arcadia* is in any case more thoroughgoing in its expression of anti-pastoral sentiment than the doubts over pastoral *otium* expressed, for instance, in Piers's May Eclogue attack upon shepherds (or pastors) who pass their time "In lustihede and wanton meryment." And while I treat the *Old Arcadia* primarily for the light it sheds on the *New Arcadia,* one of the added advantages of examining the earlier version at length is that it provides us with the best and clearest statement of exactly what anti-pastoral sentiment is; Sidney can thus do much of my defining for me. Finally, Sidney is studied here as an assertion of his importance. There has been a renaissance in Sidney studies in the past twenty years, but there is still not much indication of widespread reading of the *Arcadia* by students or critics other than those who write directly and at length on Sidney; the new interest has not spread much beyond dedicated Sidneians. Part of the reason for placing Sidney side by side with Shakespeare and Milton, then, is to suggest not only that there is a strong community of interest among the three writers but also that this is the kind of literary company Sidney deserves to keep.

The study of Sidney and Milton necessarily reveals the ways in which ethical and religious ideals find expression in English Renaissance literature. Both writers were to a certain extent ideologues, in that their minds were distinctly capable of being violated by ideas. This is not generally supposed to be the case for Shakespeare, and it is critically imprudent to accuse him of explicitly endorsing any narrowly religious or specific Humanist program. If we can with some ease and assurance identify what ideas behind their work prompted the anti-pastoralism of Sidney and Milton, Shakespeare is included here as a type of control, precisely because we cannot easily determine why he should express as much anti-pastoral sentiment as he does. As it happens, Shakespeare too does not merely explore the pastoral mode and balance opposing positions against one another in the way he is usually pictured as doing in critical literature. Rather, he takes stands on the major issues English Renaissance pastoral frequently raises, issues such as whether the active or contemplative life is the superior and whether a pastoral sojourn is wise or even possible. They are stands, finally, very close to those of Sidney and Milton. It therefore seems fair to conclude that in the opposition to the prospect of uncomplicated ease in a pastoral setting we have come upon an attitude that is enduring, pervasive, and of considerable importance in the English Renaissance.

ONE FINAL INTRODUCTORY comment needs to be made. I ought to acknowledge that what I am calling "anti-pastoral" throughout this study might as easily be called "pastoral" properly defined. In opposing what they saw as the implicit escapism of prior pastoral writing, Sidney, Shakespeare, and, in his special way, Milton also were insisting upon pastoral's ability to picture our present life in small. They were returning to the conception of pastoral shared by Theocritus and Virgil and using the pastoral mode, not to express nostalgia for a better time and better place, but to comment upon life both within and outside Arcadia. They were driving a wedge between pastoral Arcadia and customary conceptions of the Golden Age and Eden (with Milton viewing his Paradise more as a version of an anti-pastoralist's Arcadia than as a typical Eden). I have, however, retained the term "anti-pastoral" because Sidney's two *Arcadia*s, Shakespeare's pastoral plays, and Milton's *Paradise Lost* reveal these authors not so much consciously following the model of Theocritus and Virgil or insisting on a proper definition of the pastoral mode as simply opposing the assumptions they saw implicit in pictures of pastoral life in writers like a Sannazaro, a Montemayor, a Lodge, or, in Milton's case, much of the hexameral tradition before him. The argument with another vision of Arcadia or Eden is built into their works, and I have chosen to use the label "anti-pastoral" in an attempt to be true to that spirit of contentiousness.

CHAPTER II

Sidney's Old Arcadia

THREE DIFFERENT versions of Sidney's *Arcadia* have come down to us, more than enough for Sidney's, or anyone else's, benefit. My main concern is with the revised or *New Arcadia,* Sidney's highly complex and mature masterpiece published posthumously in 1590, his prose equivalent to *The Faerie Queene*. For several reasons, though, I begin my study of that work with an examination of Sidney's original version, the *Old Arcadia*. The revised version tends to resist interpretation on its own. It is patently unfinished, Sidney having completed only two and one-half books before breaking off in mid-sentence, and yet it is a work which, unlike *The Faerie Queene,* depends upon what would have been its ending for the revelation of its full meaning. Begun in the late 1570s, the *Old Arcadia* is both the earliest significant English anti-pastoral work we have and the only *Arcadia* completed by Sidney himself: it perforce presents the only fully articulated statement, albeit an interim one, of Sidney's objections to prior literary pastoralism and the assumptions he saw underlying the pastoral tradition. While the *Old Arcadia* is not simply a rough or first draft for the more capacious and overtly heroic *New Arcadia,* it is, as R. W. Zandvoort observed back in 1929, the principal source of the *New Arcadia*.[1] One of the arguments I shall be putting forward is that a finished *New Arcadia,* or at least the *New Arcadia* as Sidney still conceived of it at the point he broke off writing, would have been closer to the *Old Arcadia* than most recent criticism of Sidney has been willing to grant. Just as Sidney did, we ought to have the overall shape and argument of the *Old Arcadia* in mind

as we proceed through the *New Arcadia*. For even with all the material that was added in the revision and was apparently taking Sidney off in a different direction, there is evidence that as long as Sidney labored over a manuscript entitled "Arcadia" he never worked himself free of the shaping power and implications of the narrative structure of the original version.[2]

I shall be arguing, then, that the *Old Arcadia* is of considerable help in understanding the *New Arcadia*. And help comes from another quarter as well, though a suspect one—the 1593 *Arcadia,* that hybrid work made up of the two and one-half books of the *New Arcadia* and the last three books of the *Old Arcadia*. This composite version, put out under the direction of Sidney's sister, is not really Sidney's creation in its present form, and hence that form can tell us little about Sidney's own thought and intentions. But, as has been known since the rediscovery of *Old Arcadia* manuscripts early in this century, the action of the last three books of the 1593 version departs from that of the *Old Arcadia* at several significant points. In 1962 William A. Ringler, Jr., established through detailed critical and textual analysis which of these changes could safely be attributed to Sidney himself, rather than to the Countess of Pembroke or some other bowdlerizing editor, and we can now say with a good measure of assurance that Sidney was directly responsible for the elimination of the lovemaking between Pyrocles and Philoclea, the suppression of Musidorus's near rape of Pamela, and the alteration in the Book V account of Euarchus's journey to Arcadia.[3] These particular changes are extremely important in what they reveal about Sidney's attitude toward his narrative and its characters, and since at the time they were written or planned they were plainly intended for inclusion in the completed revision, I shall be calling upon the evidence they provide in considering Sidney's aims in the *New Arcadia*.[4]

Biographically oriented studies of Sidney suggest that he would have preferred not to have written the *Arcadia* in any version; far better, rather, to have been so busy in that active service to the state for which his Humanist training prepared him as to have had no time for such writing.[5] We ought not, though, to be misled by the nonchalance that prompted him to refer to his *Arcadia* as an "idle work" and a "trifle, and that triflingly handled." A close reading of any of Sidney's major writings would reveal that he is by no means a casual writer. The recent editorial work on the *Arcadia*s makes that point for us with a new and strengthened immediacy. The various manuscripts of the *Old Arcadia* reveal four, perhaps five, different states of composition and revision; Sidney was, it would appear, continually tinkering with his own manuscript even before he embarked on the major revision of his text.[6] This amount of revision suggests a fondness for the work, a desire to perfect what was already there, but also some measure of dissatisfaction. The changes that appeared in the last three books of the 1593 text, particularly those in the conduct of Pyrocles and Musidorus, reveal more significant dissatisfaction with important details of the plot of the *Old Arcadia*. And of course the fact that Sidney felt impelled to revise, rework, and enlarge the material of the whole of the *Old Arcadia* into what is virtually a new work suggests not simply dissatisfaction with details but a major change in purpose and direction. Yet this change in purpose, along with the immense widening of scope of the *New Arcadia* over the *Old,* does not necessarily point to a complete turnabout in Sidney's philosophy or in his attitude toward important questions which arise in both versions: questions, for instance, on the advisability of retiring to a pastoral setting, on the possibility of reconciling the demands of love with the responsibilities of life in the public, heroic world, or on what should be man's conception of his own nature and of the world around him. Amid all the changes, there is a marked consistency in the thought underlying both versions of the *Arcadia,* just the kind of consistency we might expect of an author whose active writing career spanned perhaps six years, eight years at most, before his death at age thirty-one.

"VERY BORN ARCADIANS" AND FOREIGN SHEPHERDS

In a very literal way, the starting point of Sidney's *Old Arcadia* is the pastoral tradition: his title would appear to be a direct borrowing from Sannazaro's *Arcadia,* and his opening paragraph's description of Arcadia is one that owes more to Virgil's and Sannazaro's work than to, for instance, the presumably more accurate account Polybius provides of his native land in his *History.* Sidney's Arcadia is depicted as a distinctly pleasant place, where man lives in easy accord with his natural surroundings:

> ARCADIA among all the provinces of Greece was ever had in singular reputation, partly for the sweetness of the air and other natural benefits, but principally for the moderate and well tempered minds of the people who (finding how true a contentation is gotten by following the course of nature, and how the shining title of glory, so much affected by other nations, doth indeed help little to the happiness of life) were the only people, which, as by their justice and providence gave neither cause nor hope to their neighbors to annoy them, so were they not stirred with false praise to trouble others' quiet, thinking it a small reward for the wasting of their own lives in

ravening that their posterity should long after say they had done so. [*OA*, 4]

Polybius did acknowledge the very high reputation his fellow Arcadians had for hospitality and piety; but the particular fame they had gained for music and singing Polybius attributes to a wise invention by the ancient inhabitants of the land, who saw community singing and other musical entertainment as a means of tempering the particularly harsh and austere living conditions forced upon the Arcadians by the cold and gloomy air of the province.[7] Sidney follows the pastoral tradition in viewing that fame for music simply as an extension of a quiet, unambitious life lived in accord with pleasant nature's dictates:

> Even the muses seemed to approve their good determination by choosing that country as their chiefest repairing place, and by bestowing their perfections so largely there that the very shepherds themselves had their fancies opened to so high conceits as the most learned of other nations have been long time since content both to borrow their names and imitate their cunning. [*OA*, 4]

But even with the explicit reference to the literary pastoral tradition in the mention of "the most learned of other nations," when it comes time for Sidney actually to introduce some of his Arcadian shepherds' songs, he does so with a good measure of self-consciousness, a self-consciousness which indicates discomfort with major assumptions of the pastoral convention. At the opening of the First Eclogues, he tries to explain away the relatively sophisticated nature of the poems to follow by noting that these are not your modern-day, lower-class shepherds who will be singing for us, "not such base shepherds as we commonly make account of, but the very owners of the sheep themselves, which in that thrifty world the substantiallist men would employ their whole care upon" (*OA*, 56). He goes on to inform us that the poems are not what Sannazaro claimed the eclogues in his *Arcadia* were, "rude eclogues issuing from a natural vein, set forth just as naked of ornament as I heard them sung by the shepherds of Arcadia."[8] Sidney's shepherds in effect have a secretary, who touches up and improves what he hears: "then was it their manner ever to have one who should write up the substance of that they said; whose pen, having more leisure than their tongues, might perchance polish a little the rudeness of an unthought-on song" (*OA*, 56).

Such explanations by Sidney are prompted by a rather strict sense of literary and social decorum, a feeling that true shepherds would not be capable of the artistic achievement the pastoral tradition ordinarily attributed to them.⁹ This same sense of decorum probably lies behind Sidney's choosing to present the first shepherd we encounter in the *Old Arcadia* as sleeping, and in a rather inelegant manner at that. It is Dametas, chief herdsman to Basilius, and when awakened by the song of Pyrocles (disguised as an Amazon), this shepherd proves to be no great lover of poetry:

> But so fell it out that, as with her sweet voice she recorded once or twice the last verse of her song, it awakened the shepherd Dametas, who at that time had laid his sleepy back upon a sunny bank not far thence, gaping as far as his jaws would suffer him. But being troubled out of his sleep (the best thing his life could bring forth) his dull senses could not convey the pleasure of the excellent music to his rude mind, but that he fell into a notable rage. [*OA*, 29]

Having evoked the pastoral tradition, Sidney seems determined to disabuse us right off, to inform us that the true rustic one might stumble across in the field is distinctly not one of those sensitive, self-consciously artistic figures who inhabit the pastoral landscapes of Sannazaro and Montemayor.

To be totally fair to the shepherd profession and to Sidney (lest he be accused of *outright* aristocratic snobbery), it should be noted that Dametas and his family are caricatures of shepherds, used not so much to tell us about the sensibility of actual shepherds as to indicate the drastic impairment in judgment of a duke who can raise a man like Dametas to an office of responsibility and have him serve as guardian to a princess. Yet other Arcadian shepherds, those designed to be fictive approximations of actual country people, often do not fare much better at Sidney's hands. In the First Eclogues, soon after the initial description of the pastoral pastimes that are to serve as *intermezzi* between the five books of prose narrative, there is a poetic confrontation between one of the Arcadian shepherds, Lalus, who is "accounted one of the best singers among them" (*OA*, 58) but whose name unfortunately means "babbler" in Greek, and Prince Musidorus, disguised as the shepherd Dorus. The placement alone of this singing contest has meaning, for it is the first extended poem in the eclogue sections, preceded only by a brief dance that sets the theme of unrequited love for the first of the pastoral interludes; while the poem may not bring us to love Sidney's various experiments in verse in the eclogues, it does serve to establish early on the difference between the two sensibilities of its participants and of the classes they represent. Following closely upon Sidney's expressions of discomfort with the pastoral convention's assumption of easy artistry among men of humble origin, it points up his discomfort with a related assumption, pervasive in Renaissance pastoral at least, namely, that one can place sophisticated courtier and lowly shepherd side by side and expect them to converse with one another as equals. What William Empson sees as responsible for the breakdown of the pastoral convention—when members of the upper class become self-conscious enough about their relations with members of the lower classes so that they can no longer hold to the "polite pretense" of a possible "beautiful relation between rich and poor"—is occurring here in one of the earliest examples of English Renaissance pastoral.[10]

Lalus challenges Dorus to sing of his beloved's perfection, to determine which of the two shepherds most deserves compassion. Dorus at first refuses the challenge but then enters into the contest and proceeds to defeat Lalus rather convincingly. Ringler has shown how in the seven pairs of answering stanzas that constitute the body of the singing contest, Dorus first easily follows the metrical pattern and rhyme scheme Lalus sets as part of his challenge and then proceeds to add further sophistications, for instance, that of beginning his reply with a repeat of Lalus's previous line.[11] Lalus is able to sing in terza rima, first in triple, then in feminine, finally in masculine, rhyme, and can thereafter switch to a medial rhyme pattern and more complex stanzaic forms; this ability makes him even in defeat more, certainly, than a mere country bumpkin. But Dorus's technical superiority is accompanied by a parallel distinction and superiority in language, metaphor, and sentiment. Dorus's characteristic vocabulary is latinate and his rhyme words, particularly, multisyllabic; Lalus relies more upon much simpler, monosyllabic language and easier rhymes (with frequent use of "is" as a rhyme word). Lalus tends to talk about Kala's physical qualities, and his analogies are simple and down-to-earth, sometimes so much so that they border on the outlandish: he refers to his beloved Kala as "A lily field, with plough of rose, which tilled is" (*OA*, 59.18), which comparison probably yields sense as a reference to the red and white of his beloved's complexion but which is rather awkwardly conceived nonetheless. His characteristic metaphors are monetary and proprietary: Kala's conversation is more enheartening to him "than to a miser money is" (*OA*, 59.21); he asks, "Can I be poor, that her gold hair procure myself?" (*OA*, 60.10), and follows with the suggestion that, once won, Kala would become one of his possessions: "So fair a field would well become an owner" (*OA*, 61.15). Dorus, for his part, speaks in a Renaissance courtier's Petrarchan conceits of his beloved's soul, which is already "by inward assumption" enjoyed by the gods even though that soul is still in the "body's fair possession" (*OA*, 59.28–29); the ordinary world simply cannot yield proper objects for comparison with his beloved since "She is herself of best things the collection" (*OA*, 59.36). Lalus's father has tried to discourage him from loving Kala, since long love brings no real profit (*OA*, 60.3–6); it is Dorus's own reason which tries to discourage his heart from reaching "beyond humanity" in his love (*OA*, 60.16).

Lalus does at one point offer a vision of harmony, freedom, and pastoral plenitude,[12] when he speaks of the bliss he expects to share with Kala:

> My sheep your food shall breed,
> Their wool your weed: I will you music yield
> In flow'ry field; and as the day begins
> With twenty gins we will the small birds take,
> And pastimes make, as nature things hath made.
> But when in shade we meet of myrtle boughs,
> Then love allows, our pleasures to enrich,
> The thought of which doth pass all worldly pelf.
>
> [*OA*, 62.4–11]

Dorus's parallel statement is, in contrast, a syntactically clogged and choppy description of an inner landscape of despair:

> My food is tears; my tunes waymenting yield;
> Despair my field; the flowers spirit's wars;
> My day new cares; my gins my daily sight,
> In which do light small birds of thoughts o'erthrown.
> My pastimes none; time passeth on my fall.
> Nature made all, but me of dolours made.
> I find no shade, but where my sun doth burn;
> No place to turn; without, within, it fries;
> Nor help by life or death who living dies.
>
> [*OA*, 62.18–27]

Through the contrast of these two passages we can see that in fact both sensibilities—that of disguised prince and that of true shepherd—are being criticized, but for very different reasons. Dorus may be the better poet, but he is, ultimately, the figure more deserving of our compassion. For it is the very sophistication and complexity of his vision that create what he refers to, in his final line before Lalus yields the poetic victory to him, as a "wretched state of man in self-division" (*OA*, 63.14). Praise of a beloved's soul inevitably implies distance, and a lover speaking in such terms is likely to find himself disoriented upon drawing close enough to see that it is more than a soul that he loves: if Dorus expresses his love in such a sublimated manner, well dissociated from the actual woman beloved, what is to happen when his desires prove to be just as earthbound as those of Lalus, when he wishes to possess Pamela's body as well as her soul?—a very real problem for him in the *Old Arcadia*.

Lalus does ultimately achieve his goal, and the Third Eclogue section is devoted to celebrating his marriage with Kala, a celebration which takes place while Musidorus is in the process of abducting Pamela and Pyrocles is consummating his love with Philoclea, without benefit of formal marriage. This eclogue section presents us with a picture of pastoral joy and harmony, but it is a joy that is very much dependent upon the simplicity of Lalus's desires and overall vision. Given the limited resources of Lalus's metaphors in the singing contest, it seems unlikely that Sidney intended Lalus and his country fellows to be representatives of an ideal existence his courtiers might be expected to pursue and emulate. Too much would have to be sacrificed for them to aspire to such a life. Lalus and his fellow Arcadians are, rather, included primarily for contrast with the princes and their experience in love, to show what life might be like if one simply had no obligations in, or vision of, a larger outside world.[13] The native Arcadians embody not so much a simplified and idealized version of our complex existence as a severely circumscribed version of it, a version that in any case proves (like many a pastoral existence before it) extremely fragile; any security it might claim to offer is thoroughly undermined with the apparent death of its protector, Basilius.

To satisfy his sense of decorum, then, but in order still to gain the depth of expression and feeling customary in pastoral literature, Sidney has recourse to a third type of shepherd: figures who have sought refuge in Arcadia from outside. Such figures stand between the Arcadian shepherd (Lalus) and the heroic prince disguised as shepherd (Dorus); they are not representatives of the heroic world and they have no particular responsibilities beyond their pastoral retreat, but neither are they treated in a condescending or patronizing manner. Shepherds of this type include the two "gentlemen," Strephon and Klaius; Sidney's fictionalized self-portrait, Philisides; and, in the latest manuscripts, Agelastus, a former Athenian senator whose unspecified cause of sorrow has prompted him to become an Arcadian shepherd (*OA*, 284). The reason Strephon, Klaius, and Philisides assume pastoral garb is the traditional one in Renaissance pastoral romance, an unhappy love affair. All these foreign shepherds have by virtue of office or blood some claim to be of noble or gentle caste, and their sensibility is accordingly (in Sidney's *Arcadia* at least) closer to that of the disguised prince, Musidorus, than to that of the

Arcadian rustic, Lalus. Their shepherd clothing is for them, as for Musidorus, in effect a disguise, and the landscape that Strephon and Klaius, for instance, see is not Lalus's "flow'ry field," with its myrtle boughs, but Dorus's psychological landscape:

> I that was once esteemed for pleasant music,
> Am banished now among the monstrous mountains
> Of huge despair, and foul affliction's valleys,
> Am grown a screech-owl to myself each morning.
> [OA, 329.5–8]

These foreign shepherds hail ostensibly from three different places: Agelastus from Athens, Philisides from "Samothea" (a legendary name for Britain when it enjoyed a Golden Age),[14] and Strephon and Klaius from we know not where exactly, except that it is some place other than Arcadia. We might best call them, though, not simply foreign or "stranger shepherds," as Sidney does (OA, 245), but rather "literary" shepherds since their common and real place of origin is Sannazaro's *Arcadia*, Montemayor's *Diana*, and the literary tradition lying behind those works and extending back to Virgil.

THE PLACING OF the author in his own work under an assumed name was a well-established convention of pastoral poetry. By the time of Servius's fourth-century commentary, Virgil's Tityrus was understood as a portrait of Virgil himself, and Sannazaro appears as the character Sincero in the Italian *Arcadia;* Sincero, like Philisides after him, tells his life story in prose and verse after coming to Arcadia to recover from the effects of love. Strephon and Klaius may not point as obviously as Philisides does to the pastoral convention, but their lineage is nonetheless the same. These two gentlemen are hopelessly in love with the same maid, yet their love has sparked a friendship between them "of so high a quality . . . that they never so much as brake company one from the other, but continued their pursuit, like two true runners both employing their best speed, but one not hindering the other" (OA, 328); it seems fair to say that they were modeled primarily upon Montemayor's Sireno and Sylvano, friends and rivals in love whose laments occupy the opening pages of the *Diana*. It is a debt that the opening of the *New Arcadia*, with the reappearance of Strephon and Klaius and their direct echoes of Sireno's lament, makes even more explicit.[15] There is, however, evidence of a considerable debt in Strephon and Klaius to Sannazaro's *Arcadia* as well. If Montemayor is mainly responsible for the details in the biographical account of Strephon and Klaius, their most accomplished and most widely known song, the double sestina "Ye goat-herd gods," is clearly based on Sannazaro's Fourth Eclogue; it has been best read, in fact, as a specific critique of that poem, undermining Sannazaro's easy resolutions and indeed the overall appeal of pastoral experience as it is rendered in that poem and in the whole of the Italian *Arcadia*.[16]

The fact that Sidney was indebted to both these pastoral sources is of some interest, for it suggests the full range of his discomfort with prior pastoral writing. His use of (and departure from) Sannazaro's double sestina in "Ye goat-herd gods" reveals well the extent of Sidney's uneasiness with the mood of melancholic nostalgia that is the keynote of Sannazaro's pastoral work and of Italian Renaissance pastoral generally. The same mood pervades the opening scene and much of the rest of Montemayor's *Diana*. But the *Diana* also qualifies, much more than the loosely structured Italian work, as an example of the pastoral romance form. That Sidney specifically evokes Montemayor's work in addition to Sannazaro's serves to indicate that he was uncomfortable also with the pastoral romance form; this latter discomfort was to lead to a variation upon the form which was in fact a subversion of it.

Sannazaro's Fourth Eclogue is one of those which brings its singers praise from the shepherds gathered around them. The poem is presented as a singing contest, and one of its speakers, Logisto, initially refuses to participate unless prizes are to be awarded to the winner. The judge of the contest, Selvaggio, rules that the traditional pastoral wagers—a sheep with two lambs, a goat, and a beech-wood cup—should not be offered and announces instead that it will be enough that the winner of the contest earn praise and the loser shame (p. 82). In the contest, both singers start, much as Strephon and Klaius after them do, by lamenting how often the surrounding woods, fields, and valleys, have heard their complaints. But halfway through the poem, Elpino finds some respite from his pain. A mysterious voice from amid the rocks has told him of a happier day to come which will prompt him to sing sweeter verse (lines 31–36). Thereafter in the poem Elpino's joy alternates with Logisto's continued complaint. If the promised joy were in fact to come to Elpino, he would see himself capable of Orpheus's poetic achievements, able to make the very woods and rocks move (lines 43–49). Logisto, for his part, will only keep on uttering laments until such time as the day gives no light to the happy fields and the rocks in a sheltered valley have cause to fear light breezes (lines 73–75). But despite this divergence in fates, Logisto at least gains the consolation of being judged a distinguished poet by his pastoral peers. The eclogue is heard in rapt silence by the shepherd band, every member of which with greatest admiration praises both singers; and Selvaggio, in traditional manner, judges both worthy of highest praise (p. 86).

There are three different sources of consolation for the poet-lovers of Sannazaro's eclogue: recognition as distinguished poets; the sympathy that their natural surroundings give them when they are miserable (Logisto, for instance, speaks of having moved the trees and rocks to pity with his complaints [lines 17–18]); and for Elpino, that miraculous answer to his prayers which turns his plaints to joy. Sidney's Strephon and Klaius are granted none of these consolations. Their poem is not a singing contest but rather only a recitation of their grief. They do create great music for us, but they see it in their poem only as "plaining" and "deadly swannish" music. They are distinctly out of harmony with their country neighbors:

> Long since the happy dwellers of these valleys
> Have prayed me leave my strange exclaiming music,
> Which troubles their day's work, and joys of evening.
> [*OA*, 329.21–23]

And they are even more out of harmony with their direct natural surroundings (at those points in the poem when those surroundings are not merely internalized into mountains of despair and valleys of affliction):

> I wish to fire the trees of all these forests;
> I give the sun a last farewell each evening;
> I curse the fiddling finders-out of music;
> With envy I do hate the lofty mountains,
> And with despite despise the humble valleys;
> I do detest night, evening, day, and morning.
> [*OA*, 330.7–12]

With figures as despairing as this, there can be little question of sympathy for man from nature either. There was a time when Strephon and Klaius could acknowledge themselves esteemed for pleasant music (*OA*, 329.5), but sweet music now seems to Klaius like the sound of "dreadful cries of murdered men in forests" (*OA*, 330.6). An expression such as this last and the self-hatred that Strephon's stanza just quoted betrays point to a strength of emotion much more savage than anything the suffused melancholy characteristic of Sannazaro's Fourth Eclogue and his whole *Arcadia* might admit. It is at this level of emotion that Sannazaro breaks off pastoral song completely. And there is no end to this unhappiness: neither in the double sestina itself nor in their biographical account is there any sign that Strephon and Klaius have gained any relief either through venting their grief in pastoral song or from having taken up residence in a pastoral landscape.

Sannazaro's *Arcadia,* still closely attached to its lyric antecedents, mainly evokes a mood; Montemayor's *Diana* accommodates that mood to a fully developed plot. Magic or the miraculous is at the center of this plot, as it was at the center of Sannazaro's Fourth Eclogue, and in both cases that magic comes to stand for the consolation or relief that retreat to or continued residence in a pastoral setting might ideally provide. Renaissance pastoral romance plots generally move toward a reestablishment of mental peace and harmony and, following therefrom, often a new social order instituting harmony on levels beyond the merely personal. The main characters are usually pastoral sojourners from the heroic or courtly world who progress through a series of contrasting settings: from a troubled or turbulent court, to a more peaceful and refined pastoral landscape, and then often to a yet more refined, even supernatural or sacred center of this pastoral world, before an actual or implied return to the outside world.[17] Montemayor's Sireno and Sylvano, our main concern here, are native shepherds and not foreign gentlemen, and hence their story makes use of only the middle two settings; but what happens to them serves as a paradigm for the adventures of virtually all of the *Diana*'s characters. At the sacred Temple of Diana, the Lady Felicia, whom nature has blessed with divine knowledge, administers to both unhappy lovers a magic potion. By its means Sylvano forgets about his former unrequited love for Diana and falls in love instead with the shepherdess Selvagia, who has also partaken of the potion. Sireno's draught frees him from his past passion for Diana and enables him to live in close proximity to the now miserably married Diana, and with no remembrance of his past pain. This is perhaps not an ideal resolution for Sireno—and it was probably one of the reasons why Perez and Gil Polo felt a need to provide the promised second part of Montemayor's romance—but Sireno has at least gained some relief or consolation from his journey to the sacred temple. And even this limited relief is enough to drive home the contrast with Sidney's *Arcadia* and our characters of Strephon and Klaius, for whom there is no relief whatsoever.

That Sidney has taken two native shepherds from Montemayor (and Sannazaro) and made them foreign-born sojourners in Arcadia in effect starts the normal action and attendant readers' expectations of the Renaissance pastoral romance form in motion for us—only to bring us up short, by stopping that motion abruptly. None of the foreign-born shepherds of Sidney's eclogue sections, in fact, finds the peace and consolation that a sojourn in a pastoral landscape is customarily expected to offer. In this respect these foreign-born shepherds provide us a reflection in small of the action of the main plot in the prose sections of the *Old Arcadia*. While these shepherds constitute Sidney's most pronounced and explicit borrowing from the literary pastoral tradition, the particular treatment of them conveys his doubts about prior Renaissance pastoral's assumption that residence in a natural setting might bring happiness, peace, and relief from the difficulties of a more complex and troubled outside world. To see the full expression of those doubts, though, we need to examine the main plot of the *Old Arcadia*.

DEFINING ARCADIA

The central structure of the prose sections of the *Old Arcadia* embodies a debate over definitions of Arcadia. The debate itself is rehearsed twice over in the opening pages of the work and is then repeated a third time, with a finality that leaves little room for doubt which is Sidney's preferred definition, in the concluding trial scene. The two definitions are first presented with Duke Basilius's decision to withdraw into solitary retreat and his principal adviser's opposition to such an act. Basilius envisions an Arcadia after the manner of the literary pastoral tradition from Virgil to Sannazaro. Having consulted the oracle of Delphos from a vain desire to know the certainty of things to come ("wherein there is nothing so certain as our continual uncertainty" [*OA*, 5]), Basilius has learned that there are impending threats to his daughters by "princely" and "uncouth" means, respectively; that he himself is somehow to commit adultery with his own wife; and, most important, that on his throne "a foreign state" will sit—all in the course of a single "fatal year" (*OA*, 5.15–21). His response to these threats is to make the pastoral assumption that one can best avoid fortune's blows by adopting the position of a humble figure not worth fortune's while to disturb. He delegates his princely authority and retires with his wife and daughters to a solitary place where he can "draw himself out of her [fortune's] way by this loneliness"; there, for his pleasure, "he would be recreated with all those sports and eclogues wherein the shepherds of that country did much excel" (*OA*, 6). His Arcadia thereby becomes not the whole province he has up to now governed well enough but merely the literary pastoral tradition's sparsely populated countryside, beautified by shepherd song.

Philanax, Basilius's adviser, argues for the view that Arcadia is not merely pastureland and the solitary ground Basilius intends to live on for a year but a whole province with cities and neighboring provinces threatening at its borders, a political realm, then, that must be actively governed to be kept secure. Philanax condemns both the desire to consult the oracle and Basilius's impulse to turn his back upon his responsibilities in the public, political world and retire into pastoral retreat. Since Basilius has ruled well and justly all these years, there is no reason to seek new courses now. A prince should act like a prince at all times: "Let your subjects have you in their eyes, let them see the benefits of your justice daily more and more . . . [And] whether your time call you to live or die, do both like a prince" (*OA*, 7–8). It is standing upon one's own virtue which constitutes man's best defense against fortune's blows. By withdrawing into solitude Basilius is neglecting his proper responsibility both as a father and as a prince, and by not relying upon his own virtue he is abandoning the surest means to avoid evil.

Basilius's move into pastoral solitude is clearly a mistake. Not only does Philanax oppose it, but Sidney-as-narrator comments adversely upon it as well, noting that Basilius has only "dukely sophistry" with which to oppose Philanax's argument before he makes his will wisdom and proceeds with his plan to retire (*OA*, 9). Basilius's manifest foolishness notwithstanding, much the same debate with much the same result occurs immediately thereafter, with Pyrocles' and Musidorus's entrance upon the scene and Pyrocles' desire to stay longer in a land he claims to see as possessing qualities of prior literary Arcadias. As was the case with Basilius's consultation with Philanax, just and reasonable advice is heard and rejected by a figure not interested in reasonable arguments in the first place. In this version of the debate, Sidney acknowledges the long-standing connections between pastoral Arcadia and the Golden Age or Eden, only to reject the parallel by placing it in the mouth of a figure using it to hide his true reasons for wishing to remain in pastoral surroundings. We need to examine this debate in some detail both because it has been subject to misinterpretation and because it keeps reappearing, in one form or another, in subsequent English pastoral works.

Musidorus has in a judicious and princely manner—in precisely the way that Sidney urged upon his brother when the latter was to undertake his tour of Europe[18]—informed himself fully of Arcadia's strength and riches, the nature of its people, and the manner of their laws, and he is now anxious to move on. Arcadia has been for him merely another province among many, knowledge of whose features will better enable him to understand the conditions of, and hence to rule, his own country. But he has noticed a change in his cousin of late; the Macedonian prince, instead of devoting himself in his customary way to those things which would better his mind and enable him to convert right thinking into right action, seeks solitude. Like Philanax before him, Musidorus objects both to a change in conduct which has given such past evidence of virtue and to solitariness, "the sly enemy that doth most separate a man from well doing" (*OA*, 14). Pyrocles counters with a multifaceted argument in defense of an Arcadian sojourn, the various parts of which are not in perfect accord with one another.

Musidorus has charged that Pyrocles has let his mind fall asleep (*OA*, 13), and Pyrocles at first admits that he has been relaxing, though for an ultimately salutary purpose: for "the mind itself must, like other things sometimes be unbent, or else it will be either weakened or broken" (*OA*, 14).[19] His defense begins in earnest, though, when he moves quickly from this disarming honesty to the suggestion that knowledge that leads to good action is not, in any case, all the mind can stretch itself unto. "Who knows," he asks in a rhetorical question (that often specious mode of argumentation which frequently manages to suggest without actually stating outright), "whether I feed not my mind with higher thoughts?" His claim would appear to be, then, that he is not relaxing at all, but rather is devoting his mind in his Arcadian solitude to contemplation:

> the workings of the mind, I find, much more infinite than can be led unto by the eye or imagined by any that distract their thoughts without themselves. And in such contemplations, or, as I think, more excellent, I enjoy my solitariness; and my solitariness, perchance, is the nurse of these contemplations. Eagles, we see fly alone; and they are but sheep which always herd together. Condemn not, therefore, my mind sometimes to enjoy itself, nor blame the taking of such times as serve most fit for it! [*OA*, 14–15]

Musidorus has appealed to a life of well doing or action, and Pyrocles, countering with this appeal, is reopening one of the major debates of Italian and English Humanism, whether (as the wording of Sidney's *Defence* has it) "the contemplative or active life do excell." Sidney admits in a parenthesis that Pyrocles' argument on behalf of contemplation might well have satisfied some listeners, presumably ones like Francis Bacon, whose endorsement of the contemplative life and firm association of that life with Abel's pastoral existence has already been quoted in Chapter I. But Pyrocles himself is not content with this argument and jumps to still another defense of his solitariness; he commends the Arcadian landscape, not as a place for contemplation, but simply for its beauty, enough in itself to justify a sojourn there:

> "And lord! dear cousin," said he, "doth not the pleasantness of this place carry in itself sufficient reward for any time lost in it, or for any such danger that might ensue? Do you not see how everything conspires to-

gether to make this place a heavenly dwelling? Do you not see the grass, how in colour they excel the emeralds, everyone striving to pass his fellow—and yet they are all kept in an equal height? And see you not the rest of all these beautiful flowers, each of which would require a man's wit to know, and his life to express? Do not these stately trees seem to maintain their flourishing old age with the only happiness of their seat, being clothed with a continual spring because no beauty here should ever fade? Doth not the air breathe health, which the birds, delightful both to the ear and eye, do daily solemnize with the sweet concent of their voices? Is not every echo here a perfect music? And these fresh and delightful brooks, how slowly they slide away, as loath to leave the company of so many things united in perfection! And with how sweet a murmur they lament their forced departure! Certainly, certainly, cousin, it might needs be that some goddess this desert belongs unto, who is the soul of this soil; for neither is any less than a goddess worthy to be shrined in such a heap of pleasures, nor any less than a goddess could have made it so perfect a model of the heavenly dwellings." [OA, 15]

Pyrocles' various defenses of Arcadian solitude have been rising in a crescendo, as is to be seen in the number of words devoted to each justification for his conduct and the amount of emotion poured into them. This final praise of Arcadia for its beauty constitutes not only his most impassioned appeal but indeed as much as might be said on behalf of Arcadia generally. What is claimed for Arcadia here is a return, even if necessarily brief and limited, to a Golden Age or Edenic existence when there was eternal spring and when earthly conditions reflected those of heaven. A sojourn in such a place would presumably offer, then, not simply Basilius's desired freedom from external danger but a much more significant possibility of regaining some measure of the original righteousness which characterized man in his initial ideal state; in such a setting, it is assumed, man draws near to the divine again.

Unfortunately, as eloquent as Pyrocles' praise of Arcadia is, there is much to suggest that neither he nor Sidney really believes it. Musidorus might well argue that he has seen the place Pyrocles describes before. Pyrocles' Arcadia has all of the main ingredients of the *locus amoenus,* a rhetorical set piece which had an independent poetical existence and history and could be placed in diverse contexts for varied ends. Its details had been firmly established in landscape descriptions in rhetorical and school exercises and in pastoral and erotic poetry extending from the time of the Roman Empire to the sixteenth century and beyond. Accordingly, Pyrocles waxes enthusiastic over this natural setting's meadows, flowers, trees, birdsong, and brooks, in large part because so many other poets and rhetoricians have done so before him.[20] Recourse to a rhetorical convention is of course not in itself necessarily evidence of insincerity; but any eloquence expended in it tends to be undermined when one's debating opponent refuses to play the game of accepting the convention without comment and instead points directly at its borrowed quality—which is what Musidorus proceeds to do in his answer. More damaging yet is Sidney's prior announcement that Pyrocles intended to inform Musidorus of his true reason for wishing to stay on in Arcadia and of his intention to assume the disguise of an Amazon to gain access to Basilius's younger daughter (*OA*, 12). Hence, whether Pyrocles is at all sincerely taken with Arcadia's natural beauty or is simply practicing his rhetorical skills, the Golden Age or Edenic characteristics of this Arcadian landscape are very much beside the point. The various defenses of Arcadia are in fact merely attempts to soften the blow that is to follow shortly, the confession that Pyrocles is in love.[21]

Musidorus, for his part, is inclined from the beginning to see their, and indeed any, debate over the relative merits of the active and contemplative lives as, in fact, a debate between the active and the idle lives. And here he sees not only that there are signs of perturbation in Pyrocles ("a kind of shaking unstaidness over all his body") but also that the different arguments Pyrocles has put forth do not agree with one another: "[Musidorus] might perceive in him store of thoughts rather stirred than digested . . . and the tenor of his speech (though of his wonted phrase) not knit together to one constant end but rather dissolved in itself, as the vehemency of the inward passion prevailed" (*OA*, 16). He has an argument prepared to counter Pyrocles' claim for contemplation's superiority to action, an argument which is traditional and predictable enough in its turn. It is, however, less susceptible to dismissal as mere rhetoric than Pyrocles' opposing argument because it is not actually delivered aloud:

> that in action a man did not only better himself but benefit others; that the gods would not have delivered a soul into the body which hath arms and legs (only instruments of doing) but that it were intended the mind should employ them; and that the mind should best know his own good or evil by practice. [*OA*, 16]

But because he sees Pyrocles as more passionate in his praise of Arcadia's natural (even supernatural) beauty than in his defense of the contemplative life, he moves directly to Pyrocles' final justification and proceeds to demonstrate that he is as conversant as Pyrocles with the various *topoi* a rhetorician might draw upon. It is here that he shows his recognition of the conventional quality of Pyrocles' praise and calls his cousin to task for it:

> But I marvel at the excessive praises you give to this desert. In truth, it is not unpleasant; but yet, if you would return into Macedon, you should see either many heavens or find this no more than earthly. And even Tempe, in my Thessalia, where you and I (to my great happiness) were brought up together, is nothing inferior unto it. But I think you will make me see that the vigour of your wit can show itself in any subject; or else you feed sometimes your solitariness with the conceits of the poets whose liberal pens can as easily travel over mountains as molehills, and so (like well disposed men) set up everything to the highest note—especially when they put such words in the mouth of one of these fantastical mind-infected people that children and musicians call lovers. [*OA*, 16–17]

Ernst Robert Curtius notes that even for the ancients Tempe had become the generic name of a variety of *locus amoenus*.[22] That *topos* was often used to set the scene in erotic poetry, and Musidorus reveals his knowledge of one of the more common uses of such scene painting by suggesting what would ordinarily come next. His mention of those "fantastical mind-infected people that children and musicians call lovers" is designed, then, to smoke Pyrocles out. And his wit has precisely that effect, as Pyrocles now confesses outright that he has fallen in love, an occurrence he refers to not in the high-flown, rationalizing terms of his earlier defenses of an Arcadian sojourn but merely as "the fatal overthrow of all my liberty" (*OA*, 17).

Pyrocles and Musidorus have had the same upbringing and heretofore have shared the same system of moral values. At their initial entrance it was noted that, with their increase in years, they had taken it "very timely into their minds that the divine part of man was not enclosed in this body for nothing" and hence had given themselves "wholly over to those knowledges which might in the course of their life be ministers to well doing" (*OA*, 10). Thus Pyrocles might well be able to predict what his cousin's reaction will be to his confession of love. And Musidorus reacts much as Pyrocles feared he would (although perhaps with more humor), first interrupting Pyrocles' confession with a cry of mock horror, "Now the eternal gods forbid," and then continuing in the same vein with an exaggerated refusal to believe the evidence of his own senses: "And is it possible that this is Pyrocles, the only young prince in the world, formed by nature and framed by education to the true exercise of virtue?" (*OA*, 18). As his reference to Pyrocles' education suggests, Musidorus has put on the robes, howsoever lightly, of his and Pyrocles' moral tutors and indeed Sidney's own Humanist mentors. To divert one's thoughts from the way of goodness and give oneself over to love is "to lose, nay to abuse your time," an abuse that becomes particularly heinous when one is sorely missed by one's father and native country (*OA*, 19). In such an appeal, Musidorus perhaps echoes, perhaps anticipates (depending upon the date of composition of this debate), Hubert Languet's rebuke of Sidney himself for his lengthy rustication at Wilton in 1580: "Consider well, I entreat you, how far it is honourable to you to lurk where you are, whilst your country is imploring the aid and support of her sons."[23] And even with its greater measure of humor, Musidorus's argument promotes precisely the set of values which Philanax gave expression to in counseling Basilius and which Euarchus is to evoke again at the work's conclusion. Duty to the state has highest claim and certainly supersedes satisfaction of one's merely personal desires; and virtue, to be considered virtue at all, must be constantly maintained: "for . . . there is no man suddenly either excellently good or extremely evil, but grows either as he holds himself up in virtue or lets himself slide into viciousness" (*OA*, 19).

Once Pyrocles admits that he is in love and Musidorus calls upon the standards of their joint education and training, the debate deteriorates sharply and need concern us little further. Pyrocles' defense of love itself, even more than his specious defense of an Arcadian sojourn, is a ragbag of miscellaneous points, an occasional good stroke (women are not necessarily incapable of virtue) offset by a large number of quibbles and, as one critic has aptly noted, an occasional old chestnut (women must be virtuous and honorable because mother was a woman).[24] Pyrocles makes a feint toward climbing a Platonic ladder of love, up which several critics have followed him, in fact passing him along the way: he divides the heavenly love Musidorus has spoken of into two, love itself and the excellency of the thing loved, and suggests that he will get to raising his sights to heavenly objects later; in the meantime he has work to do on the first, on making himself a proper instrument for any kind of love (*OA*, 22). As we might expect, love is finally not to be defended by reasonable argument at all, and the whole debate is resolved by an emotional bribe: if Musidorus forsakes his cousin now he will have to bear the onus of having abandoned a friend at time of greatest need.

The debate thus ends in highly unsatisfactory manner, as far as the princes' (and Sidney's own) moral tutors would be concerned. Musidorus's initial conception of Arcadia as a province one visits to gain knowledge of a political and social nature that can prove serviceable in ruling one's own land has been countered and in effect overcome by a conception of Arcadia as a natural shelter where one can find *otium* and, after the manner of Renaissance pastoral particularly, devote oneself to love and to poeticizing about that devotion. And matters do not get any better when, in what can be considered a coda to the debate, Musidorus finds that it is easier to condemn love than to resist it. He quickly falls in love with Pamela and disguises himself as (of all things) a shepherd, in order to be near her. His single-mindedness in the debate, his misogynism, and his refusal to see any virtue at all in Pyrocles' earthly love of a woman were in part preparation for the moment when with chagrin he would have to endure Pyrocles' revenge: "Why, how now, dear cousin . . . you that were even now so high in the pulpit against love, are you now become so mean an auditor? Remember that love is a passion, and that a worthy man's reason must ever have the masterhood" (*OA*, 42).

The full extent of Musidorus's recantation is shown nicely by his song in praise of solitude and the contemplative life, at the end of the Second Eclogues:

> O sweet woods, the delight of solitariness!
> O how much I do like your solitariness!
> Where man's mind hath a freed consideration
> Of goodness to receive lovely direction;
> Where senses do behold th'order of heav'nly host,
> And wise thoughts do behold what the creator is.
> Contemplation here holdeth his only seat,
> Bounded with no limits, borne with a wing of hope,
> Climbs even unto the stars; nature is under it.
>   [*OA*, 166.9–17]

The poem is cast in asclepiad meter, and very imperfectly so. Ringler has accordingly concluded that it represents one of Sidney's early experiments in measured verse and was only later placed in the *Old Arcadia*, in a context where it does not reside at all comfortably. For its praise of retired country life where no external danger or hidden treason exists is particularly inappropriate to the Second Eclogues, which are performed immediately after the rebellion of the Phagonian townspeople has disrupted the tranquil life of the rural lodges and forced Pyrocles and Musidorus to take up arms in defense of the royal family.[25] But Musidorus's praise of Arcadian solitude for the opportunity it presents for contemplation is in fact no more legitimate than Pyrocles' earlier similar argument. Musidorus is no more interested in the contemplative life than Pyrocles was, and once again the connection between pastoral Arcadia and the contemplative life is shown to be, in this work, a specious one. Musidorus's ostensible praise of Arcadian solitude turns out to be, finally, a means of bestowing praise on his beloved; in the third stanza he reveals a willingness to part with that blessed solitude in order to be with Pamela:

> O sweet woods, the delight of solitariness!
> O how well I do like your solitariness!
> Yet dear soil, if a soul closed in a mansion
> As sweet as violets, fair as a lily is,
> . . . .
> Oh! If such a one have bent to a lonely life,
> Her steps glad we receive, glad we receive her eyes.
>   And think not she doth hurt our solitariness,
>   For such company decks such solitariness.
>   [*OA*, 167.3–6, 13–16]

And Musidorus, like Pyrocles and Basilius before him, now assumes that he can afford to leave his obligations in the outside heroic and political world behind him and dwell for a while in a landscape he rather willfully sees as, in the words of the poem's earlier lines, "veiled in innocence," where "wrong's name is unheard" and where "Naught disturbs thy quiet" (*OA*, 166.25, 34, 18).

IF MUSIDORUS does not hold true to the principles he expounded in the debate with Pyrocles, the structure and argument of the *Old Arcadia* as a whole do. Though Pyrocles and Musidorus are still capable of some heroic action—they save the princesses from a lion and a bear and defend Basilius and the whole royal family from the rebellious mob from the town of Phagona—their love prompts them to acts which, while perhaps not appearing terribly serious in themselves, are punishable by death in Arcadian law, and for which they are brought before the bar. Both princes succumb to passion. After arranging the bed trick whereby Basilius and Gynecia sleep with one another instead of their desired Cleophila, Pyrocles proceeds to Philoclea's bedchamber, where the two spend the night in passionate lovemaking. Musidorus meanwhile, having persuaded Pamela to run off with him and be married in Thessaly, has stopped en route in another *locus amoenus* (*OA*, 197–98) so that she can rest; after twice swearing that he will offer no force to her before their marriage, Musidorus looks down upon the sleeping princess and immediately forgets his promise. "Overmastered with the fury of delight," he is about to attack the bulwark of her chastity, when the remnant of the rebel band enters and halts the near rape. In the trial scene which marks the culmination of the *Old Arcadia*, the princes are asked both to face up to the full seriousness of these actions and to acknowledge the dangers implicit in their original decision to stay on in Arcadia. Blinded by their love, our heroes prove unable to do so in any convincing manner.

The dominant figure in the trial scene, the character most responsible for the moral direction it takes, is its judge, Euarchus, father of Pyrocles and king of Macedon, who has not seen his son and nephew for some twelve years. The name "Euarchus" means "good ruler" in Greek, and Euarchus is Sidney's portrait of the ideal prince and a consistent and authoritative spokesman for the active life. His definition of Arcadia is clearly that which Philanax and Musidorus put forward at the work's beginning. He has come to Arcadia to draw Basilius from "this burying himself alive" and persuade him to return to an active life of doing good, not only because that is "the only happy action of man's life" but because the safety of Arcadia and indeed all of Greece depends upon it (OA, 359). With his insistence upon fulfilling one's public responsibility and upon relying on one's own virtue as a source of strength, Euarchus in effect follows Philanax's opening advice and serves as a corrective to Basilius and as a model for that (or any) ruler, both as a man and as a prince:

> Euarchus did not further exceed his meanest subject with the greatness of his fortune than he did surmount the greatness of his fortune with the greatness of his mind; in so much that those things which oftentimes the best sort think rewards of virtue, he held them not at so high price, but esteemed them servants to well doing, the reward of virtue being in itself; on which his inward love was so fixed that it never was dissolved into other desires, but keeping his thoughts true to themselves, was neither beguiled with the painted gloss of pleasure nor dazzled with the false light of ambition. This made the line of his actions straight and always like itself, no worldly thing being able to shake the constancy of it. [OA, 357–58]

Although Euarchus no doubt was conceived primarily as a public figure, such a description reveals Sidney's belief that there is not, or at least ought not to be, any breach between the private and the public man.

Euarchus's principled dedication to an active life of well doing makes him a stern judge. Philanax at the opening of the Old Arcadia advised Basilius to live and act like a prince at all times; Euarchus lives in such a manner and expects other princes to live that way as well. Hence he cannot allow Pyrocles' and Musidorus's claim to immunity from the laws because of their royal blood, for they "not only left to do like princes but to be like princes" when they entered into Arcadia in disguise and as private persons (OA, 404). He disallows as well Musidorus's plea that the princes' past honorable actions should influence his decision. Their honorable services are worthy of great reward, but cannot countervail their subsequent wickedness. Indeed, one who commits evil after earlier good deeds deserves even more to be punished, since he has shown that he knew what good actions were and then intentionally acted differently (*OA*, 405). Proceeding on such principles and still another fair-minded one, that "in equality of conjectures we are not to hold of the worst, but rather to be glad we may find any hope that mankind is not grown monstrous," Euarchus is able to acquit the princes of direct responsibility in the murder of the duke; yet "the fact . . . is nakedly without passion or partiality to be viewed" that Pyrocles does not deny offering violence to Philoclea and that Musidorus has admitted persuading Pamela to fly her country—both of which acts are punishable under "all the Grecian laws" with the death penalty (*OA*, 405).

It is important that we see how full is Sidney's endorsement of Euarchus's actions and statements in the trial scene, since a proper estimation of him helps to determine not only Sidney's purposes in the *Old Arcadia* but the likely use of that prince in the *New Arcadia* as well.[26] Admittedly, Euarchus does have a strict view of the law in general, and he does defend the law's severity: in opposition to Musidorus's attractive definition of laws as sea marks which enable ignorant passengers to avoid shipwreck (*OA*, 402), Euarchus proposes his own more limiting and conservative definition of them as "bounds" beyond which man should not go lest his nature range infinitely (*OA*, 404). He resists lengthy theoretical discussion of the nature and purpose of laws, confining himself instead to judgment according to the laws of Greece and the "municipal statutes" of Arcadia (*OA*, 404). But this last was the agreement he made with Philanax and the Arcadian people when he took on the position of protector (*OA*, 361); and the Arcadian penal code is, of course, not of Euarchus's making. Sidney himself would appear to be attempting to free Euarchus from the accusation of undue severity, by having him observe explicitly each time he hands down a death penalty that this particular punishment is required by Arcadian or all Greek statutes (*OA*, 383, 405, 406).

In the case of the princes, we know from having seen the action of the earlier books that Euarchus's conclusion about their guilt is essentially correct; if Pyrocles did not, as he confessed, attempt to rape Philoclea, he had his way with her nonetheless; and Musidorus did attempt to abduct Pamela (and added to that crime an attempt to violate her). Gynecia's case, however, is more complicated. The duchess's own remorse prompts her to confess to Basilius's murder without pausing to explain that his death was in fact accidental, that the apparent poison he drank was, she thought, a love potion and not intended for him in any event. That Euarchus may need greater judicial flexibility might appear to be suggested not simply by the apparent miscarriage of justice in Gynecia's conviction for murder but also by explicit comments to that effect from Pyrocles and Sidney himself as narrator.[27] Pyrocles' opinion is that Gynecia has prosecuted herself "more like the manner of passionate than guilty folks" and hence that condemnation may have been passed too quickly on her (*OA*, 393). Sidney's own earlier comment similarly takes note of the fact that she has overhastily condemned herself:

> Thus the excellent lady Gynecia, having passed five and thirty years of her age even to admiration of her beautiful mind and body, and having not in her own knowledge ever spotted her soul with any wilful vice but her inordinate love of Cleophila, was brought, first by the violence of that ill-answered passion, and then by the despairing conceit she took of the judgement of God in her husband's death and her own fortune, purposely to overthrow herself, and confirm by a wrong confession that abominable shame which, with her wisdom, joined to the truth, perhaps she might have refelled. [*OA*, 384]

But Pyrocles' sympathetic grasp of the truth in Gynecia's case is in large part neutralized by the benefit brought to his own case should Gynecia be thought innocent: he is attempting to combat Philanax's suggestion of the likely collaboration between a confessed murderer and a confessed rapist with the contrary suggestion that not only is he innocent of murder but he believes Gynecia to be so as well. And Sidney's own comment on Gynecia is not directed toward any failure in Euarchus's judgment or method of arriving at the truth but rather simply toward noting the effect that passion and despair can have on ordinarily good people. Given Gynecia's desire to condemn herself there is little any human judge could do to find out the true circumstances of Basilius's death.

Euarchus looks upon justice as a never-changing pattern which man must strive to understand and imitate by the use of reason, freed from the effects of passion and partiality. He is not guilty of any undue pride or overconfidence in his ability to achieve such justice (as we shall see, quite the opposite is the case). And there is no valid appeal in the *Old Arcadia* to any quality attainable by man higher or more pervasive than his concept of justice. There is, for instance, no explicit plea for Christian mercy, nor for a concept of equity which would allow a governor to alter the written law when it is itself unjust or overly harsh in its rigorous adherence to general principles rather than individual circumstances. This is perhaps a limitation in the *Old Arcadia* and in Sidney's thought generally, but any argument we have on this account is with Sidney and not with Euarchus. Even if Euarchus's judgment proves wrong, there is every indication that

Sidney wishes us to honor him for his effort to bring peace and justice back to a land that has been becoming increasingly disordered since Basilius's original act of retirement into pastoral solitude.

When Euarchus agreed to become protector of Arcadia, he was warned by Philanax that his Arcadian stay was likely to be a test of his virtue: "this country falls to be a fair field to prove whether the goodly tree of your virtue will live in all soils" (OA, 361). By the time Euarchus adheres to "sacred rightfulness" and never-changing justice and orders the defendants he now knows to be his son and nephew to be led away to execution, it is clear both that he has passed the test Arcadia has set for him and that the princes have failed theirs. Our favorable estimation of Euarchus is in fact largely determined by the contrast between his steadiness and the more erratic conduct of the princes. On the night before the trial the princes have every appearance of having made considerable progress. In their confinement, the two fortify their courage with the "rampire of patience" and console themselves, finally, by raising their sights toward heaven and "that second delivery of ours when, void of sensible memory or memorative passion, we shall not see the colours but lives of all things that have been or can be" (OA, 373). But the very end of the trial scene particularly reveals how much moral distance the princes still have to travel. Just as Musidorus earlier fell away from the principles he advanced on behalf of reason and the active life against passion and an extended Arcadian sojourn, so again he fails to keep to the noble resolution of the prison scene. Enraged by having his hopes for survival and recovery of Pamela so suddenly dashed again, Musidorus denounces Euarchus as a tyrant and a murderer, in the process plainly giving in to passion once again, which act suggests little overall change or improvement in his character. And even while Pyrocles rebukes his cousin for his diatribe, "willing him to consider it was their own fault and not his [Euarchus's] unjustice" which brought them to this pass (OA, 413), he reveals how much he too falls short of Euarchus's model and ideals. In making his own final plea for his cousin's life, Pyrocles accepts Euarchus's principle that rulers must always serve as models to their people: he argues that Euarchus's execution of his own son will provide a sufficient example of justice to the populace. But he warns his father to "take heed . . . lest seeking too precise a course of justice, you be not thought most unjust" (OA, 414). His argument here is limited to terms of what others are to think of Euarchus's action, and he thereby betrays that he has learned only half of what Euarchus might wish to teach him; he shares no part of Euarchus's vision of a never-changing justice. Sidney's own final approval of Euarchus's conduct and ideals, on the other hand, is made explicit in a comment, immediately following Pyrocles' final plea, on the reactions of the spectators at the trial:

> most of them, examining the matter by their own passions, thought Euarchus (as often extraordinary excellencies, not being rightly conceived, do rather offend than please) an obstinate-hearted man, and such a one, who being pitiless, his dominion must needs be insupportable. But Euarchus, that felt his misery more than they, and yet loved goodness more than himself, with such a sad assured behaviour as Cato killed himself withal, when he heard the uttermost of that their speech tended unto, he commanded again they [Pyrocles and Musidorus] should be carried away. [*OA*, 414]

But if Euarchus is as faultless as I have been claiming, we might well ask why Sidney and Euarchus himself have been insisting, from the time of Euarchus's first entrance, on the limitations of man and his powers of reason. When Philanax first saw Euarchus, the Macedonian king was "taking his rest under a tree with no more affected pomps than as a man that knew, howsoever he was exalted, the beginning and end of his body was earth" (*OA*, 355–57). The first words we hear from Euarchus's own mouth—"Although long experience hath made me know all men (and so princes, which be but men) to be subject to infinite casualties, the very constitution of our lives remaining in continual change . . ." (*OA*, 362)—acknowledge how little control man has over his own life. Such statements tend to suggest that any claim to ideal conduct or adherence to principles of never-changing justice cannot help but be suspect. And one expression of Euarchus's humility would appear to be preparing us directly for some mistake in his judgment: "But remember," he says to the Arcadian people, "I am a man; that is to say, a creature whose reason is often darkened with error" (*OA*, 365). But the only possible error that he falls victim to is in the conviction of Gynecia, and that "error" arises not as a result of a mistake or fault in his logic or mode of reasoning but from a necessary inability, because he is only a human being, to see into the hearts and minds of other human beings. These statements by Euarchus and Sidney are no more directed toward criticism of Euarchus than are the statements, already cited, on the evident miscarriage of justice in Gynecia's case; they are better seen, rather, as preparation for a final turn in the action and some intervention by a higher power, one without Euarchus's human limitations. The faculty of reason that Euarchus relies on and praises is to be seen as the best human guide, as far as it can reach. But man, while remaining fully responsible for his own actions, must recognize not only a system of abstract laws—justice—outside himself but also the existence of a moving power, whose ways man cannot always comprehend.

In defending Euarchus's action at the trial, Sidney likens the judge's bearing to that of Cato when he killed himself (*OA*, 414). But there is in Euarchus's conduct more than a Stoic reliance upon reason and insistence on one's integrity as the way to withstand the blows of irrational fortune in a hostile world. In Book IV, Philoclea opposed Pyrocles' determination to commit suicide with an argument of a distinctly un-Stoic cast: it is not for us to determine for God when he will help us; to leave early, "to prejudicate his determination," is "but a doubt of goodness in him who is nothing but goodness" (*OA*, 297). Euarchus's recognition of his own humanity, and hence frailty, is another expression of that essentially Christian cast of mind. For the recognition of human frailty postulates a belief in a higher power which can toss a man about like a tennis ball from its racket if it so wishes, but which, whether man can comprehend its purposes or not, operates above and independent of even the finest of human actions. And hence it is, just as Pyrocles and Musidorus are to be led away to execution, after Euarchus has held to ideals that Sidney himself would approve of and has judged in the best manner possible for a human being, Basilius awakens and overturns Euarchus's judgment. "Considering all had fallen out by the highest providence" (*OA*, 416), Basilius sees that the oracle's words have been fulfilled, pardons the princes, and, to the great joy of Euarchus, agrees to the marriage between them and his daughters.

The explicit recognition of human frailty and its concomitant implication of the existence of some higher power suggest that we do not need to apologize for, or explain away, the often maligned ending of the *Old Arcadia*. The sudden reversal of fortunes for the princes is not merely a structural characteristic taken over by Sidney from the Greek romances;[28] nor are we forced to conclude that the final pardon of Pyrocles and Musidorus undercuts Euarchus's heroic adherence to "sacred rightfulness."[29] The figure insisting on rightfulness and justice would himself approve of the overturning of his judgment, and the change in the princes' fortune is fully prepared for by Sidney and desired by us. It is true that Sidney does not give the princes much firm ground to stand on in the trial. Their every excuse and objection is explicitly and reasonably overruled by Euarchus. And their motives in the course of the trial are often not of the highest nature: contributing to Pyrocles' delight when he heard that Philoclea would live, though in a convent, was the knowledge that no one after him would enjoy her (*OA*, 381); Musidorus's later tirade against his judge was in part induced by his intense desire to live, and to live with Pamela, regardless of the interests of justice (*OA*, 412). It is quite understandable, but nonetheless still true, that the princes do not pay much attention to the idealistic principles Euarchus is enunciating throughout the trial. And they have been guilty of misconduct. The evidence at the trial may not have shown that they let their passion get the better of them, but we have witnessed it, and it is enough to convince us that some kind of chastisement or punishment is in order.

But, of course, the death penalty is much too harsh a one. For, despite their faults, we never lose sympathy with Pyrocles and Musidorus, and it is very important for the success of Sidney's work that we do not. We must both be prepared to accept Euarchus's judgment upon them as just and, in order to accept the sudden turnabout at the end, want the princes to be pardoned. And there is much in the *Old Arcadia* which ensures our continued liking for the two princes. As rather conventional chivalric heroes, they perform appropriate heroic deeds both in Arcadia and earlier, in Asia Minor. Pyrocles, in his willingness to confront the Phagonian rebels and convince them that they love their duke after all, demonstrates both his bravery and his shrewdness. And because they are rather conventional chivalric heroes, their expressions of both love and friendship are suitably exalted and ingratiating, even if their actions do not always correspond to those sentiments. Pyrocles' desire to commit suicide in order to preserve Philoclea's reputation, for instance, is noble, even if misguided. A less conventional trait, and one therefore probably more likely to stir our affections on their behalf, is the strong sense of humor in both princes. While indulging themselves in their conventional praise of their mistresses or the ground these mistresses walk on, they often show an awareness that they are mouthing clichés, as in, for instance, that debate in which they match *loci amoeni*. And we are no more likely than Musidorus to turn against someone who defends himself from the charge that love of a woman is making him effeminate by announcing that he wants nothing more than to prove himself a man in the venture (*OA*, 22–23).

Most of all, though, we want the princes to survive their Arcadian adventure because we, as part of Sidney's implied audience, have been thoroughly compromised by the figure speaking to us as narrator. This compromise takes the form both of expressed enthusiasm for the princes and princesses and of incidental comments on the extent and power of love. Sidney, his Preface tells us, wrote the *Old Arcadia* primarily for his sister, the Countess of Pembroke, but the audience implied would appear to include a small group of friends, mainly female, since there are frequent references within the text to the readers as "fair" or "worthy ladies." These direct addresses to the readers usually accompany a reference to experience shared by the readers and the characters in the tale—and the shared experience is usually love. In commenting, for instance, on how love even in the solitary woods infected both Gynecia and Basilius with passion for the same Amazon lady, Sidney pauses to say:

> it seems to myself I use not words enough to make you see how they could in one moment be so overtaken. But you, worthy ladies, that have at any time feelingly known what it means, will easily believe the possibility of it. Let the ignorant sort of people give credit to them that have passed the doleful passage, and daily find that quickly is the infection gotten which in long time is hardly cured. [*OA*, 49]

Again, in the First Eclogue section, Sidney moves away from a discussion of the love afflicting the various royal characters, and especially Gynecia, with:

> But another place shall serve to manifest her agonies; this, being dedicated only to pastorals, shall bend itself that way, and leave all those princely motions to their considerations that, untold, can guess what love means. [*OA*, 57]

And at the first extended mention of love in the *Old Arcadia*, when Pyrocles falls in love with Philoclea's portrait, the emotion is described in a manner that is far from disparaging:

> As the most noble heart is most subject unto it, from questions grew to pity; and when with pity once his heart was made tender, according to the aptness of the humour, it received straight a cruel impression of that wonderful passion which to be defined is impossible, by reason no words reach near to the strange nature of it. They know it which inwardly feel it. It is called love. [*OA*, 11–12]

Love throughout the *Old Arcadia* is seen as something which is powerful, sometimes wonderful, often dangerous, but which in any case cannot be controlled. If we have all felt the force of this passion, as Sidney asserts, then we cannot look too harshly upon Pyrocles and Musidorus for succumbing to it also. Though events in the tale force us to take a more cautious and dispassionate view of the effects of love, we have by these appeals to common experience been implicated in the princes' fortunes enough certainly not to wish them killed off in the work's final pages.[30]

WE RETAIN OUR sympathy with Pyrocles and Musidorus, then, but see their sojourn in Arcadia as far from a triumph. The frame provided by Philanax's and Musidorus's opening arguments and Euarchus's judgment and conduct in the trial scene makes sure of that latter observation. And judged along with Pyrocles and Musidorus, and adversely so, is the conception of Arcadia they subscribe to when they decide to abandon the principles of their education and devote themselves instead to what they incorrectly envision as a quiet, retired life. This conception plainly comes to them, and to Sidney, by way of the prior literary pastoral tradition: the safety and peace, the harmony between man and nature, that Pyrocles and Musidorus (and Basilius before them) think they are gaining are the Arcadian charms suggested in the opening paragraph of the work and in conventional pastoral poems and romances before it. And once in their Arcadia, all three figures devote themselves almost exclusively to the major Renaissance pastoral activity, love. Although perhaps not consistently aware of it themselves (the princes have to be reminded of it in their trial), all three act in their pastoral pursuits under the assumption that they are only private, not public, figures. This would be legitimate behavior in previous pastoral, a mode concerned with the cultivation of the inner as opposed to the public man. But here, figures wishing to pursue a pastoral life find themselves confronted with a judge who defines Arcadia as an actual province, a part of the public, political world, no different from any other country one might wander into; Arcadia is not, for him, a realm of special conditions established by a literary convention, where one is allowed to disregard normal responsibilities of the day-to-day world in order to concentrate on something else.

And this judge has, as well, definitions of love and marriage which are decidedly public in their orientation. Marriage, for him, is far more than a mere private agreement between two consenting parties. It involves a commitment to society and its continuance as a whole (much as it does in Shakespearian comedy). Hence Euarchus justifies the death penalty for Pyrocles' confessed rape, on grounds that a "general ruin" follows upon the taking by force "that which, being holily used, is the root of humanity" (*OA*, 406). And he sees love as rightly called love only when it remains within the bounds of morally and socially responsible conduct: "That sweet and heavenly uniting of minds, which properly is called love, hath no other knot but virtue; and therefore if it be right love, it can never slide into any action that is not virtuous" (*OA*, 407). Pyrocles and Musidorus might wish to object that Euarchus oversimplifies the problems love presents. But given their faults and the actions they have confessed to, the only response they might justly give to his definition is that they have been unable to reconcile their own private desires with the demands that adherence to an active life of well doing, governed by the principles of reason, places upon them.

The *Old Arcadia* does not work out any accommodation between these private and public demands. The final scene is concerned with judgment and then with providential intercession, with recognition of one's failings, and not with reconciling opposites. This makes for a very unusual use of the pastoral romance form. For we have that form's crucial sojourn in a pastoral setting, but the Arcadian sojourn ends by intensifying personal difficulties rather than resolving them. Sidney is plainly not using Arcadia to bring man back into harmony with nature or to bring about a harmony within the human psyche. Nor, as I suggested in my first chapter, is he being necessarily fair to the previous pastoral tradition while evoking it. He has systematically deprived pastoral experience of any ethical underpinnings, refusing to let stand as legitimate, for instance, its claims to provide spiritual renewal or opportunity for development of the inner man; and he has placed retreat into a pastoral setting in a context in which it appears irresponsible, while ignoring entirely the possible drawbacks that might result from commitment to an active life of service to the state (for instance, the compromise of one's ideals that involvement in day-to-day governing often seems to entail). The final book, with its introduction of Euarchus's vision and definitions, simply reasserts a hierarchy of values in which responsibility in the public, political world holds precedence over satisfaction of personal desires. Such responsibility allows little time for and accords little value to the pastoral life practiced by the main characters in this *Arcadia* or to the life pictured, and implicitly praised, in prior Renaissance pastoral works. The noblest prospect that this particular Arcadia offers its sojourners is the high road that leads them toward Macedonia.

CHAPTER III

Sidney's New Arcadia

THE PROCESS OF REVISION

WHY DID Sidney revise the *Old Arcadia* into the *New*? Since 1935 and Kenneth Orne Myrick's influential study, *Sir Philip Sidney as a Literary Craftsman*, answers to that question have been almost invariably bound up with consideration of the genres of the two versions. Myrick argued that the *New Arcadia* (but not the *Old*) was explicitly designed by Sidney as a heroic poem, in accord with dictates set down by Minturno and reflected in Sidney's own *Defence of Poetry*.[1] It is generally agreed today that the *New Arcadia* is indeed a heroic poem in prose, written after the manner of Xenophon's *Cyropaedia* and Heliodorus's *Aethiopica* as those works are described in the *Defence;* the *Old Arcadia,* on the other hand, is usually seen as belonging to some other genre, for instance, the comic novel, tragicomedy, Terentian comedy, something akin to tragedy, or simply pastoral romance. The effect of this generic distinction between the two versions has been to widen the gap between them and in the process particularly to present the princes Pyrocles and Musidorus in two very different lights. They tend to emerge from critical studies of the *Old Arcadia* (as they have from the preceding chapter) rather tarnished figures and from studies of the *New Arcadia* as fully admirable heroes, to be considered in much the way Sidney himself in the *Defence* views Aeneas, as direct models for heroic and moral conduct.[2]

And it is not simply the two princes who are transformed by asserting a generic distinction between the two *Arcadia*s: the Arcadian landscape the princes inhabit is likely to be altered as well. There was a strong insistence in the *Old Arcadia* that any figure desiring to be honorable or virtuous could not afford to let down his moral guard and indulge in the dreams of ease or personal gratification that the pastoral setting of the work inevitably seemed to encourage. If the princes are conceived as intended by Sidney to leave the *New Arcadia* indisputably heroic figures, inherently good rather than sharply divided or flawed, the animus against a pastoral sojourn for them could reasonably be expected to be toned down. Even Arcadia might serve as a setting for the display of the princes' exemplary nature, and there ought to be no particular harm, and perhaps even some advantage, in abandoning for a while that adherence to the active life of well doing which the *Old Arcadia* affirms is the only source of true virtue.³

Certainly there is much in the *New Arcadia* to support an argument for an altered conception both of the two princes and of the genre in which they are placed. A vast majority of the material added to that taken over from the *Old Arcadia* involves heroic action of some sort, and in this new action the princes themselves are the major participants. But the idea that Sidney simply changed genres implies both a definite decision made at some specific time and a sharp alteration of (among other things) the "*Idea* or fore-conceit" of his work. Yet the little we know, or are able to construct, about Sidney's methods of composition tends to run counter to such an assumption. What I propose to do as preparation for the discussion of the *New Arcadia* itself is to leave aside both the question of genre and the terms of the *Defence,* both of which have I believe had a role in clouding our perception of what actually happens in the *New Arcadia;* instead I should like to pursue the implications arising from what we do know about Sidney's working methods in the process of revising the *Old Arcadia* into the *New.* In such an enterprise, the nature and very existence of those changes in the 1593 *Arcadia* that we can attribute to Sidney himself tell us a great deal.

One of the two most extensive changes in the last three books of the 1593 *Arcadia* that we can confidently assign to Sidney's own hand—and the most important for the present purpose—is in the treatment of the scene in Philoclea's bedchamber which in the *Old Arcadia* culminates in the sexual union between Pyrocles and Philoclea. The 1593 changes eliminate that sexual union and, along with it, Pyrocles' plan for seduction beforehand. In the *Old Arcadia* it was clear that Pyrocles expected to be still in Arcadia after his night with Philoclea. In the 1593 version of this scene, Sidney explicitly states several times that Pyrocles goes to Philoclea's chamber so as to encourage her to flee with him to Macedonia and be married. She agrees, but overcome by the emotion consequent upon her discovery that Pyrocles loves her after all, falls asleep. The two are discovered lying side by side, but it is clear to us that physical consummation of their love has not taken place. This change eliminates Pyrocles' most morally questionable act in the *Old Arcadia* and would leave him available for much greater admiration in a completed *New Arcadia*. We do not know if Sidney would have had Pyrocles claim later in the *New Arcadia* (as he does in the *Old*) that he attempted violence on Philoclea and was rebuffed, but Pyrocles would be free in any case to proclaim the highest of motives and conduct both in Philoclea and himself, whether in a trial scene or under other circumstances, and not have us look askance on such claims because we know better.

The ten pages describing the bedchamber scene in the 1593 *Arcadia* are a mosaic of new material and passages carried over from the *Old Arcadia*, joined in a manner typical of Sidney's method in much of the *New Arcadia*: two lines of new material are followed by five from the *Old Arcadia;* seven lines that ensued in the *Old Arcadia* are omitted at this point (and reinserted later in the account); then fifteen lines of material from the *Old Arcadia* are included, along with a slight new qualification in the middle of them; they are followed by six lines of new material, two pages of old, then a changed brief phrase; and so on until two and one-half pages of primarily new writing close Book III.[4] The freedom with which the material from the *Old Arcadia* is handled—consecutive sentences are taken from widely separated contexts in the *Old Arcadia,* and material that was originally used to describe Musidorus and Pamela is here transferred to Pyrocles and Philoclea—argues convincingly for Ringler's conclusion that these pages are not the work of an editor or even simply part of a "direction" Sidney may have left with his friend Fulke Greville or someone else, but were in fact fully written out by Sidney himself.[5]

We do not have the same kind of direct verbal evidence pointing to Sidney's own authorship of the changes in Musidorus's conduct which similarly exculpate that hero from his worst *Old Arcadia* faults. All reference to Musidorus's near rape of Pamela is eliminated, but this is a change which involves merely cutting some twenty-five lines of text and thus could be the work of an editor as easily as of Sidney himself.[6] Yet in view of the close friendship between the two princes, their common upbringing and shared system of values, and the similar plight in which they find themselves—both are in disguise and attempting to woo a daughter of Basilius—it is unlikely that Sidney would have drawn a sharp distinction between the two by improving and ennobling Pyrocles while leaving Musidorus his old self. Sidney's own 1593 changes, we can conclude then, were likely to involve both princes and would have eliminated their most grievous faults; and this alteration in turn would have had the effect also of making us more sympathetic toward the princes. If Sidney planned to have Euarchus appear at the end of a completed *New Arcadia*—and as we shall see, there is good reason to think he did—the princes would presumably have greater claim to his, and our, respect than they do throughout the trial scene of the *Old Arcadia*.

The princes were plainly, as critical studies insisting on the differences between the two versions of Sidney's work claim, undergoing a change for the better in Sidney's mind as he moved from the *Old Arcadia* to the *New*. The 1593 edition's alterations in their conduct are fully of a piece with all the new added heroic material of Books I–III of the *New Arcadia*. The princes *were* going to be more admirable in a completed *New Arcadia*, on both moral and heroic grounds. But the 1593 changes attributable to Sidney point to something in addition to an ennobling of the princes. The three major changes by Sidney in the 1593 version—the two already described dealing with the princes and the account of Euarchus's journey to Arcadia in Book V—appear to have been written after the completion of Book II of the *New Arcadia* but before Sidney was very far into the revised Book III; both the revised bedchamber scene and the new account of Euarchus's journey refer directly to, or build upon, events taking place in Books I and II of the *New Arcadia,* but neither passage reveals any awareness whatsoever of events of the new Book III.[7] Written at that relatively late date in the course of his revising, Sidney's 1593 changes show us an author thinking in the terms of the material and plot line of the *Old Arcadia,* making significant changes in that material to be sure, but nonetheless intending to make whatever use of that old material he could in the future. While he is in the process of expanding that material's scope and adding considerably to it, he is also looking back to the context of the *Old Arcadia*. And this conclusion in turn suggests a *New Arcadia* in effect growing out of the *Old Arcadia,* not a sharp, conscious decision made before undertaking the revision to change utterly the genre of his work and along with it the way he viewed his major characters and the landscape in which they act.[8]

Simply placing the *Old* and *New Arcadia*s side by side and comparing them, whether or not such comparison is accompanied by assumptions about genre, tends to lead to a concentration only on the differences between the two versions. But as in all comparisons of a work with its main source, while we note that additions to and departures from the original material might reveal the direction in which a writer was moving, we have also to determine why the author was attracted to the source to begin with—or in the present instance, why he chose to stay with the original material rather than strike off toward something totally new. The decision to rework, expand, and add to the old material in this instance may well reflect a change in Sidney's thought; alternatively, it may just as easily reflect a desire to enlarge and deepen, to delve into the full implications of what was already there. A completed *New Arcadia* would of course help greatly in judging between these two alternatives. Failing that, we do have means (besides the mere comparison of the two versions) of estimating Sidney's overall intention in the *New Arcadia*. We can, for instance, examine the *New Arcadia*'s additions in themselves and not simply as departures from the first version, to see if they project a pattern of their own which might reveal Sidney's purposes. Accordingly, in the sections that follow, I shall look first at some of the revised version's new material—heroic material primarily in the episodes—to see what it can tell us about the princes of the *New Arcadia* and the world they inhabit. Next I shall consider that part of the *New Arcadia*'s action which might more properly be called pastoral, to determine how much of the *Old Arcadia*'s overall thought and sentiment, particularly in regard to a sojourn in a pastoral setting, is carried over into Sidney's revision. Only then, I believe, will we be able to make full sense of both Sidney's continued attachment to his *Old Arcadia* material and his apparent change in emphasis from heroic action to Christian patience in the incomplete Book III of the *New Arcadia*.

HEROIC ACTION

The opening scene of the *New Arcadia* is new material and bears much the same relation to the main action of the princes' adventure in Arcadia as do the detachable episodes that follow in Book I. The only thing in it forwarding the main plot is that it brings Musidorus to the shore. Otherwise it has a static, emblematic quality and is concerned primarily with presenting initial forays into the two realms that are to be the main subject of the *New Arcadia:* love and heroic action. Strephon and Klaius in the *New Arcadia* are Arcadian shepherds and not foreign gentlemen, but they are still set apart from the other shepherds "by so much as learning commonly doth add to nature" (I.27).[9] They claim it is love which has raised up their thoughts so that clerks do not disdain their company; Kalander finds it "a sport" to hear them impute their strength of mind to love (I.27). Given the unfinished state of the *New Arcadia,* we may never know Sidney's own opinion on this question, but in any case the opening with Strephon and Klaius on the shore of Laconia establishes a background for the action to follow. Their lament expresses an ideal love which moves in the opposite direction from the love Pyrocles and Musidorus experienced in the *Old Arcadia;* it imposes reason on desire, and there are suggestions of a rise up a Neoplatonic ladder of love. But it is just as significant that Urania, who threw reason on their desires and made friends of rivals—be she, as has been variously suggested, Christian muse, heavenly love, or the principle of natural harmony in the world, as well as earthly woman—has left them, in the manner of Astraea leaving the earth. It is on a note of loss that we are introduced into the world of the *New Arcadia*.

The celebration of an idealized love ends abruptly with the appearance of a figure from outside the Arcadian world, the abruptness perhaps implying that idealized Arcadian love and figures from the heroic world do not go very well together. Strephon interrupts the rapturous eulogy on Urania, to point out "a thing" floating in on the waves (I.8). The difficulty Strephon and Klaius have in determining the exact nature of Musidorus as a human being, rather than a lifeless object borne along by the elements, is repeated shortly afterward when they and the Laconian fishermen they hire as a search party catch their first glimpse of Pyrocles. Here the mistake is the opposite of the shepherds' first: the mariners stop, amazed before what they think is not a man but a god, and thus they fail to rescue him as he drifts past, mounted on the ship's mast as if on horseback and waving a sword in his hand (I.10). But both Pyrocles and Musidorus are of course men, and the first view we are given of them represents Sidney's preliminary step in defining the nature and limits, not simply of a hero, but of man. Their respective entrances present us images of man on the two fringes of a wide range of human possibilities: man as completely helpless object at the mercy of outside forces and the evil that is capable of consuming other human beings, and man in godlike manner holding to a heroic stance and insisting on his ability to act in the midst of adversity.

Just as the opening sequence had two parts, dealing with love and heroic action, respectively, so does the first "episode," which presents the story of Argalus and Parthenia. This tale is not a completely separable unit, detached from the main action. What starts as an isolated account of the love between Parthenia and Argalus, an interpolated tale told to Musidorus for its "strangeness" (I.37), leads to events fully involving Pyrocles and Musidorus, the Helot War. And the story of the love of Parthenia and Argalus and the account of the Helot War are closely related, not simply because the accounts are interwoven, but because they present ideal conduct and perfect solutions of problems raised in their respective realms. For convenience of discussion I shall refer to the love story and the account of the heroic action of Pyrocles and Musidorus in the Helot War as a single episode.[10]

The story of Argalus and Parthenia presents us pictures of self-sacrificing love, in Parthenia's refusing to marry Argalus when her beauty has been ruined by Demagoras, and of true loyalty, in Argalus's loving and wishing to marry only Parthenia despite her changed appearance. For his devotion and loyalty, Argalus is eventually rewarded with marriage to a miraculously restored and beautiful Parthenia. True reciprocal love leads to happiness after triumphing over the various obstacles set up by an ambitious mother, a vicious rejected lover, and the chances of war. But in order for love to triumph inside Arcadia, a battle has to be fought outside its borders. Argalus, seeking revenge for the destruction of Parthenia's beauty, killed Demagoras but was himself captured by Demagoras's followers, the Helot rebels who for two years had been laying waste to Laconia. After Clitophon, the son of Musidorus's Arcadian host, has also been captured, Musidorus leads a band of Arcadians to a Helot stronghold and is soon engaged in individual combat with the new Helot leader, who turns out to be Pyrocles. After a brief fight of "delightful terribleness" (I.42), the two recognize one another, embrace, and bring the fighting to a halt. The two princes have so distinguished themselves and gained the admiration of their respective parties that their word alone is enough to end the hostilities between the two forces, to reunite Clitophon and Kalander, and to establish a peaceful political settlement between the Helots and the nobles of Laconia.

When Pyrocles, having set Laconian politics in "perfect order" (I.47), comes into Arcadia with Argalus and the latter is married to Parthenia, the two incidents within the realms of love and heroic action appear settled and stand as completed units. This first two-part episode, then, shows how much can be achieved both in the heroic world and in the realm of personal feeling by virtuous men and women. It is all very neat. But there proves to be something wrong: the perfect resolutions do not stay resolved. In Book III the happy marriage of Parthenia and Argalus is destroyed by a call to public duty from Basilius. Argalus answers the call and meets his death at Amphialus's hands; Parthenia follows him to a similar death. And it appears that Sidney also intended the "perfect" peace worked out by Pyrocles in Laconia not to last very long. Before the Helots would allow Pyrocles to leave them, he had to swear, in what looks like rather specific preparation for a return to this subject by Sidney, that he would resume his position as their captain should the Laconian king and nobility ever break their agreement to treat the Helots as free men and full citizens (I.47). And in the second lengthy passage of the last three books of the 1593 *Arcadia* attributable to Sidney on stylistic grounds, the Book V account of Euarchus's journey to Arcadia, we learn that the Laconian king did precisely what the Helots feared he would. As a result, immediately upon Pyrocles' departure fighting had broken out "more violently than ever before" (*OA,* 357, Textual Apparatus; II.152). We are informed of this fact in the middle of a four-page passage which, like the bedchamber scene, contains considerable departures from its parallel passage in the *Old Arcadia* and yet is made up of a mosaic of new and old phrases and sentences. There appears little doubt that Sidney himself wrote the passage and that, at the time he wrote it, he intended it for inclusion in his completed *New Arcadia,* for it contains not only this reference to the Helot War but several other references which correspond to events or details found only in the first two books of the *New Arcadia* and not in the *Old*.

That the ideal resolutions of the first episode do not stay resolved is corroboration of, or a variation upon the theme of, the lament which opened the *New Arcadia*. The disintegration of the results of this episode implies a world in which an ideal can be postulated and even achieved temporarily, but only temporarily. Heroic action can achieve definite good, but that achievement is subject to qualification and even denial by fortune or the acts of unvirtuous men who refuse to adhere to a system of values that respects virtue and right action. The preliminary perfect resolution and eventual dissolution of the achievements in the first episode of the work provide an understated expression of a pattern which extends through the whole of the *New Arcadia*—understated because of the great expanse of text between the episode itself and the final disintegration of its solutions. The most direct presentation of this pattern, as we shall see, is in the progression of heroic episodes in Book II.[11]

Sidney makes twofold use of the account of the Helot War. Not only are the effects of ideal conduct and solutions eventually undermined, but the episode, being placed so early in the narrative, serves as a standard against which subsequent action can be gauged. If the world pictured in the new episodes of the *New Arcadia* is a world of uncertainty, where completed incidents do not stay completed, it is also a world in which most human action is far from ideal or prompted by virtuous motives. The ideal, even charmed, nature of this initial instance of heroic action is expressed in the fight the princes have with one another:

> and so drawing themselves to be the uttermost of the one side, they began a combat which was so much inferior to the battle in noise and number as it was surpassing it in bravery of fighting, and (as it were) delightful ter-

ribleness. Their courage was guided with skill, and their skill was armed with courage; neither did their hardiness darken their wit, nor their wit cool their hardiness; both valiant, as men despising death; both confident, as unwonted to be overcome, yet doubtful by their present feeling, and respectful by what they had already seen; their feet steady, their hands diligent, their eyes watchful, and their hearts resolute. [I.42]

The oxymoron of "delightful terribleness" indicates that this fight, like many that are to follow in the *New Arcadia,* is seen as having a type of beauty, a beauty in part expressed here by the care Sidney took in his balanced phrasing: courage against skill, hardiness against wit. That balance suggests not only precise, ballet-like, mastery of the art of war but equality between the two combatants in the fight. And this equality, in turn, leads to the eventual neutralization of the two fighting forces, which will occur immediately after the combatants recognize one another: peace will come out of balanced combat. But while there is, for Sidney, undeniable beauty in the combat, the fight itself is not mere pageantry. Both combatants are fighting for a cause, and the fight itself is at every stage a meaningful one, since the whole battle's outcome depends upon the outcome of this individual conflict.

We can compare this combat with one in Book III, when war comes into Arcadia itself. This later contest shows a significant departure from the ideal conditions and conduct of the match between Pyrocles and Musidorus in the Helot War. In the midst of the siege of Amphialus's castle, a Black Knight (presumably Musidorus) comes to the aid of Basilius's troops, and soon there begins a combat between this new knight and Amphialus, "worthy to have more large lists, and more quiet beholders" (I.393)—wording which suggests that the fight merits being viewed as a joust, a public entertainment designed primarily to display skill in arms. This is in fact how Amphialus himself looks upon the combat, considering it as a legitimate opportunity for showing off his skill and winning the admiration of the woman he loves but has imprisoned. But he is rebuked for this conception by an unnamed "old governor" who acts as a kind of adviser and protector and who is described as "always a good knight, and careful of his charge"; this figure disrupts the individual combat by wounding the unwary Black Knight and killing his horse. When Amphialus complains that he has been dishonored by such an act, the old governor turns back the complaint with the charge, "You say well . . . to stand now like a private soldier, setting your credit upon particular fighting, while you may see Basilius with all his host is getting between you and your town" (I.393)—an occurrence that Amphialus, upon observation, sees is indeed taking place. The fight between Pyrocles and Musidorus in Book I was in perfect harmony with their responsibilities as leaders of their respective parties; here in Book III, Sidney places individual combat in a context which throws doubt upon its efficacy or wisdom. The issue is not simply that Amphialus is wrong for seeking merely personal glory—although he certainly bears a good measure of blame for concentrating too exclusively on glory—but that this war demands policy and strategy of a more complex and realistic kind. Amphialus finds himself in those new military conditions which, Lawrence Stone tells us, took the fun out of war for the aristocracy of Sidney's generation.[12] "Particular fighting," which was a perfectly legitimate means of determining the outcome of a general battle early in Book I when Sidney wished to provide a statement of ideal possibilities, can no longer be accepted. Heroic action by an individual does *not* automatically lead to the solution of problems, either immediate or long term, and the now behind-the-times Amphialus (like Hector in Shakespeare's *Troilus and Cressida*) is criticized for believing that the world he lives in is simple enough so that it still does.[13]

WHILE THE INDIVIDUAL combats of Books I and III reveal a movement away from ideal human conduct and solutions and a growing complexity within or near the borders of Arcadia in the present, Book II shows much the same processes having taken place well outside Arcadia in the past. Book II, with its crowded and complex account of the past heroic action of Pyrocles and Musidorus, probably bears more responsibility than any other section of the *New Arcadia* for confusing and alienating the new or half-hearted reader of the work. Despite the difficulties that Book II presents, or perhaps because of them, there have been several impressive attempts at uncovering the principles on which Sidney arranged this mass of heroic material, the first back in 1913 by Edwin A. Greenlaw and the others in the burst of Sidney studies of the last twenty years.[14] Greenlaw observed a difference in subject matter and narrative method between the tales Musidorus delivers and all those that follow. He saw Musidorus's account of Euarchus, the princes' upbringing, and their initial adventures in Asia Minor as modeled on Xenophon's *Cyropaedia* and providing, as part of the princes' education, examples first of an ideal and then of tyrannical and unjust governors; the other tales, beginning with those which treat of Erona and Plangus, present examples of sins against love; the overall movement, then, is from public to private virtues and vices. The most helpful and convincing recent discussion of Book II, that of Nancy Lindheim, divides the narrative of past adventures into three parts rather than two and considers the movement from the tales of Musidorus's narrative to those of Pyrocles' as marking a change in emphasis from moral action to moral choice. The intervening episodes dealing with Erona and Plangus, narrated by Philoclea and Pamela (and later completed by Basilius after Pyrocles has finished his account), are seen to bear only indirectly on the princes' education. These other tales remain, though, an integral part of the whole Asia Minor history, since they point to increasing moral confusion in a world in which it is more and more difficult to distinguish good from bad actions and in which virtuous action has less and less of a lasting effect.

Lindheim's analysis of Book II's episodes alerts us to the pattern of decline and increasing complication I have already noted extending over the heroic material of Books I and III. For the purpose of tracing that pattern briefly in the very complex Book II, we might best look first at Erona's story, an episode which is centrally placed in between the lengthy accounts by Musidorus and Pyrocles and which is an epitome of all the other episodes.[15] It presents a demonstration not only of heroic action by the princes but also of the limitations of such action. As far as Pyrocles and Musidorus knew at the time, their action in Erona's Lycia was exemplary and successful. Only now in Arcadia do the princes learn how others looked upon their acts and what in fact were the ultimate results of those acts. In order to save Erona's beloved Antiphilus from death, the princes resorted to a night attack, not realizing that Erona had, in exchange for Antiphilus's life, already agreed to let Tiridates enjoy her. Philoclea (and hence Sidney) in narrating the adventure is careful to point out that Pyrocles and Musidorus knew nothing of the private agreement between Erona and Tiridates (I.236); yet it is with some justification that Tiridates' sister can look upon the night attack and subsequent death of her brother as a "most abominable treason" on the princes' part. From the point of view of the people attacked, it does look as if the agreement of Erona was a trick designed to put Tiridates and his camp off guard.

A military trick is not in itself necessarily bad in the *New Arcadia*. In the Helot War of Book I, the Arcadians (at the suggestion of Musidorus) employed a ruse to gain entrance into an enemy town. And although Artaxia's interpretation of the incident happens to be incorrect, by providing the full questionable circumstances of the night attack and then following that with Artaxia's objection, Sidney is qualifying and casting some doubt upon the heroism of the princes' action. From the beginning of their *New Arcadia* tour of duty in Asia Minor, the princes assume that the world around them is a stage designed for the demonstration of their own heroic virtue, which everyone will recognize and admire as heroic;

Pyrocles, for instance, hopes that "his doings might send his praise to others' mouths, to rebound again true contentment to his spirit" (I.206). That the degree of heroism seen in any given act is dependent upon the point of view of the person judging it says more about the world in which the action is performed than it does about the action itself. But it does mean that the princes' task is not as easy and simple as they think. This is not a world in which well-motivated heroic action will automatically lead to the establishment of justice and respect for principles based on goodness.

In addition, the princes' adventure in Lycia did not end as happily as they had thought, with the marriage of Erona and Antiphilus. As in the case of the Helot rebellion, a "finished" incident in their lives simply will not stay finished. We learn from Basilius, when he takes up the narrative in the concluding chapter of Book II, that the new king the princes helped to put on the throne of Lycia proved to be the very opposite of a Euarchus; Antiphilus "made his kingdom a tennis court where his subjects should be the balls, not in truth cruelly but licentiously abusing them, presuming so far upon himself that what he did was liked of everybody" (I.330). And seeking even more power for himself, he eventually betrayed Erona into the hands of her enemy, Artaxia. The princes' heroic action, then, has ultimately left Erona in straits no better, if not worse, than those in which they found her in the first place.

The account of the princes' past action begins with Musidorus's description of Euarchus and the education of the two young princes. The presentation of Euarchus here is similar in its purpose and tone both to the brief description of him early on in the *Old Arcadia* (*OA,* 10) and to the lengthy treatment of him when he enters upon the Arcadian scene in Book V. Here, as there, he is pictured as the ideal prince and good man: "A prince that indeed especially measured his greatness by his goodness, and if for anything he loved greatness it was because therein he might exercise his goodness" (I.185). Possessing the virtues of justice and magnanimity, he made his life the example of his laws, and was, because of his virtue and love for his subjects, loved in turn by them. The princes were educated to become like such a man. From an early age, their inborn virtue was encouraged to show itself forth, just in the way Sir Thomas Elyot prescribed: ". . . the delight of tales being converted to the knowledge of all the stories of worthy princes, both to move them to do nobly and teach them how to do nobly, the beauty of virtue still being set before their eyes, and that taught them with far more diligent care than grammatical rules" (I.190).[16] Their bodies were exercised, as was that of Euarchus before them, in "all abilities both of doing and suffering." When Pyrocles reached the age of sixteen and Musidorus that of nineteen or twenty, they desired to join Euarchus at the siege of Byzantium, where "they would needs fall to the practice of those virtues which they before learned" (I.191). The princes themselves, then, intended that the siege of Byzantium should be a type of apprenticeship in virtuous action and the art of ruling, according to the model of Euarchus. Fortune and the sea take them to Asia Minor, and they serve their apprenticeship there instead.

The progression of the episodes dealing with the princes' Asia Minor adventures itself reenacts an educative process. After being shown the example of Euarchus and having his ideals and principles presented to them, the princes go out and try to apply those principles in their own actions. At first they meet with relatively easy success. Their initial acts—in overthrowing the kings of Phrygia and Pontus and the giants of Pontus—recall the conditions of the Helot rebellion in Book I. The princes demonstrate unequivocally heroic action, which leads to ideal results. But once Sidney has shown us that the princes have mastered their early lessons, he forces us and them to take a closer second look at the principles they act upon and the world they act in. The episodes of Pyrocles' narrative which follow those of Musidorus's account imply a world more complex than that of the initial episodes. This complexity is in part expressed in the difference in narrative method between Pyrocles' set of tales and Musidorus's set before it.[17] The individual adventures in Musidorus's narrative stand as discrete, separable units; we can talk of a Phrygian episode, a Pontus episode, and a Paphlagonian episode in which the princes oppose tyrannical or usurping rulers of those respective lands and install new and better princes in their places. In Pyrocles' narrative, the individual episodes interweave and impinge upon one another; it becomes difficult to determine where one action leaves off and another begins. Characters of supposedly finished episodes ride in or engage the princes' attention once again. Pyrocles goes off to fight Anaxias, on the way has to save the loose-loving Pamphilus from Dido and her cohorts, then proceeds to meet Anaxias, only to have to break off that fight in order to rescue Dido from Pamphilus and his followers.

Further, in the tales Musidorus narrates, it is relatively easy for the princes and for us to tell who the oppressed and who the villains are, who should be saved and who opposed. The villains of Musidorus's account in effect carry placards announcing themselves as such; the villains of Pyrocles' account merely smile. Pyrocles, whom nature in any case did not make "apt to suspect," is deceived both by the false courtesy of Chremes (Dido's avaricious father), who accompanies him on a second search for

Anaxias, and later by Plexirtus's apparent repentance and officious furnishing of a ship for the princes' journey to Greece. No longer can the princes simply go out and overthrow a figure like the melancholic and suspicious king of Phrygia, who makes their work morally easy for them by trying to kill them first. And as part of this added complication, the princes find themselves increasingly in situations in which they cannot react single-mindedly to threats against themselves and their allies; they must choose between the relative merits of two different and sometimes morally questionable actions.[18] Pyrocles must decide whether it is better to continue his fight against Anaxias or risk ridicule by abandoning that fight and rescue Dido, a figure more worried about her reputation for beauty than her chastity and hence hardly the typical maiden in distress. When both Pyrocles and Musidorus are imprisoned by the Iberian queen Andromana, they have to choose between denouncing publicly that queen's lust for them and continuing to endure unworthy bondage to protect the reputation of a woman who loves them in a disreputable manner. And later, Pyrocles has to choose between helping his cousin in what looks to be an unequal fight with Otanes and two giants or honoring his pledge to the dying Zelmane by rescuing her evil father, Plexirtus, a man he knows to be not worth saving.

The closer second look at the efficacy of Euarchus's principles reveals definite limits to what a hero acting on the basis of those principles can achieve. But this inefficacy is not attributable to any inadequacy in Euarchus's ethical system; rather, it results from the conditions of a world which is more complex and confusing than a textbook statement of ethical principles implies. That there are people in the world like a Plexirtus or an Antiphilus who, no matter what good is done for them, do not respond appropriately to the best of human actions and thus continue to be threats to peace and order after the princes have dealt with them is not a criticism of Euarchus's ethical system or of the princes themselves. And though the world around the princes proves to be rife with moral confusion, a confusion which at times can be seen affecting the princes as well, this does not mean that Sidney would have us or the princes abandon the ethical system that has been handed down to them. Two sets of paired episodes at the end of Pyrocles' narrative would appear to be explicitly designed to prevent us from drawing such a conclusion, for they present us with a balanced picture of the effect of virtuous action in a complex world. We are not witnessing simply a world in progressive decline in which it is useless to try to stay the confusion that is all too prevalent and becoming more so.

After the princes escape from Andromana, they embark upon an adventure in Bithynia which might appear relatively insignificant since Sidney assigns it only a short paragraph. The episode is, however, a replica of the princes' action in the Helot rebellion and hence calls to mind the ideal conditions of that adventure. In two months' time the princes bring to an end the war long maintained between the king of Bithynia and his brother: "For my excellent cousin and I (dividing our selves to either side) found means (after some trial we had made of ourselves) to get such credit with them as we brought them to as great peace between themselves as love towards us for having made the peace" (I.292). The princes are as successful here as they were in their first heroic action in Book I. But this action, in which they successfully reconcile two brothers who had long been at war with one another, is followed immediately by an episode in which the princes are forced to stand by helplessly and watch two brothers, Tydeus and Telenor, the friends and chief supporters of the now suspicious Plexirtus, kill each other. The princes, unable to intercede and stop the fight resulting from a new instance of Plexirtus's treachery toward those to whom he is most indebted, have to accept the incident simply for the moral lesson it provides: the dying Tydeus and Telenor warn them not to base their good will or friendship upon any other ground than proof of virtue (I.294). But the princes find themselves incapable of any action that might have prevented or softened the effects of Plexirtus's villainy.

There is a similar balance in the last two Asian actions of the princes, when they must separate because of Pyrocles' vow to the dying Zelmane. The successful action, again, receives only brief mention. Musidorus proceeds toward Pontus to take on Otanes and two giants, the former the brother of Barzanes, whom Musidorus had killed in Lycia, and the latter the sons of the Pontus giants whom the princes had conquered near the beginning of their Near Eastern adventures (again, apparently closed earlier episodes have ways of opening up again, and their aftereffects continue to trouble the princes in the present). Musidorus, aided by two of the good rulers he and Pyrocles helped to their thrones (the king of Pontus and Leonatus of Paphlagonia), quickly accomplishes his goal. The giants are killed and Otanes is taken prisoner, to which happy result is added the further boon that Otanes is converted to a figure of good and becomes a friend to Musidorus: "To whom [Otanes] as he gave his life, so he got a noble friend, for so he gave his word to be, and he is well known to think himself greater in being subject to that than in the greatness of his principality" (I.301). No such enheartening conversion follows upon Pyrocles' action, recounted immediately before. Pyrocles succeeds in conquering a monstrous beast of most ugly shape ("armed like a rhinoceros, . . . as fierce as a lion, as nimble as a leopard, and as cruel as a tiger" [I.300]) in order to save what Plexirtus's jailer rightly calls a "worst monster," Plexirtus himself (I.301). Plexirtus seems grateful for his deliverance and for a second time appears repentant for his past actions, but proceeds to plan yet another treacherous act by arranging to have Pyrocles and Musidorus killed on shipboard while en route to Greece.

The pairing of these final episodes, with two of the four ending as successfully as the princes might wish, suggests then that the episodes of Book II were not designed simply to show a steady decline in the princes' effectiveness or even in the efficacy of the set of principles learned and inherited from Euarchus. Rather, the fact that properly motivated heroic action can achieve positive good, but does not necessarily do so, attests to the need to hold actively to those principles at all times. After the success of their first Asian adventures, those occurring in Phrygia and Pontus, Pyrocles had announced an intention to keep to a life of active well doing: "But as high honour is not only gotten and born by pain and danger, but must be nursed by the like or else vanisheth as soon as it appears to the world, so the natural hunger thereof (which was in Pyrocles) suffered him not to account a resting seat of that which ever either riseth or falleth, but still to make one action beget another" (I.205–6). But the need for continued dedication to active heroism is much more intense than Pyrocles could know at the time or even than Musidorus seems to realize when he gives his account to Pamela in Arcadia. For the very action that this statement of intention prefaces—the Paphlagonian episode, the source for the Gloucester subplot of *King Lear*—is itself a type of transitional episode: while it is the last of the adventures Musidorus narrates and a discrete unit in which the princes' own action is unequivocally right and impressive, it is the first of the completed episodes to open up again immediately after the princes turn their attention from it. As soon as the princes leave Paphlagonia for Erona's Lycia (and another open-ended episode), the Edmund-figure Plexirtus persists in plotting against his good-hearted and forgiving brother, just as he did before the princes entered the scene; and the further continuation of his villainy occupies the princes twice more in their subsequent adventures. There can be no resting upon one's laurels at the completion of an act, not simply because fame itself is an infirm plant, but because the accomplishments of past acts are always in danger of being upset and reversed by men acting without moral principle.

The princes' achievements in Asia Minor are impressive: they have installed new and good kings in Phrygia and Pontus; killed the Pontus giants; placed the deserving Leonatus on his throne in Paphlagonia; saved Erona from the assaults of Tiridates; brought peace to Bithynia; and converted Otanes to a man of honorable motives. But just as noteworthy would be a list of situations which they have left unresolved or have been unable to change for the better: Tydeus and Telenor are dead; Andromana has committed suicide after the death of her good son Palladius; peace between Pamphilus and Dido was never brought about and hence Dido is dead, Pamphilus is married to a whore, and Chremes has been hanged for the wrong reason; Anaxius is still at large, defaming Pyrocles' character; Erona has been left in prison as a result of new outrages by Antiphilus and Artaxia; and Plexirtus, still unrepentant and unconverted to principles of good, continues to scheme for more and more power in Asia Minor. Although Pyrocles' set of tales may move the emphasis in the princes' acts from heroic action to moral choice, the need for heroic action clearly does not cease to exist. And even when the princes make the correct moral choices, the world around them does not thereby automatically become a better place. The inability of Pyrocles and Musidorus, acting by right principles, to achieve all their goals in the external world of heroic action makes even more meaningful their debate, carried over from the *Old Arcadia* to Book I of the *New Arcadia,* on the significance and appropriateness of a sojourn in Arcadia. For it is not simply Philanax, Euarchus, and in that debate Musidorus who insist on the need for constant moral activity and preparedness; the very nature of the world the princes find themselves in demands it.

ARCADIAN SOJOURN

The *Old Arcadia* was concerned primarily with what happened to the princes when they experienced love in Arcadia; upon falling in love they found themselves unable to reconcile their passion with their reason and their duty in the public, heroic world. Were they good students (which they do not appear to have been) and had they listened carefully to what Euarchus had to tell them, their trial at the conclusion of that work would have taught them that they were but men, limited by human frailty and forced to act in a world which they could not control or order according to their own desires. Their songs throughout the *Old Arcadia* implied that they were out of their own element, experiencing difficulty in the new realm of love in which they found themselves, "Transformed in show," as Pyrocles in his Amazon costume put it, "but more transformed in mind" (*OA,* 28.30). The more heroic mold of the *New Arcadia* enables the princes to show to better advantage, but the new heroic material, even without the influence of love on their actions, does not in itself imply a significant change in their world. That world is certainly as complex and uncontrollable as was the merely pastoral world of the *Old Arcadia*. In addition, it is a world whose complexity the princes are not as keenly aware of as we are. Pyrocles tells his stories as part of his courtship of Philoclea and tells them as a record of his achievements, not of what he could not do. We see as strong an emphasis on the latter, for we witness the contrast between Musidorus's and Pyrocles' narratives; and we have the benefit of hearing all the tales with their increasing complication and moral uncertainty, extending from the relatively straightforward narrative of heroic successes that Musidorus provides to Basilius's concluding account of the unfortunate events taking place in Erona's kingdom after the princes have departed.

I have suggested that the picture of a world in which supposedly solved problems refuse to stay solved makes the debate between Pyrocles and Musidorus on the wisdom of staying in a place called Arcadia as important to the *New Arcadia* as it was to the *Old*. Equally important ought to be the princes' reason for entering Arcadia in the first place. Yet while we are provided a flurry of reasons, the princes' full motivation is never actually revealed to us. Back in Asia Minor before the Paphlagonian adventure, the princes proceeded under the belief that high honor and fame could only be maintained by the constant exercise of heroic virtue; their thirst for honor took the form of deciding not to return to Greece yet but "to see more of the world and to employ those gifts esteemed rare in them, to the good of mankind" (I.206). By the time of their Bithynian adventure they are intending to return toward Thrace "to ease the care of our father and mother" (I.292), and at Pontus, at the completion of their adventures in Asia Minor, they "hasted to Greece-ward," prompted partly by desire to see their respective parents but principally now because they understood that Anaxias was proceeding through the courts of the Peloponnesus defaming Pyrocles (I.302). Arcadia was to be one of their intended stops, renowned as it was both because of its "ancient praises" and because it boasted two such rare knights as Argalus and Amphialus and its two incomparable princesses. Pyrocles adds that he and his cousin decided not simply to take in Greece and its Arcadia on their journey but to do so secretly, that is, in disguise, "determining as soon as we came to Greece to take the names Daiphantus and Palladius, as well as for our own promise to Zelmane as because we desired to come unknown into Greece" (I.303).[19] They thus had two reasons for their disguise, but why, besides their promise to the dying Zelmane, they wished to come into Greece "unknown" is never explained.

But if the princes' own reasons for going to Arcadia are not fully articulated, Sidney's for taking them there are relatively clear. Their apprenticeship as princes in Asia Minor took the form of a series of tests, and tests which became progressively more difficult as the world they took place in was examined more closely. The placement of the entrance into Arcadia at the end of a series of tests suggests that Arcadia is to provide yet another test for the princes and perhaps their hardest yet. Book II's episodes are primarily an examination of the princes as heroes, as public figures; that they come into Arcadia in disguise and without their own names suggests that their Arcadian adventure, their final test, is to be an examination of them on a different level, not as established heroes, but more simply and radically as men. Their performance in Arcadia will in effect define them, a process of definition which begins, as we have seen, with the initial entrance of Musidorus and Pyrocles in the *New Arcadia* as "thing" and "god." And the primary means by which they are to be defined, of course, is love. Love of woman was not assigned much place in the account Musidorus gave of Euarchus. The Macedonian king's own marriage was barely mentioned, and that of Musidorus's parents was described as subordinate to, and an expression of, the friendship between Euarchus and Musidorus's father, Dorilaus: "He [Euarchus] had only one sister, a lady . . . of whom it may be justly said that she was no unfit branch to the noble stock whereof she came. Her he had given in marriage to Dorilaus, prince of Thessalia, not so much to make a friendship as to confirm the friendship betwixt their posterity, which between them by the likeness of virtue had been long before made" (I.187). Once in Arcadia, the princes' task is to add romantic love to the moral code handed down to them by Euarchus and to make the two part of a single, coherent ethical system.

The truncated state of the *New Arcadia* makes it difficult to say with certainty whether the princes would succeed in that goal and hence reconcile their public duties with their private desires. But if there is to be no final, definitive answer, there may be some consolation in knowing that we seem to be asking the right question; or so we can presume from looking at the treatment of material carried over from the *Old Arcadia* into the early part of the revision. There is evidence to suggest that Sidney, initially at least, wanted the question of the princes' ultimate success or failure to remain an open one in our minds: we are not to come to any conclusion too easily or quickly. Several changes in narrative technique make our reading of the opening book particularly a more problematic experience than it was in the *Old Arcadia*.

One such change is in the elimination of that chatty, intrusive narrator who guided us through the *Old Arcadia*. In the place of that often helpful, sometimes unhelpful (because confusingly ironic) figure, we hear in the *New Arcadia* a more distant, omniscient voice, one which draws no attention to itself and is not particularized enough to tempt us into thinking that it is Sidney himself speaking to us. Those often witty comments, on the nature of love particularly, are now either assigned to the various characters in the tale or cut completely; and gone along with them are those direct addresses to an audience of fair ladies, experienced in the pains of love and thus well able to appreciate the princes' or Gynecia's plight. Myrick considered these changes one of the signs that Sidney was attempting to write a heroic poem according to the instructions of Minturno, who would have his epic poet delegate as much of the narration as possible to characters in the fable.[20] Whatever the motivation behind these changes, their effect is to involve the reader more directly and immediately in the narrative. The reader of the *Old Arcadia* is cajoled or, I have said, compromised into being interested in the outcome of the princes' Arcadian adventure; here the reader is forced to work his way through a given episode or debate and determine for himself what the adventure means and where truth in the debate is to be found.

This new mode of involvement in the narrative is particularly evident in the first, now two-part, debate between Pyrocles and Musidorus. In the *Old Arcadia,* the narrator gave the game away before the debate began: he presented a lengthy account of the first stirrings of love in Pyrocles and told us of Pyrocles' intention to inform his cousin of his new affliction (*OA*, 11–12). In the *New Arcadia,* Sidney puts the account of the "fatal overthrow" of Pyrocles' liberty in Pyrocles' own mouth and has him present it only after the debate is finally concluded (I.84–95). Thus it is from Pyrocles himself now, and not the narrator, that we hear (and this time without its earlier hint of slightly mocking bathos) how his heart "received quickly a cruel impression of that wonderful passion which to be defined is impossible, because no words reach to the strange nature of it. They only know it which inwardly feel it. It is called love" (I.85). We know the princes are in a land called Arcadia and can easily guess what kind of experience they are to undergo there, but before the debate itself the only definite indication we now have that Pyrocles has been struck down by love is his exclamation upon seeing Parthenia, "O Jupiter . . . how happens it, that beauty is only confined to Arcadia?" (I.54). Instead of being in effect warned beforehand that any statement by Pyrocles other than an immediate confession of his love is likely to be a rationalization or a feint, the reader must sift through Pyrocles' rhetoric and establish for himself that the arguments for contemplation and for Arcadia's beauty are in fact specious and beside the point. The humor is certainly still there in the *New Arcadia*'s version of the debate, but it is less overt, since we have not been alerted to the discrepancy between Pyrocles' real reason for wanting to stay in Arcadia and what he claims in high-flown language are his reasons. The reader thus proceeds relatively unaided, without benefit of the narrator's reassuring good humor, which in itself suggested that no matter what the outcome of this or any subsequent debate or adventure, everything would eventually work itself out to the princes' advantage.

BUT WHILE THERE may be distinct changes in the narrative technique in the move from the *Old* to the *New Arcadia,* the further we proceed through the revision the less it looks as if there are major changes in Sidney's essential thinking—particularly on our questions of the wisdom of a sojourn in a pastoral setting and the possibility of reconciling one's public duties with private desires there. The reigning definition of Arcadia in the *Old Arcadia* proved to be the conception of that land as a political unit, an actual Greek province at all times in need of active governance by a responsible ruler. This definition was put forward at the expense of one suggested by the literary pastoral tradition and epitomized in the image of the *locus amoenus,* an idealized natural setting, suited to dedication to poetic song and to love. Much in the *New Arcadia* suggests that Sidney has not changed his terms or definitions and still has not lost his distrust of ideal natural settings.

Arcadia is first presented in the revised version as a haven. Musidorus enters the province only after his shipwreck and a journey through the ravaged landscape and wasted soil of Laconia, with which the "delightful prospects" of Arcadia are in sharp contrast:

> There were hills which garnished their proud heights with stately trees; humble valleys whose base estate seemed comforted with refreshing of silver rivers; meadows enamelled with all sorts of eye-pleasing flowers; thickets which, being lined with most pleasant shade, were witnessed so to by the cheerful deposition of many well-tuned birds; each pasture stored with sheep feeding with sober security, while the pretty lambs with bleating oratory craved the dams' comfort; here a shepherd's boy piping as though he should never be old; there a young shepherdess knitting and withal singing, and it seemed that her voice comforted her hands to work and her hands kept time to her voice's music. As for the houses of the country (for many houses came under their eye) they were all scattered, no two being one by the other, and yet not so far off as that it barred mutual succour: a

shew, as it were, of an accompanable solitariness and of a civil wildness. [I.13–14]

There is perhaps a slight note of warning in the phrase "as though he should never be old," which is gratuitously included and hence implies the possibility of its opposite, that the shepherd's boy will in fact grow old; Musidorus is evidently not entering into a timeless realm. But the irony intended in this particular initial glimpse of Arcadia will be on a much more obvious level and more extensive than that conveyed by a small qualifying phrase. Musidorus is just as impressed with this landscape as Pyrocles later shows himself to be in their debate and asks why there is such a contrast between the two lands he has seen. He is told by Klaius that Laconia is "not so poor by the barrenness of the soil (though in itself not passing fertile) as by a civil war" which had been waged for two years and had "disfigured the face of nature" there (I.14); Arcadia on the other hand is "decked with peace and (the child of peace) good husbandry." Its people live a life of pastoral calm and joy: "a happy people, wanting little because they desire not much" (I.14). The full ironic intent in this picture of Arcadia as a peaceful haven is demonstrated when Sidney takes peace away from it, with the outbreak of the peasant rebellion and the more serious civil war waged against Basilius by Amphialus and Cecropia; Arcadia will subsequently prove to be little different from its neighboring Laconia.

By presenting Arcadia as an apparent resting place after the shipwreck and the harsh landscape of Laconia, Sidney sets a trap for Musidorus and for us. He invites us to look upon Arcadia as a haven by calling up the familiar picture of the pastoral convention's *otium,* and then proceeds to show that it is a mistake to look upon this particular landscape in that way. Many times over in the course of the narrative, Sidney plays much the same trick, using the beauty of a natural setting to provide a false sense of security. In their search for the missing Pyrocles in Book I, Musidorus and Clitophon come upon a *locus amoenus:*

> As they passed in a pleasant valley (of either side of which high hills lifted up their beetle-brows as if they would overlook the pleasantness of their under-prospect) they were by the daintiness of the place and the weariness of themselves invited to light from their horses; and pulling off their bits that they might something refresh their mouths upon the grass (which plentifully grew, brought up under the care of those well-shading trees) they themselves laid them down hard by the murmuring music of certain waters which spouted out of the side of the hills, and in the bottom of the valley made of many springs a pretty brook, like a commonwealth of many

families. But when they had a while hearkened to the persuasion of sleep, they rose and walked onward in that shady place, till Clitophon espied a piece of armour and, not far off, another piece. [I.63]

Red Cross Knight, in Spenser's variation upon Ovid's tale of Salmacis and Hermaphroditus, stops at a stream, disarms, and then succumbs to sexual passion, in the process becoming metaphorically indistinguishable from, in fact metamorphosed into, the stream whose water he drank.[21] Nothing quite that disastrous happens to Musidorus personally as a result of his stopping to rest in a beautiful setting, but his sojourn in a pleasant place prefaces both trouble for him and a demonstration of the effect of passion in men's lives. Picking up Amphialus's cast-off armor involves Musidorus in a fight with Helen's guards and thereafter an account of Helen's destructive love.

And later, when Philoclea and Pamela go swimming in another beautiful spot wherein nature speaks of love—"The banks of either side [of the river] seeming arms of the loving earth that fain would embrace it" (I.216)—the natural setting serves as a background not only for the princesses' beauty but again for a display of passion, this time in Pyrocles. The sexual excitement that has been welling up inside him as a result of looking upon the naked Philoclea is vented in his uncontrollable rage against Amphialus, who is discovered hiding in the bushes. And later yet, when Nature puts on another show for her spectators, in "a pleasant valley . . . like one of those circuses which in great cities somewhere doth give a pleasant spectacle of running horses" (I.292), Pyrocles and Musidorus discover Tydeus and Telenor fighting one another. The scene provides evidence of human maliciousness at work even in such settings, since Plexirtus has appointed this as the place to rid himself of the very people to whom he owes most in the world.

These incidents in *loci amoeni* (all three of them new to the 1590 *Arcadia*) have a cumulative effect. As they unfold one after another, they cause us to be wary of beautiful natural settings, and thus they provide a background of uneasiness which reflects upon the princes' decision to stay in Arcadia, itself initially introduced as a peaceful place of natural beauty. They begin to look like possible images in small of what might well become the princes' whole Arcadian experience. And it is not only the conventional pastoral setting, as epitomized in those recurrent images of *loci amoeni,* which is viewed with continued distrust in the *New Arcadia;* a similar aura of uneasiness and distrust also hovers over the conventional pastoral entertainments associated with such settings. The eclogues, which are announced in the text as imminent (I.125, 338) but which Sidney did not get to revising, are placed in contexts casting some doubt on the wisdom of Basilius's and the princes' attendance at them. The First Eclogues, for instance, are scheduled to take place, as they were in the *Old Arcadia,* in yet another version of a *locus amoenus:*

> It was, indeed, a place of delight, for through the midst of it there ran a sweet brook which did both hold the eye open with her azure streams and yet seek to close the eye with the purling noise it made upon the pebblestones it ran over, the field itself being set in some places with roses, and in all the rest constantly preserving a flourishing green. . . . About it, as if it had been to enclose a theatre, grew such a sort of trees as either excellency of fruit, stateliness of growth, continual greenness, or poetical fancies have made at any time famous. In most part of which there had been framed by art such pleasant arbours that, one answering another, they became a gallery aloft from tree to tree almost round about, which below gave a perfect shadow, a pleasant refuge then from the choleric look of Phoebus. [I.118–19][22]

As was the case also in the *Old Arcadia,* no sooner are the princesses, Gynecia, and the princes seated in this spot than a lion and a bear emerge from the forest. But while the spot described and the events occurring there are essentially the same in the *Old* and *New Arcadia*s, there are several significant differences in the handling of the scene. In the *Old Arcadia,* the attack of the wild beasts is presented in a flashback, after we have seen the shepherds fleeing from the place where the pastorals were to be held; in the *New Arcadia,* we go along with the princesses and princes, perceive the beauty of the spot, and then are as surprised as the royal figures are by the appearance of the beasts. Here too the reader is more directly involved in the narrative, and Sidney's intention would appear to be to lull us into thinking that there is no danger in relaxing and enjoying oneself in such pleasant surroundings, only to show us, once again, that such an assumption is wrong.

Further, the danger or threat to the royal family is not simply eliminated in the *New Arcadia,* as it was in the *Old,* when the beasts have been killed. In the earlier version we are told only that such beasts had never been seen before in Arcadia (*OA,* 46); in the revision, a servant of Cecropia enters to apologize for the escape of several of Cecropia's animals. This is the third reference to Cecropia in the *New Arcadia,* the first two telling of her dislike of Basilius, her atheistical pride, and her lack of regard for love, courtesy, gratefulness, and friendship (I.68, 98). Thus, when we hear that the animals belong to this woman, we tend to give credence to Gynecia's conjecture that the appearance of the animals "proceeded rather of some mischievous practice than of misfortune" and to think it might be better for Basilius to have some other commonwealth on his mind than the late-conceived one of love that we are told is his only present interest (I.125).[23]

Sidney's continued uneasiness with the conventional pastoral setting and activities is perhaps best revealed, though, by the rather thorough study of geography we know him to have undertaken in the process of revising the *Old Arcadia* into the *New*. The Arcadia of the literary pastoral tradition was usually perceived as a landscape of the mind, more a way of life than a place one might try to locate on a map. For both Virgil and Sannazaro, Arcadia was a place, any place, where one could find *otium* and write poetry. Virgil's Greek Arcadia merges easily with the countryside around his birthplace, Mantua, and the most important geographical fact about his Arcadia is simply that it is not Rome. In the Twelfth Prose section of Sannazaro's *Arcadia,* Sincero proceeds from Arcadia through the underworld to the hills outside Naples; geographical accuracy is plainly not a relevant consideration. But the Sidney of the *New Arcadia* was evidently concerned to locate his Arcadia in a rather precise way and hence establish it as a geographical entity. William Ringler has shown that one of the things Sidney did in the process of composing the *New Arcadia* was to consult recent maps of ancient Greece and Asia Minor, the maps in question being Mercator's 1578 Map X of Europe and Map I of Asia prepared for an edition of Ptolemy's *Geography*.[24] Even with the definition of Arcadia as an actual Greek province in the *Old Arcadia,* there was evidence of vagueness in geographical details and an occasional inaccuracy. Arcadia itself, for instance, was credited with having a seacoast: Euarchus sailed there early in Book V (*OA,* 359). But with the information gained from his study of recent authoritative maps, Sidney introduced some thirty new place-names in the revision and was able both to be more precise in establishing which countries bordered on which others and to correct many of the outright errors of the earlier version. His new, more precise geographical knowledge is shown at virtually every turn in the action: the need to pass through the coastal province of Laconia in order to arrive in Arcadia (which gives rise to the early contrast between the two provinces) is one expression of it; and Arcadia is this time rightly shown as landlocked, with four of its six neighboring provinces explicitly named when Musidorus goes on his search for the love-stricken Pyrocles (I.74).

But Sidney did not simply consult historical maps; he evidently sought help from an ancient prose geography as well, that of Strabo.[25] For only if we envision Sidney as writing with both an edition of Strabo and the recent maps before him can we account for the full range of geographical detail in the *New Arcadia*. Musidorus's search for Pyrocles, for instance, takes him not only to the neighboring provinces which Sidney could see plainly marked on the new maps but also through a number of Arcadian cities: first Mantinea and then "Tegea, Ripa, Enispae, Stimphalus, and Pheneus, famous for the poisonous Stygian water" (I.63). Of these six cities, only Mantinea is mentioned in the *Old Arcadia,* and only three—Mantinea, Tegea, and Stimphalus—are to be found on any of the late sixteenth-century maps of ancient Greece that Sidney might have consulted; all six, however, are mentioned in Strabo's chapter on Arcadia (Book VIII, Chapter viii) as once existing but now difficult to locate because of the devastation that had been visited upon the province by the time Strabo himself was writing.

The significance of Sidney's reliance on both an ancient geography and recent authoritative maps is suggested by the recently discovered letter of Whitsunday (May 22) 1580 from Sidney to Edward Denny. The letter offers advice on the books Denny should read while performing military duty in Ireland, and as John Buxton suggests, its principal interest probably lies in the evidence it provides of Sidney's own wide reading.[26] But when Sidney gets to the study of "historical matters," he urges his friend before undertaking such study to read (among other items) "the geography of some modern writer . . . and provide yourself of an Ortelius, that when you read of any place you may find it out and have it, as it were, before your eyes." "An Ortelius" here refers to Abraham Ortelius's popular atlas, *Theatrum Orbis Terrarum,* a collection primarily of modern maps which began to appear in 1570 but which by the 1579 Antwerp edition also contained several maps of the ancient world (including one of Greece), with their appropriate ancient place-names. As it happens, it is most likely that Sidney used the maps Ringler suggested, the 1578 Mercator maps, and not the historical maps of Ortelius (at one of the few points where the relevant maps differ in their details, Sidney follows Mercator).[27] But no matter which particular maps Sidney consulted, what his reliance upon both a map and a geography means is that in his study of ancient Greece and Asia Minor in preparation for the *New Arcadia,* he was in effect following the advice he himself gave to Denny for the study of presumably more modern history (since the letter refers to a "modern" geography). And what this in turn would mean is that Sidney conceived of the places he was writing about in the *New Arcadia* as actual and historical, not merely fictional, settings. He was clearly, then, not thinking of his Arcadia in the same way Virgil and Sannazaro and other earlier pastoral writers thought of theirs. His attention to geographical detail and concern for geographical accuracy constitute renewed, in fact intensified, endorsement of the definition of Arcadia as a land, like any other, that needs to be watched over at all times by a responsible ruler, a land that must be governed.[28]

THE HEROIC MATERIAL of Books II and III discussed earlier pictures a world becoming increasingly difficult to live in. To this evidence of what was happening to the princes in the heroic world and on the battlefield we can add what happens to them once they have experienced love in Arcadia. As in the Old Arcadia, they remain still capable after their entrance into Arcadia of some genuinely heroic action, and heroic action which love inspires: here too they kill the lion and the bear that threaten Philoclea and Pamela, and they manage to quell the peasant uprising that threatens Basilius and his family. But there is evidence also of a deterioration in their heroic and moral conduct, and it is love which is responsible for this deterioration.

The princes had gained some measure of experience with love in their earlier heroic adventures, and that experience did not represent an encouraging start. Pyrocles and Musidorus were not affected directly by love the first two times they witnessed its effects, although the passion of Erona and Dido might well have provided warning that this love is something to be approached only with caution. Their encounter with Andromana marks the first time that the princes are at all personally involved with someone in love, and this episode represents the point of greatest moral uncertainty for them in Book II. When imprisoned by the Iberian queen who lusts after them both equally, the princes find themselves, as Pyrocles tells it, "in a great perplexity, restrained to so unworthy a bondage and yet restrained by love which (I cannot tell how) in noble minds by a certain duty claims an answering" (I.280). Given the fact that Andromana's is a totally shameful love and completely unreciprocated, this recourse to an extravagant chivalric and *stilnovisti* view of love, which one associates most perhaps with Dante's Paolo and Francesca, appears rather quaint. "But that which did, as it were, tie us in captivity was," Pyrocles continues, "that to grant had been wickedly injurious to him that had saved our lives, and to accuse a lady that loved us of her love unto us we esteemed almost as dishonourable." Even if we take into account that Pyrocles is courting Philoclea and feels compelled to voice respect for love in its every manifestation while he presents his narrative, we might well wonder whether it would have been "almost as dishonourable" to expose Andromana's passion as to accede to her lustful desires and cuckold their host. The princes' quandary in this episode serves to suggest the kind of difficulty this new emotion of love will entail for them.

Love in others, then, is one of the forces making the work of the princes more difficult in the heroic world outside Arcadia. Their difficulties become even more intense when they fall victim to love themselves within Arcadia. Their first martial act after they have both been stricken with love is their participation in Phalantus's tournament, and their conduct there reveals them as major contributors to the general decline in chivalry seen extending through the whole of the *New Arcadia*. The tournament, somewhat debased to begin with because introduced by a figure who reduces chivalric ideals to mere pageantry without real meaning, soon disintegrates into a brawl with accusations being hurled in all directions and three knights all striking each other at the same time. Pyrocles as the Ill-Appointed Knight and Musidorus as the Black Knight both want ardently to fight for their respective mistresses, and their love prompts them not to high-minded chivalrous action but to ill-mannered, indecorous squabbling. The easy and direct connection between love and heroic action which is the mainstay of much chivalric literature is denied here: love appears too disruptive to fit within any hierarchical scheme or code which subordinates it to any higher value or action; rather, it threatens to upset such a hierarchy completely and become the complete master of the man experiencing it.

Consistent with the princes' conduct in Phalantus's tournament, and a matter handled with similar humor by Sidney, is that enraged and uncontrollable attack by Pyrocles upon Amphialus for being guilty of much the same thing as Pyrocles himself—spying upon the naked Philoclea while she bathes in the river Ladon. A far more seriously treated, and more troublesome, departure from controlled chivalric conduct, though, comes near the point the *New Arcadia* breaks off. Pyrocles, still dressed as the Amazon Zelmane, has just been forced to suffer the sexual advances of Zoilus (an incident Sidney does not let pass without appropriate humor), and the disguised prince gets his revenge by tripping Zoilus, seizing his sword, and killing the would-be lover before he can get help from his brothers. Lycurgus then seeks revenge for Zoilus's death, and there follows another of Book III's individual combats, though a brief one: "And so between them, for a few blows, Mars himself might have been delighted to look on" (I.514). Pyrocles quickly gains the upper hand, and Lycurgus, realizing he is about to be killed, begs for mercy: "Enough, excellent lady . . . the honour is yours. . . . As you have taken from men the glory of manhood, return so now again to your own sex for mercy. I will redeem my life of you with no small services, for I will undertake to make my brother obey all your commandments. Grant life, I beseech you, for your own honour, and for the person's sake that you love best" (I.515). Pyrocles pauses briefly, "either disdaining to be cruel, or pitiful and therefore not cruel," and begins to incline toward mercy for the figure on the ground before him. But unfortunately for Lycurgus, one of the arms he holds up to Pyrocles in supplication has tied to it a jewel taken from Philoclea and given to her by Pyrocles himself. The sight of that jewel destroys "all conceits of mercy" in Pyrocles' mind, and with remembrance of the injuries Philoclea suffered adding fuel to his wrath, he kills Lycurgus despite the appeal.

Pyrocles' killing of Lycurgus is modeled closely upon the final scene of the *Aeneid*, when Aeneas stands over the injured Turnus, who, among his other misfortunes, happens to be bearing on his shoulder the belt of Aeneas's beloved Pallas. Renaissance interpretations of the *Aeneid* almost invariably emphasized Aeneas's virtue, and he was generally viewed as a figure who, except perhaps for the stay with Dido, could do little or no wrong. Sidney himself throughout the *Defence of Poetry* speaks of him as a totally virtuous figure likely to prompt readers of Virgil's poem to heroic action of their own. Modern readings of the *Aeneid* which view this final scene in the poem as revealing an Aeneas succumbing to impulses of violence and irrationality when he kills the helpless Turnus would, I suspect, appear rather alien to most Renaissance readers. More familiar would be an interpretation along the lines suggested by Servius's often-reprinted comment on the conclusion, that all the poet's efforts are directed toward the glory of Aeneas, who is to be considered dutiful first for thinking of sparing his enemy and then dutiful as well for slaying him and thereby avenging the death of Pallas for Evander's sake.[29] But Sidney has added one important phrase to all he has taken from Virgil. As Pyrocles stands over the fallen Lycurgus, inclining for a moment (like Aeneas before him) toward mercy, Sidney notes that "the image of the human condition began to be an orator unto her [Zelmane] of compassion" (I.515). That image is evidently Lycurgus's position of prayer as a suppliant. Despite all the borrowing from Virgil, it does not seem likely that Sidney would present this picture of a man in a position of prayer or supplication, and call that position an image of the human condition generally, if he meant us to approve unequivocally of Pyrocles' angered killing of Lycurgus.

Love, then, would appear to have made Pyrocles capable of a cruel and inhuman act, as it earlier made him commit indecorous and unchivalric ones in Phalantus's tournament. Love does seem to be on the verge of inspiring Pyrocles to defeat Anaxias at the point where the *New Arcadia* stops; but the probable success in that more considerable and equal fight would have to be matched against the enraged killing of the suppliant Lycurgus right before it. This particular pairing of encounters is similar in its effect to the pairing of episodes we have seen at the end of Pyrocles' Asia Minor narrative. And such a pairing of incidents this late in the *New Arcadia* does not imply a Sidney who, at the point the work breaks off, conceived of himself as working toward a conclusion which the chivalric code, with its view of love as an inspiration for honorable heroic action, might provide.

We certainly feel as warmly toward the princes in the *New Arcadia* as we did in the *Old*. The account of their past heroic action enhances their character, even while it shows some limitations in what heroism can accomplish in a recalcitrant world. As already suggested, the 1593 edition's change in the scene in Philoclea's bedchamber reveals that Sidney intended to eliminate the princes' most serious faults; and the kiss that Musidorus attempts to steal from Pamela at the opening of Book III is only a pale reflection of his rape attempt of the *Old Arcadia*. But that kiss is nonetheless described as an act prompted by love "that never stayed to ask reason's leave" (I.355). And Pyrocles, in adopting female attire, is just as aware of the embarrassing straits in which he finds himself as he was in the earlier version. At the point Musidorus discovers him in his Amazon dress, he is singing the same song of lament assigned him in the *Old Arcadia:*

> Transformed in show, but more transformed in mind,
> I cease to strive, with double conquest foiled;
> For (woe is me) my powers all I find
> With outward force and inward treason spoiled.
>
> [I.76]

And much later, in captivity in Amphialus's castle, Pyrocles in "a wild fury of desperate agony" over the apparent death of Philoclea attempts suicide, "carried away with the madness of anguish" (I.483). In all that has been considered so far at least, there is as little indication in the *New Arcadia* as there was in the *Old* that Sidney is having the princes benefit from a pastoral sojourn to bring the warring parts of their souls into harmony.

DOING AND SUFFERING

One of the reasons why it is difficult to accept Pyrocles' killing of Lycurgus as an unqualifiedly heroic act is that much of Book III has been devoted to promoting the position of prayer Lycurgus appropriates when faced with death. With Book III there is the often-noted shift in the narrative's primary focus from Pyrocles and Musidorus to the princesses, and with that change we move from a central concern with the problem of reconciling love and heroic action to a demonstration of a rather explicitly Christian posture of patience. Pamela, who opposes the atheistic Cecropia with the argument that there is an infinitely wise and good ruling power in the universe and who in times of crisis simply puts her trust in that higher power, emerges as the chief embodiment of virtue in the book. And this change in focus has the potential, at least, for redeeming Arcadia's landscape, since an apparently new type of virtue is now being put forward for our consideration, one thoroughly appropriate to life in retirement from the heroic or public world. It would appear that *pastoral* Arcadia need not be viewed solely as a place of enervating relaxation, to be left as soon as possible lest one be lulled into letting down one's moral guard.

John F. Danby, for one, has referred to this new focus on patience as a last and exciting turn in Sidney's thought. He finds this new and more overt expression of essentially Christian thought necessarily superior to what has been Sidney's explicit ideal before this point, Euarchus's more classical magnanimity of soul and insistence upon active service to the state. For this new virtue of patience "leans on and demands the transcendent."[30] But we ought to note, and here is where keeping the *Old Arcadia* firmly in mind as we read the *New Arcadia* is particularly helpful and important, that the new emphasis on Christian patience does not constitute a turn in Sidney's thought as much as an extension and deepening of it. It was Euarchus in the *Old Arcadia* who was initially presented to us as "taking his rest under a tree with no more affected pomps than as a man that knew, howsoever he was exalted, the beginning and end of his body was earth" (*OA*, 355–57). And it was Euarchus who, even with his insistence upon the exercise of active virtue at all times, was most aware of human frailty and hence of the need to look, finally, to heaven to extricate man from difficulties which even the most active virtue is not always able to overcome. Why there should have been such a direct connection between adherence to the active life and recognition of human frailty was only slightly hinted at in the *Old Arcadia*, though. The outright need for, as differentiated from the mere wisdom of, constant moral preparedness and action is made much more explicit in the *New Arcadia*, particularly in those new heroic adventures in Book II: in a world in which finished incidents refuse to stay finished and in which figures like Plexirtus continue to hold power, man can never be confident enough to think that his work is finished and thus allow himself to stop and rest.

The only proper response to such a world is to keep doing all that one can and then leave the rest to heaven. Pamela's virtue is simply the next step after Euarchus's in that response. She is placed in an environment dominated for the moment by the evil of Cecropia; the princess can do little herself to improve her plight, and her reaction to her situation is simply to appeal to heaven for strength and have faith in the far-reaching plan of God.

The respective virtues of Euarchus and Pamela are, then, complementary. Just as the princes' formal education included exercise in all abilities "both of doing and suffering" (I.190), so Euarchus and Pamela stand before the princes as examples of perfected virtue in those respective realms of doing and suffering. They serve as moral tutors from whom the princes can learn virtue and with whom we can compare the princes to estimate their progress. The two types of virtue imply one another, and there is no need to choose one type over the other or to assume any essential change in Sidney's thinking as a result of Book III's new focus on the virtue of patience. Indeed, there are indications, some even after the full exemplification of Pamela's virtue, that Sidney intended Euarchus to make an appearance at the end of the *New Arcadia,* presumably to reassert once again the claims and values of the active life. The oracle in the *New Arcadia,* presented late in Book II, still predicts to Basilius that "In thy own seat a foreign state shall sit" (I.327). And rather late in Book III, Cecropia sends a message to Basilius threatening to behead Pamela, Philoclea, and Zelmane if the king does not raise the siege of her castle. The war council that follows this demand has a familiar look about it. Kalendar appeals to Basilius's feelings as a father, arguing that Basilius should comply with Cecropia's demand, while Philanax counters with the argument that Basilius is a ruler as well as a father: "In sum, you are a prince, and a father of people, who ought with the eye of wisdom, the hand of fortitude, and the heart of justice to set down all private conceits in comparison of what for the public is profitable" (I.468). Philanax bases his argument on sound logical and political principles: "But indeed a prince of judgement ought not to consider what his enemies promise or threaten, but what the promisers and threateners in reason will do; and the nearest conjecture thereunto is what is best for their own behoof to do" (I.467). All wisdom in the debate in fact appears to be on the side of Philanax, an appearance which is borne out when Basilius characteristically makes the wrong decision, prompted less by fatherly concern for his daughters than by his lust-inspired fear for the safety of his beloved Zelmane. The whole debate here looks strongly like preparation for some example of conduct similar to that of Euarchus in the trial scene of the *Old Arcadia,* when that prince put his responsibilities as a judge before his feeling as a father and adhered to his conception of never-changing justice even though it was his son and nephew who happened to be on trial.

This is not to claim that there would have been a trial scene at the end of the *New Arcadia* like the one at the end of the *Old,* in which the princes would have been first condemned by an ideal Euarchus and then providentially saved. We cannot speculate with any confidence on how Sidney would have continued his narrative, or if in fact he would have continued it. Book III of the *New Arcadia* was plainly taking his narrative (but not, I would argue, his thinking) off on an uncharted course. His work was changing so much under his pen that it is likely that he would have had either to abandon the *Old Arcadia* as a source for future material (something he appeared very reluctant to do) or to discard much of the *New Arcadia*'s Book III, which he had just written. Book III puts both the princes and the princesses through such trials and reveals heroism, particularly in the princesses, of such a nature that subsequent mere lapses into passion, in the manner of the *Old Arcadia,* would become either insignificant or impossible. Given the full exposition of Cecropia's atheism, it does not appear likely that Sidney could return to the *Old Arcadia*'s conception of a sexual lapse as the chief manifestation of wrong.[31] And on the workaday level of mere plotting, it is difficult to see how Sidney could have Pamela consent to flee Arcadia with Musidorus, as she does at the end of Book III of the *Old Arcadia,* after she has so adamantly asserted to Cecropia that to marry without her father's permission "should offend God" (I.405).

But if we cannot speculate with assurance on how Sidney would have or could have continued and how he might have treated the princes at the end of the completed *New Arcadia,* we can speak with better authority of how he viewed his narrative and its main characters up to the particular point at which he evidently stopped writing. The fact that as late in the work as Book III's war council (only fifty pages before the text ends in mid-sentence) he still held in the back of his mind the model Euarchus provided in the trial scene of the *Old Arcadia* suggests that he was still thinking in terms dictated by his *Old Arcadia* material. And such thinking suggests a Sidney still not viewing the princes as untarnished, or even potentially untarnished, figures. While they did in Book II attain a good measure of Euarchus's virtue, they did not fully understand the need for holding firmly to what they had achieved: they were not completely aware of the growing complexity in the world around them nor of their own growing confusion in accomplishing their deeds. Their attempt to add love to their active virtue has resulted, in that part of the *New Arcadia* which we have, in only mixed success. And they do not appear to be far along toward mastering Pamela's virtues of patience and control. Pyrocles' love for Philoclea brings him not to place his faith in God as his primary help in adversity but rather to make a suicide attempt in which he indicts heaven in far from patient terms: "O tyrant heaven, traitor earth, blind providence; no justice, how is this done? How is this suffered? Hath this world a government?" (I.483). That the princes achieved only partial success in the external world before they entered Arcadia suggests, further, that they would probably not be completely successful here inside Arcadia either. But even if the princes were to achieve the faith and patience of Pamela or the resolute and consistent dedication of Euarchus, their achievement would, at best, still bring them to a recognition of human limitations and of the need for divine help in a world that refuses to conform to human wishes. For that is the cornerstone of Pamela's virtue, as it is of the virtue of Euarchus.

The recognition of human frailty is, in fact, what heaven itself explicitly demands of man in the *New Arcadia,* and very close to the point the work breaks off. As part of his revised version's greater emphasis on man's need for higher help, Sidney altered his use of the oracle. In the first version, the narrator, speaking for Sidney, described Basilius's opening consultation of the oracle as a "vanity" arising from a mistaken desire to know the future; the priestess of Apollo was "furiously inspired" and appointed to an "impiety" (*OA,* 5). Ten pages from the end of the *New Arcadia,* we find that same priestess spoken of as possessed with a "sacred" fury (I.510). At this late point in the work Basilius, confronted with the choice of marrying Pamela off to Anaxius or resuming armed conflict, sends Philanax to Delphos once again. Basilius's desire to hear the oracle's words is criticized, as it was in the *Old Arcadia,* but for a totally different reason; the narrator this time tells us that Basilius "took the common course of men, to fly only then to devotion when they want resolution" (I.510). Basilius, then, looks to heaven as a way to avoid making a decision he ought rightly to have made on his own.

But the oracle has a message not only for Basilius but for Philanax as well. If Basilius looks to heaven in order to avoid his own responsibility, Philanax does not regard heaven enough. Near the end of Book II, when the material that opened the *Old Arcadia* was finally presented, Philanax gave as one of his reasons for opposing Basilius's retirement from public duties the fact that Basilius conceived of the idea after consulting an oracle: "all oracles holding (in my conceit) one degree of reputation, it sufficed me to know it was but an oracle which led you from your own course" (I.326–27). When the oracle is consulted a second time, here in

Book III, the spirit possessing the priestess answers Philanax even before he has a chance to pose his question ("as if it would argue [that is, accuse] him of incredulity"), advises that Basilius should not agree to the marriage, and concludes with a command that Philanax should on his part thenceforward "give tribute but not oblation to human wisdom" (I. 510). This last phrase is clearly a response to Philanax's earlier refusal to look upon oracles as anything but superstitions; but it also constitutes a generalized warning against human pride. What heaven, finally, would have Philanax, Basilius, or any other human do is to rely as much as possible on his own abilities but to recognize that he cannot rely totally upon them. For heaven sees a need for the practice of both Euarchus's and Pamela's virtue in the human journey through this world: both types of virtue are needed to respond adequately to the conditions of a world in which well-meaning men and women are more than likely to be hampered by their own limitations as human beings and by the real evil outside them.

Book III's focus on this apparently new type of virtue, Christian patience, does not, then, denote any softening in Sidney's insistence upon adhering to the active life or in his animus toward a life of merely pastoral retirement. He does allow now for the exemplification of virtue within Arcadia, but by the time he reveals that virtue fully in the *New Arcadia,* Arcadia is no longer the setting of the pastoral tradition, the land described in the opening pages of the *Old Arcadia* and by Klaius near the beginning of the *New Arcadia* as "decked with peace and (the child of peace) good husbandry," a place wherein live "a happy people, wanting little because they desire not much" (I. 14). When rebellion and the disruptive ambition and atheism of Cecropia enter Arcadia, there is little to differentiate that land from neighboring Laconia or the rest of the world, with its figures like Plexirtus or Antiphilus. Life may perhaps be simplified in Arcadia so that Sidney can examine man as man, as distinguished from a heroic or political being, and can educate the princes in their own nature. But there is no such place as the Arcadia of the literary pastoral tradition and hence no cause or opportunity to abandon the principles that ought to govern man's conduct under normal circumstances, the principles of the active life.

TO SEE THE EXTENT of Sidney's preoccupation with human limitations and hence the strength of his continued insistence upon the need to adhere to the active life, we might glance finally at another Renaissance work concerned at its best and most serious point with the education of princes, Castiglione's *Courtier.* It is a work frequently called an Arcadia, since it pictures what its author views as an ideal society set off from a more complex and harsher world outside its bounds.[32] If it is to be considered a version of pastoral, though, it is definitely of the Italian rather than the English sort, for through it runs a strong strain of that suffused melancholy we have seen to be the dominant mood of Sannazaro's *Arcadia*. Castiglione wrote the work over a long period and in a number of different stages, and by the time he agreed to publish it in 1527–28 he was writing of what was for him a very special gathering of people upon whom time and subsequent political events had taken a particularly heavy toll. In both his Prefatory Letter and his remarks opening Book IV, he paused to comment at length on the number and personalities of the companions who joined together for those wondrous evenings in 1507 and who had since died, their like not soon to return. But whatever sorrows Castiglione might bear over the loss of his ideal gathering at Urbino, there are signs as well of an idealizing optimism in the work, some of which merely reflects the views of individual speakers in the discussions and some of which is the author's own—to be seen especially at the point where Castiglione's work draws closest to Sidney's.

In Book IV, Ottaviano Fregoso objects to his peers' relatively shallow description of the ideal courtier as a figure of elegant and easy nonchalance whose main purpose in life seems to be to please his prince and the ladies of the court; and he proceeds to describe his own ideal courtier as a moral and political adviser to his prince, a conception closely resembling the early English Humanist ideal adviser and the type of figure Sidney himself no doubt aspired to be in proffering advice on such matters as Queen Elizabeth's marriage. Ottaviano's ideal courtier, he frankly admits, is a teacher to his prince, and Ottaviano is rather sanguine over the probable success of his ideal courtier's efforts. He holds to the Socratic and Platonic tenet that a man who truly knows the Good will never deliberately choose to do evil, a position that Gaspare Pallavicino and Pietro Bembo (himself a Platonist, as it turns out) commonsensically take issue with as being oversimple: men have been known to struggle against what they knew to be an evil desire and then, despite the struggle, to succumb to their worser instincts (IV.xiii–xv).[33]

What Bembo probably would not disagree with is Ottaviano's answer to the question whether the active or contemplative life is most fitting for the properly taught ruler he describes. The ruler needs to lead both lives, but especially the contemplative, and Ottaviano then divides the two lives each into two parts: contemplation for a ruler entails both the attaining of clear insight and judgment and the proper issuing of commands; and his action consists of often being present to see that his orders are carried out and even at times performing them himself (IV.xxvi). Ottaviano, sanguine once again, envisions relatively easy movement back and forth between the two lives, but has no doubt that the contemplative is ultimately the superior: "the end of the active life ought to be the contemplative, just as war leads to peace and work to rest" (IV.xxvi). His own emphasis rests most heavily perhaps on the active life and what he defines as the second part of the contemplative life, the issuing of lawful commands ("il commandar è sempre il principal officio de' prìncipi"). But the first part of contemplation, right knowledge and judgment, is rendered its full due in what follows in Book IV, with Bembo's demonstration of the joys of the contemplative life in his ecstatic rise up the Platonic ladder of love to a dwelling place in the realm of pure Ideas, the ultimate goal, we are led to believe, of courtier and prince alike. It is presumably through such a rise that the ruler gains the insight and ideas with which to issue his orders; but the contemplative state Bembo describes and momentarily enjoys is also clearly an end in itself, for it is in such a state that one draws closest to the divine, in fact, is united with God.[34]

The contrast with Sidney in all of this is striking. In the 1593 account of Euarchus's actions prior to his journey to Arcadia, Sidney's ideal prince is described as "being none of them who think all things done for which they have once given direction," and hence he "followed everwhere his commandment with his presence" (*OA*, 356, Textual Apparatus; II.150). What for Ottaviano Fregoso was "often" a necessity is viewed as a neverending responsibility by Euarchus, and Sidney's ideal ruler never gets beyond what Castiglione's speaker considers mere action. Sidney would not, of course, deny his ideal prince the insight which gives rise to correct commands. But he plainly does not share the optimism that enables Castiglione to have Ottaviano see easy movement between the complementary lives of action and contemplation or allows Castiglione himself then to provide an example of the contemplative state in which man rises above earthly concerns and reaches ultimate human fulfillment in the realm of pure goodness and Ideas.

Sidney's vision is a good deal darker than Castiglione's, even with the latter's melancholy. The only type of life Sidney views as complementary to Euarchus's dedication to "doing" or activity is Pamela's suffering; and although the latter might draw one's sights toward God's plan for man, it can hardly be considered a mode of contemplation encompassing man's highest happiness. It is merely, as we have seen, the line of conduct one pursues when no longer able to act effectively on one's own to achieve virtuous aims. The active life constitutes an ideal for Sidney: his Euarchus looks upon doing good as "the only *happy* action of man's life" (*OA*, 359; 1593 version: *OA*, 357, Textual Apparatus, or II.152; my emphasis). Yet that type of life is also the only course of conduct possible in the particular world Sidney envisions. That world simply does not allow a prince or anyone else opportunity to take time off from immediate, everyday concerns in order to climb to those contemplative heights Castiglione (and Plato and Aristotle and mystics in the specifically Christian tradition before him) would consider man's ultimate fulfillment and highest degree of happiness. It is a world we must, in the end, use the explicitly Christian term of "fallen" to describe, despite the pagan setting of Sidney's work. For the confusion and evil the young princes encounter in the world outside Arcadia arise from the very source that makes it difficult for them to reconcile their passions with their reason—man's fall from grace. There may well be instances of legitimate human achievement, as in the cases of Euarchus and Pamela. Such achievement must be viewed, though, in light of the recognition that not everyone is going to follow the examples of virtue put before him or her and that there is constant danger of falling away from one's own highest level of achievement. And one certainly cannot talk then, as Castiglione's Ottaviano does, of a new Golden Age to be ushered in once the manner and method of good government have been established by properly educated princes (IV.xviii). Man has to struggle so much with his own recalcitrant nature and with that of his uncooperative fellowmen that he cannot allow himself the luxury of such dreams. Sidney's anti-pastoralism may have manifested itself at first as a relatively minor, even snobbish, discomfort with a literary convention's assumption that simple and sophisticated people are cultural and social equals; but it is this view of life as a constant struggle, finally, which constitutes his major objection to the pastoral mode and what he saw as its idealized vision of man at ease.

CHAPTER IV

Shakespeare's "Golden Worlds"

he *Two Gentlemen of Verona* provides good evidence that anti-pastoralists are made and not born, that an anti-pastoral stance arises from continued thinking on the literary use and meaning of a sojourn in a pastoral landscape. *The Two Gentlemen* is the earliest and least successful of Shakespeare's plays to utilize a structure that Northrop Frye has labeled the "drama of the green world," comedies whose action "begins in a world represented as a normal world, moves into the green world, goes into a metamorphosis there in which the comic resolution is achieved, and returns to the normal world."[1] This structure, which Frye derives from popular medieval romance and folklore, is also the basic structure of pastoral romance we have seen suggested in Sannazaro's *Arcadia* and then subjected to Sidney's anti-pastoral purposes in the *Old Arcadia*. Walter R. Davis's several studies on explicitly pastoral romances—that is, works that insist upon their connection with the earlier pastoral tradition, as differentiated from Frye's more popular sources—have elaborated upon Frye's scheme and emphasized its psychological dimension. The pastoral sojourner retreats from the pain and turmoil of the actual world, experiences love and undergoes calm self-analysis in Arcadia, and then returns to the outer world in harmony with himself.[2] Shakespeare was to turn to this scheme, either in this psychological or in Frye's more general form, which encompasses a play's whole society, some eight times in his career,[3] and it is in the use of this particular comic structure as opposed to that of a history play or a tragedy that we might best determine the degree of the playwright's pas-

toralism or anti-pastoralism. For when Henry VI in the midst of battle expresses a desire "To be no better than a homely swain" (*3 Henry VI*, II.v.22), he is turning his back upon his responsibilities in the public, heroic world; such a wish is more likely to be expressing Shakespeare's judgment upon Henry than upon the pastoral ideal. But in the drama of the green world Shakespeare had at hand a structure in which characters might legitimately seek refuge in a pastoral landscape in order to escape fortune's blows or regain emotional balance, with no opprobrium being cast on their act of retreat; it is when and if Shakespeare shows himself unwilling to accept the full implications of that structure that we can with some assurance talk of his being anti-pastoralist in the way I have been using that term.

The full implications of the pastoral romance structure might best be understood as those assumed by Charles the Wrestler of *As You Like It* when he says that Duke Senior and his band "fleet the time carelessly as they did in the golden world"; they are a reflection of the merging of Arcadia with the Golden Age or prelapsarian Eden discussed in my opening chapter and are implications that Frye, with his interest not simply in literary structures but in the archetypal patterns or myths lying beneath those structures, might be expected to seize upon. And in the scheme Frye (and Davis after him) postulates, the green or pastoral world is a realm where special conditions are in effect, a realm of wish-fulfillment closer than the normal world to the ideal life of the Golden Age or Eden:

> The forest or green world, then, is a symbol of natural society, the word natural here referring to the original human society which is the proper home of man, not the physical world he now lives in but the "golden world" he is trying to regain. This natural society is associated with things which in the context of the ordinary world seem unnatural, but which are in fact attributes of nature as a miraculous and irresistible reviving power.[4]

Frye's green world is thus qualitatively different from normal life outside its bounds, in effect morally purer since it is a more direct reflection of Eden. Contact with that purer realm must, as if of necessity, prove morally or psychically therapeutic, an assumption which might well account for the apparently miraculous events that tend to occur in Shakespeare's green worlds (for instance, the immediate conversion of villains as soon as they enter a forest).

One of the troublesome characteristics of *The Two Gentlemen of Verona*, yet one which makes the play instructive in a consideration of Shakespeare's attitude toward pastoral, is that in its green-world scenes it adheres unequivocally to the form and concomitant implications that Frye has sketched for us. It is, in fact, the only Shakespearian green-world play to do so, and it thereby becomes vulnerable to the charge of escapism. It does not impose the limits upon the pastoral impulse toward retirement that Shakespeare's later pastoral plays do, and unlike those later plays it does not insist upon a realistic vision of, or fallen quality in, the forest in which the characters take refuge.

The particular appeal of the forest of this early play is suggested by Valentine in the soliloquy which opens the final scene:

> How use doth breed a habit in a man!
> This shadowy desert, unfrequented woods,
> I better brook than flourishing peopled towns:
> Here can I sit alone, unseen of any,
> And to the nightingale's complaining notes
> Tune my distresses, and record my woes.
> O thou that dost inhabit in my breast,
> Leave not the mansion so long tenantless,
> Lest growing ruinous, the building fall,
> And leave no memory of what it was.
> Repair me, with thy presence, Silvia:
> Thou gentle nymph, cherish thy forlorn swain.
>   [V.iv.1–12][5]

The first six lines especially do little but present a very conventional statement of the country's superiority to the court, the only doubt of this superiority being expressed in the initial line's suggestion that Valentine has had to learn to enjoy the country, that he at first held a courtier's prejudice against it. The country, here, holds much the same appeal for Valentine as it did for Sannazaro's Sincero. This green world is a place where a "forlorn swain" can indulge himself in grief and not worry overmuch about most of life's responsibilities; the country is being viewed, to use Panofsky's phrase again, "through the soft, colored haze of sentiment," and that view is symptomatic of the handling of the forest scenes throughout the final two acts of the play.

We are otherwise told relatively little about the forest of *The Two Gentlemen*. Silvia in the final scene wishes that she had been seized by a hungry lion rather than saved by the false Proteus (V.iv.33–35); but there are no hungry lions in this particular forest. In lieu of other evidence we are forced to accept the outlaw existence of the exiles who inhabit the forest as representative of life there generally. And if life at court in the play proves to be characterized by petty squabbles, below-stairs plotting, and flamboyant and unrealistic speechifying, the Robin Hood life that the forest scenes present hardly serves as a more viable alternative. Upon one brief meeting, the outlaws consider Valentine "a man of such perfection" (IV.i.57) that they elect him their leader, simply on the basis of his "goodly shape," his own claim that he knows languages, and his announcement that he has killed a man. The whole sequence of events in the forest scenes—from the moment when the exiled Valentine in effect applies for membership in the outlaw band by inventing an offense far more serious than the intended elopement of which he was guilty (IV.i.26–29) to his final request that the Duke pardon those companions "full of good, / And fit for great employment" (V.iv.154–55)—is merely wish-fulfilling fantasy. The humor with which Shakespeare handles his pasteboard outlaws, who equate an outright murder with an attempt to elope with a Duke's daughter, calling both "petty" crimes (IV.i.47–52), reveals that the playwright himself is looking upon the green world of this play as a realm where society's everyday rules do not apply and do not need to.

What is perhaps most startling about this treatment of life in the forest is that the forest scenes come at the end of a play that has in every other respect been moving its characters to a realistic perception of themselves and the world around them. The play as a whole is structured around the education of the two gentlemen of the title, an education which Proteus's guardians see as designed to make a young man "perfect," by which is meant early in the play simply "tried and tutor'd in the world"; the young gentlemen are to become courtiers, adept in the social arts (I.iii.17–23). Their full education takes them, though, both to the court at Milan and to those "unfrequented woods" where both young men are brought to understand that true human perfection would involve unfallen virtue and hence that there is slight possibility of actually achieving that state. It is Proteus himself who ultimately corrects Valentine's and Julia's earlier descriptions of him as possessing "angel-like" and "divine" perfection (II.iv.61; II.vii.13), when he admits fully to what has been his own very imperfect conduct:

> O heaven, were man
> But constant, he were perfect. That one error
> Fills him with faults; makes him run through all th' sins;
> Inconstancy falls off, ere it begins.
> What is in Silvia's face but I may spy
> More fresh in Julia's, with a constant eye?
> [V.iv.109–14]

Just as Shakespeare has Proteus speak here in terms of a generalized man, not simply of personal offenses, a proper view of any man in the world of this play has to take into account the ways in which man is not perfect but rather quite flawed and fallen.

If we can speak of accepting full responsibility for one's own bad actions in a tarnished world as part of an anti-escapist ethic, *The Two Gentlemen of Verona* presents an unusual instance of an author proposing such an ethic before realizing that an attitude toward a pastoral retreat might in some way be related to it. The play reveals a disharmony between the realistic vision toward which the action as a whole moves its characters and the quite unrealistically portrayed green world in which that vision is finally achieved. There is little reason why Proteus's final recognition of himself and all men as imperfect and fallen should take place in this particular forest. While using the Renaissance pastoral romance's sojourn in the green or pastoral world in order to resolve complications arising at court, Shakespeare fails to take full advantage of a natural setting which might better have served to mirror more explicitly the fallen state of the men going into it; the setting might thereby have enhanced the education in man's own nature which was the main concern of the play.[6] The woods of *The Two Gentlemen* can be said to have been unfrequented, then, not only by figures in the play's normal court world, but by the playwright himself: Shakespeare simply did not bring the force of his whole imagination to bear on the forest he was using, and the result was an unthinking or automatic acceptance of a pastoral romance structural scheme he adopted from pastoral writers before him, most likely from Montemayor, whose *Diana* was one of the sources of the play.

The Two Gentlemen's forest scenes represent what we can consider a missed opportunity for Shakespeare, but one he would not miss again. In his later green-world comedies, and particularly his two most overtly pastoral plays, *As You Like It* and *The Winter's Tale,* the playwright does focus fully upon the assumptions embodied in the pastoral romance form, and the outcome of this new concentration is an attitude toward a pastoral sojourn similar to, if less assertive than, Sidney's. Life in Sidney's Arcadia proved to be virtually indistinguishable from life outside its boundaries, and his Arcadia provided no escape from the normal cares and responsibilities of the outside heroic world. Sidney was able to call upon pastoral's traditional function of examining man as man—as an individual as opposed to a prince or public figure—and yet still nursed in both versions of his *Arcadia* an objection to the requirement of placing such an examination in a pastoral setting. The pastoral worlds of *As You Like It* and *The Winter's Tale* are, similarly, only simplified reflections of the normal world outside their bounds, not qualitatively different from it; they provide only limited relief from the concerns of everyday life.

Shakespeare is, to be sure, less grudging than Sidney in granting his characters a sojourn in Arcadia, but the force of his pastoral plays' arguments is either to insist upon the need to leave Arcadia again or at least to cure characters of wrong ways of thinking about Arcadia and the idea of retreat generally. While Shakespeare uses the pastoral sojourn to educate his characters, those characters emerge from Arcadia and their education, much like Pyrocles and Musidorus before them, not closer to man's unfallen state but more fully aware of the ways in which they themselves and the world around them are time-bound, fallen, and limited. The pastoral plays, like all of Shakespeare's comedies, are directed not toward any past or even future more perfect life but toward full participation in life in the present.

THE FOREST OF ARDEN

As You Like It is the most self-consciously literary of Shakespeare's pastorals and among the most literary of all his plays. Like Sidney's *Old Arcadia,* it takes its start from an argument with conventional literary pastoralism, in this case as that mode is represented by the play's main source, Lodge's *Rosalynde*. While relying heavily upon Lodge for his characters and action, Shakespeare uses his inherited material in such a way as to undermine many of the basic assumptions of Lodge and other pastoral writers like Sannazaro and Montemayor, particularly the belief in Arcadia as a special land of ease and escape from worldly responsibilities.[7] If Shakespeare paid too little attention to the pastoral setting of his first green-world play, in this one he may well have paid it too much; for the play is, as critical studies have frequently pointed out, particularly lean in dramatic action. In place of any dramatic complication or plot, we have in the middle acts especially a series of apparently casual encounters or debates between various characters in which they discuss their views primarily on two closely related subjects, romantic love and pastoral life.[8] But no matter what the appearances, those encounters in the forest are not so casual after all. Shakespeare uses them to mold, burnish, and refine his version of an ideal human sensibility, the sensibility embodied in the play by the central, controlling figure of Rosalind. It is a sensibility that can, among other things, take full advantage of the freedom a pastoral sojourn might offer without succumbing to the belief that life in Arcadia is significantly different from life elsewhere.

THE FOREST OF ARDEN is no Eden.[9] While apparently miraculous conversions of evil men to good do occur in the Forest of Arden, those conversions warrant close examination to determine how miraculous they actually are. That they are in the play at all is an indication that the connection between Arcadia and Eden or the Golden Age was a part of Shakespeare's consciousness in writing a pastoral work; yet the thrust even of those conversions, and particularly Oliver's, which is described in most detail, is to remind us of the difference between present Arcadia or Arden and past Eden. Oliver is rendered a true brother again and fully confesses to his former "unnatural" behavior in seeking to kill Orlando (IV.iii.123–37).[10] Such wording might appear to mark a return toward man's original condition when his actions and desires would have been totally in accord with God's design for him, before man's true nature was obscured by the fall. But Oliver's conversion did not just occur as if by magic in the forest: it was the result of considered, human action on Orlando's part, and action that involved ridding Oliver of the threat of a serpent and a lioness. This is plainly not a realm in which lions lie down peacefully next to lambs, or men; and serpents also have already become dangerous. If Oliver has entered into a "better world" (LeBeau's phrase of I.ii.274) in the forest, it is an entrance made with full recognition both of human sinfulness and of animal savagery.

That Arden is a fallen landscape we learn initially from Duke Senior, who at his first appearance defines both himself and his immediate surroundings for us:

> Now my co-mates and brothers in exile,
> Hath not old custom made this life more sweet
> Than that of painted pomp? Are not these woods
> More free from peril than the envious court?
> Here feel we not the penalty of Adam,
> The seasons' difference, as the icy fang
> And churlish chiding of the winter's wind,
> Which when it bites and blows upon my body
> Even till I shrink with cold, I smile, and say
> "This is no flattery. These are counsellors
> That feelingly persuade me what I am."
> Sweet are the uses of adversity.
> [II.i.1–12]

The Duke is saying, not that he escapes from the effects of the fall in Arden, but that he is fully conscious of those effects and yet they do not bother him (hence there is no need for Theobald's famous emendation of line 5's "not" to "but"). But if the Duke is apparently clear-sighted in his observation of Arden as fallen and demonstrates some familiarity with his natural surroundings, he is nonetheless an unreliable witness; for there is much in his opening speech to suggest that he has never left the court and been in a state of nature after all.[11] Like Valentine's forest, the Duke's Arden is perceived very much after the manner of earlier Renaissance pastoral poetry and romance. He expresses the view that country life is superior to life at court, and in finding his present life "more sweet / Than that of painted pomp" and the woods "More free from peril than the envious court," he thinks he sees a definite difference between court and country. He is assuming the view of the country as a place of relief from worldly cares, a view common in pastoral poetry written at court but not nearly so common among actual country people.

The play's most explicit connection between the Duke's point of view and literary pastoralism is to be found in Amiens's lovely and extremely conventional pastoral song of II.v; the courtier is an extension of the Duke himself, and his song is essentially a restatement of the Duke's opening speech:

> Under the greenwood tree,
>   Who loves to lie with me,
> And turn his merry note
>   Unto the sweet bird's throat,
> Come hither, come hither, come hither.
>   Here shall he see
>   No enemy,
> But winter and rough weather.
>
> Who doth ambition shun,
>   And loves to live i' th' sun,
> Seeking the food he eats,
>   And pleas'd with what he gets,
> Come hither, come hither, come hither.
>   Here shall he see
>   No enemy,
> But winter and rough weather.
>
> [II.v.1–8, 35–42]

The tradition has been Anglicized in the song's reference to the greenwood tree of English ballads rather than to the more specific beech of Virgil, but the posture of a man lying beneath a tree and gaily singing or piping to the birds overhead is one that looks back ultimately to Virgil's First Eclogue and, beyond that, to Theocritus's *Idylls*. With the important qualification which admits once again that there is a winter season in Arden and hence that the forest is not actually part of an Edenic or "golden world," this song's evocation of traditional pastoral *otium* bears out at least the substance of Charles's remark about Duke Senior's life in the forest: while the Duke, Amiens, and the rest of the gentlemen-foresters there sing, hunt, talk, and feast, they *do* "fleet the time carelessly."

The Duke and Amiens come by their conception of country life most directly from Lodge's *Rosalynde*. But there, the view of the country as a place essentially free from care is ascribed to a country figure rather than an exiled courtier, and this difference accounts in large part for the considerable differences in tone and attitude between the play and its source. Lodge fully endorses the attitudes expressed by the Duke and by Amiens's song; since a shepherd ought to be able to speak authoritatively about the country in which he has spent all his life, there is little reason to question the picture of country life Coridon provides:

> and for a shepheards life (oh Mistresse) did you but live a while in their content, you would saye the Court were rather a place of sorrowe, than of solace. Here (Mistresse) shall not Fortune thwart you, but in meane misfortunes, as the losse of a few sheepe, which, as it breedes no beggerie, so it can bee no extreame prejudice: the next yeare may mend al with a fresh increase. Envie stirres not us, wee covet not to climbe, our desires mount not above our degrees, nor our thoughts above our fortunes. Care cannot harbour in our cottages, nor doo our homely couches know broken slumbers: as we exceede not in diet, so we have inough to satisfie: and Mistres I have so much Latin, *Satis est quod sufficit*.[12]

Lodge is assuming for the purposes of his fiction that the literary conception of pastoral *otium* presents an accurate view of country life, and his *Rosalynde* is throughout marked by just such a strict, unquestioning adherence to the assumptions of the pastoral convention.[13] Lodge's Arden is an artificial, idealized realm of special conditions, one in which courtiers and shepherds can converse with one another on equal terms, in fact, in exactly the same terms; all the lovers in the work, regardless of class, speak the same elegant, Petrarchan language. The sheep that most need tending here are thoughts or passions, and few of the normal concerns of everyday country life enter within its borders.

Shakespeare's distance from the assumptions of his source is shown most directly in his character Corin, the figure in the play who corresponds in his actions, but not in many of his opinions, to Lodge's Coridon. Corin presents a much more down-to-earth picture of life in the country, and his overall function in the play is to act as a corrective to the Duke's and Amiens's view of pastoral life. He later is to announce that he (like Coridon) envies no man and is satisfied with little (III.ii.71–75), but his first words to a court figure attest that a shepherd's life is by no means necessarily an easy or happy one, that very real misery exists in Arden:

> CORIN.   Who calls?
> TOUCH.   Your betters sir.
> CORIN.   Else are they very wretched.
>   [II.iv.64–66]

And he goes on to provide evidence that, quite contrary to the implications in the Duke's thinking, people in the country can be just as selfish and greedy as those at court: Corin can provide little aid for the travel-weary Aliena because he is not master of his own sheep but is subject to the rule of a churlish country master who "little recks to find the way to heaven / By doing deeds of hospitality" (II.iv.78–80). An actual shepherd does not simply lie beneath a greenwood tree and play upon his pipe as Amiens's song might have us believe, but rather has to make a living, even in Arden. Like the Duke, Corin recognizes a difference between court and country, but in contrast with the Duke's assumption that court people are envious and malicious while country people are not, the distinction he points to is a real one. The difference between court and country people is merely a difference in manners and customs, rather than one in man's nature:

> Those that are good manners at the court are as ridiculous in the country as the behaviour of the country is most mockable at the court. You told me you salute not at the court, but you kiss your hands: that courtesy would be uncleanly if courtiers were shepherds. [III.ii.44–49]

It is Corin's direct knowledge of the greasy quality of a sheep's fleece which prompts him to make such an observation. And his direct knowledge of country life enables him to point out for us the discrepancy between country life as it really is and idealized country life as it is envisioned by Duke Senior, Amiens, and Thomas Lodge.

Shakespeare's treatment of the other shepherds in his play shows a similar movement away from Lodge's pastoralism. Silvius, like Montanus, his counterpart in Lodge, is through much of the play pursuing the proud and pitiless Phebe, claiming in Petrarchan manner that he bears invisible wounds from love's keen arrows (III.v.30–31). Phebe has a more critical sensibility than does Lodge's shepherdess of that name—she points to the exaggeration in Silvius's complaints—but she also has considerably less beauty. Instead of a figure who in Lodge was the fairest shepherdess in all Arden, we have in *As You Like It* one who needs to be told by Rosalind that she should sell when she can (III.v.60). Such a figure can have little claim to occupy the idealized realm of conventional Renaissance pastoralism she aspires to in her Petrarchan disdain. Even less appropriate in such a realm would be the two rustics Shakespeare added to his source, William and Audrey. Lodge's Montanus was bilingual (one of his songs was in French); Shakespeare's William has barely mastered English. The longest single word he speaks is his own name. He and Audrey are caricatures of country figures, Shakespeare's equivalent to Sidney's Dametas and his family, and (it is to be hoped) as far removed from actual shepherds as are Silvius and Phebe. Shakespeare has given us in Corin a country figure with a good measure of dignity and intelligence; in the literal-minded William and Audrey he shows that living close to nature does not necessarily provide even a modicum of good sense, much less refinement.

Corin, Silvius and Phebe, William and Audrey, all provide what we can call unconscious criticism of Duke Senior's and Lodge's pastoralism. They help Shakespeare establish a realistic picture of pastoral life and love, but in doing so are unaware that they serve such a function. Corin, for example, does not intentionally correct the Duke; he simply speaks of his life as he lives and sees it. To all these unwitting critics, Shakespeare added two others not to be found in Lodge, both of whom consciously set themselves up as critics of Duke Senior's attitude. Touchstone and Jaques are directly familiar with both court and country, and both hold to the belief that country life is no better than life at court; in fact, in several respects it is decidedly worse. Both see that the country is by no means necessarily a place of ease and relief. Touchstone bemoans the lack of simple creature comforts there, and Jaques, in effect agreeing with Corin's realistic picture of country life, counters Amiens's song praising the country with his own verse asserting that only an ass or stubborn-willed fool (like the courtiers circled around him as he speaks) would leave the court's "wealth and ease" to take up life in the forest (II.v.47–54); if *otium* is to be found anywhere, it is only in the aristocratic life at court where there are servants and courtiers of lower rank to do one's bidding.

It is Jaques's claim that there is a close affinity between himself and Touchstone, so close that he wishes to assume a suit of motley and set himself up as a professional fool. But whereas the two do have a good deal in common, both having been added by Shakespeare to his source material to puncture the illusions of their fellow characters and to help in the criticism of more conventional literary pastoralism, the two actually serve very different purposes in the play. As professional fool, Touchstone acts very much as his name suggests. Through parody and mimicry he tests the assumptions of the play's other characters in order to expose their illusions, but without necessarily suggesting what should be substituted in their stead. His comments do reveal a rather conservative estimate of what is real, as he customarily disregards whatever he does not break his shins against. But beyond that, there is not much consistency to his opinions: he simply assumes one perspective and then another—for instance, when in conversation with Corin he tries at the same time both to mock the affected snobbery of a courtier and yet to bring Corin to admit that the country is inferior to the court (III.ii.31–83). He holds to what Richard Lanham has called the rhetorical view of life.[14] Merely a rhetorical being, he has, finally, no substantive existence in the play's world, and although we should be very sorry to see him go, Touchstone is thus not strictly necessary to the play's central argument. Jaques, on the other hand, *is* necessary to that argument and represents a much more significant addition to Shakespeare's source than all the others combined. Accordingly, it is necessary to examine Jaques and his position in the play in detail.

JAQUES, QUITE UNLIKE Touchstone, speaks and acts from a fixed point of view, one that is consistently negativistic and pessimistic. A generation ago James Smith accused him of posing as a skeptic, an adherent to what is in fact an inconsistent doctrine, a belief that denies the possibility of belief and of meaningful human action.[15] We need not necessarily posit a whole philosophic system to Jaques or label it, but we should note that his point of view is pronounced enough to put him at odds with virtually every other character in the play. And because of his negativism Jaques cannot be included in the celebration at the play's end: as all the other characters proceed to the marriage feast presided over by Hymen, who "peoples every town" (V.iv.143), as they thus take active steps toward ensuring the continuance of the race and building a society that is to endure into future generations, Jaques is forced not only by his own desires but by the play's comic logic as well to retire to a more remote part of the forest and to absent himself from the new society taking shape at the play's conclusion.

At the point Jaques announces his desire to become a professional fool, he receives the strongest of several rebukes he has to endure in the play:

> Most mischievous foul sin, in chiding sin.
> For thou thyself hast been a libertine,
> As sensual as the brutish sting itself,
> And all th' embossed sores and headed evils

> That thou with license of free foot hast caught
> Wouldst thou disgorge into the general world.
> [II.vii.64–69]

This speech is somewhat out of character for the basically good-natured Duke, who has earlier confessed that he actually enjoys coping with Jaques in the latter's sullen fits (II.i.67). And we are by no means obligated to accept its charges as fully true; there is little direct evidence within the play that Jaques was once a libertine. But the lines do indicate that the period of Jaques's activity—if it ever did exist, and whether it was good or bad—is in the past. The position he now holds is that of someone tired of action and of life. The melancholy man, Thomas Overbury tells us, "thinkes businesse, but never does any: he is all contemplation, no action."[16] And the melancholy Jaques is merely an observer, one who goes around gaining knowledge and experience and doing nothing with them. When he looks back at the society he detaches himself from, he expresses distaste for everything he sees: both court and country life, love, lovers, even the name of Rosalind. Everything human is alien to him. He urges Orlando to sit down with him and "rail against our mistress the world and all our misery" (III.ii.272–74), an invitation Orlando refuses to accept, since he finds no cause to chide anything in the world besides himself. The celebrated speech on the seven ages of man, with its focus only on woeful pageants (II.vii.139–66), of course presents a very one-sided picture of human life. The speech conveys not only Jaques's essential dislike of human life but his detachment from it: the metaphor of the world as stage suggests that any given human being is only playing at a part and thus is not a figure one need sympathize with fully in his joys and sorrows.

Donning a suit of motley would enable Jaques to express his dislike of the world around him at will: he says he wishes to "Cleanse the foul body of th' infected world" (II.vii.60), but he is willing to do so only under the condition that no one consider him wise, and hence serious (II.vii.44–47). The statement of this rather contradictory desire is of interest on several counts. One is that it reflects a basic misunderstanding of the role of professional fool in a society. A fool has a special status, occupying a position both inside and outside society at the same time. He is permitted to mock, to parody, to criticize in ways that others are not, but he does so as part of an established social function: he allows for the release through laughter of emotions that would under normal circumstances be repressed by society. He is, then, ultimately a source of social cohesion and remains, like Touchstone at the end of *As You Like It,* a part of the society he criticizes. Jaques, from an alienated vantage point that can see only an "infected world" around him, wants the fool's freedom but fails to recognize the fool's concomitant responsibility of playing an active (if indirect) part in the construction of an enduring, cohesive social group.[17] More important yet is the fact that Jaques's desire to take up motley betrays a wish to avoid moral as well as social responsibility. In desiring the fool's traditional immunity from prosecution (or, alternately, freedom of the press for satirists), Jaques would also gain unlimited opportunity to vent his spleen without ever being called to account for his words. This indulgence, if granted, would place him not simply in the social no-man's land he already occupies in his detachment but in a moral no-man's land as well. And the desire to avoid full moral accountability for what one says or does betrays what we can label as escapist tendencies.

As we might expect, any escapist desires Jaques might have are revealed most fully in his attitude toward pastoral life. One of Duke Senior's lords remarks that Jaques, in ruminating on the fate of an injured deer, pours forth invectives not only against the country, city, and court but even against the particular type of pastoral existence the Duke and his followers are experiencing in the forest:

> Thus most invectively he pierceth through
> The body of country, city, court,
> Yea, and of this our life, swearing that we
> Are mere usurpers, tyrants, and what's worse,
> To fright the animals and to kill them up
> In their assign'd and native dwelling-place.
>
> [II.i.58–63]

Peter G. Phialas has observed that Jaques here is holding to an extreme form of pastoralism,[18] the most extreme voiced in the play. Jaques is totally opposed to man's occupancy of the natural world. By implication he is looking back for his ideal to a benign period before man was forced to hunt and kill animals, even before there was such a thing as human society at all. He yearns, then, for the distant past and for impossible conditions, and with such an attitude he can only observe and attack the world he sees in motion around him. He must be totally outside life that moves in time—precisely the position in which he chooses to remain at the play's conclusion when he decides to stay on in the forest. His claim is that he will observe and learn from the habits of the new monk, Duke Frederick: "Out of these convertites, / There is much matter to be heard and learn'd" (V.iv.183–84). But by this point in the play, it is clear that

Jaques will only be gaining more experience and, as Rosalind has suggested earlier, doing nothing with it but make himself sad (IV.i.20–27). Remaining in the forest will enable him to make permanent both his stance as an observer outside society and his refusal to take up meaningful action of any sort.

In fairness to Jaques, we should observe that while alienated and melancholic, he is not at all a malicious figure. There is a considerable measure of goodwill and humor in the blessings he doles out to the other characters as he takes his leave:

> [*To Duke Sen.*] You to your former honour I bequeath,
>   Your patience and your virtue well deserve it.
> [*To Orl.*] You to a love that your true faith doth merit:
> [*To Oli.*] You to your land and love and great allies:
> [*To Sil.*] You to a long and well-deserved bed:
> [*To Touch.*] And you to wrangling, for thy loving voyage
>   Is but for two months victuall'd. So to your pleasures.
>   I am for other than for dancing measures.
>   [V.iv.185–92]

But while not in fact a villain, Jaques assumes the *role* of villain in the thoroughly comic world of the forest, a world in which true villains are converted to goodness as soon as they enter. For Jaques puts forward the point of view that must be cast out before the life-affirming philosophy of Rosalind and Orlando can reign supreme. By his very existence in the play's world, Jaques helps to define the positive ideals which the play embodies. He favors solitude, detachment, and inaction; he looks back longingly toward the distant past and thus wishes to stop time and to escape from a world governed by it. His whole world view thereby stands diametrically opposed to that held initially by Rosalind alone and finally by Rosalind and Orlando together, an opposition Shakespeare objectifies nicely by his staging when he has Jaques exit right before each of the two great wooing scenes in the forest (at III.ii.289 and IV.i.36).

What precisely Jaques is opposed to in the play can be seen from examining Rosalind's (and ultimately Orlando's) very different response to time.[19] Once Rosalind establishes that Orlando is listening to her, the first question she asks of him in the forest is "I pray you, what is't o'clock?" (III.ii.294). The question proves significant, since it is asked by someone very aware of time's passing and of a figure for whom time is not yet consistently important. Orlando earlier expressed considerable dismay over the enforced idleness resulting from his brother's neglect of him (I.i.32–34), and he showed a distaste for wasting time when he first encountered Duke Senior in the forest and observed that the Duke and his followers "Lose and neglect the creeping hours of time" (II.vii.112). But here in III.ii, Orlando answers Rosalind's query with the assertion that "there's no clock in the forest" (295–96). Rosalind's response in turn is that if Orlando were the kind of lover his poems claim he is, he himself would be the forest's clock: "Then there is no true lover in the forest, else sighing every minute and groaning every hour would detect the lazy foot of Time, as well as a clock" (297–99). Were Orlando to become the kind of lover she suggests, he would of course become even more like the ridiculous Silvius than he already is. But Rosalind's humor covers serious concern: despite his claim to be "love-shaked," Orlando does not yet seem to have a committed lover's consciousness of time, or of anything else. He misses his next appointment with his mock-Rosalind, rather casually excusing himself by saying that he has come within an hour of his promise (IV.i.40–41).

Rosalind meanwhile has been very conscious of the time passing when Orlando is away, and while her high spirits consistently temper her concern with a note of mock sentimentality, she reveals a true lover's distress and dedication when she asks Celia, "But why did he swear he would come this morning and comes not?" (III.iv.17–18) or announces, "I'll tell thee Aliena, I cannot be out of the sight of Orlando" (IV.i.205–6). It is largely because she is aware of the true identity of the man she has been speaking to that time trots hard for Rosalind when Orlando is absent. And he is, no doubt, to be excused for his lack of punctuality and for his ability to part for two hours calmly because he does not realize that Ganymede is his real Rosalind. But one of the ways that Shakespeare has of showing that Orlando is worthy of the love of the generally more witty Rosalind is to bring him to her consciousness of time. On the second occasion that he misses an appointment with Ganymede, Orlando has a valid excuse, his fight with the lion which threatened his brother. And despite his wound, he remembers this time to send a messenger to his mock-Rosalind to explain his absence. It is when Orlando finally expresses impatience with the masquerade with Ganymede, when a mock-Rosalind will no longer serve his turn for the real one, that she acknowledges that Orlando has passed his test and is ready to receive her. Rosalind has used a game as a way of showing Orlando that his earlier claim to be a lover was also only a type of game or pose, merely borrowed Petrarchanism. When Orlando now announces that he can "live no longer by thinking" (V.ii.50), Rosalind responds with, "I will weary you then no longer with idle talking," a line which in itself ought to promise fair for Orlando, given his own earlier stated concern over idleness. Mere game playing is now a thing of the past.

Rosalind has been asserting consistently that time is, or should be, important to a lover. But even in the two wooing scenes in the forest when she has been discussing this importance, all movement has in effect stopped while their love is allowed to blossom. It is in these scenes that Shakespeare allows his characters (and us) to relax, to enjoy their pastoral existence more than Sidney's heroes ever could. Orlando may have his obligations to the Duke and he has his fight with the lion, but these are offstage; when onstage the two lovers return over and again to the question whether Orlando is truly in love. Although Rosalind is actually using these encounters to educate Orlando and is not herself idle in them, the two scenes convey a general impression of timelessness, an impression we may in fact not be fully or immediately conscious of as the scenes themselves progress; what points it out forcefully is the abruptness with which the concern for events offstage is reasserted toward the end of IV.i. With no preparation whatsoever, following a speech in which Rosalind discusses the use women make of their wit, Orlando announces: "For these two hours Rosalind, I will leave thee" (168). Orlando's outburst of impatience in V.ii dispels that impression of timelessness and has the effect of bringing their pastoral sojourn to an end. By his impatience Orlando is expressing a desire that time move on so that he might devote himself to action, action in this context being defined as genuine loving as opposed to a life of pretense or mere thinking about love. Rosalind's own interest in a life of such action is to be seen in the complex yet very direct speech which continues from her statement that she will weary Orlando no longer with idle talking:

> Know of me then—for now I speak to some purpose—that I know you are a gentleman of good conceit. I speak not this that you should bear a good opinion of my knowledge, insomuch I say I know you are; neither do I labour for a greater esteem than may in some little measure draw a belief from you to do yourself good, and not to grace me. Believe then, if you please, that I can do strange things. I have since I was three year old conversed with a magician, most profound in his art and yet not damnable. If you do love Rosalind so near the heart as your gesture cries it out, when your brother marries Aliena, shall you marry her.[V.ii. 52–64]

Even though Rosalind is still in disguise as she says this, she shows a desire to get beyond ulterior motives in conversation, to communicate precisely and completely what she means. Language here is stripped bare of any possible ambiguities of expression. In a work with so much play upon and criticism of style, and particularly style in courting, this speech is a breakthrough. In its unambiguous directness it acts out a commitment to action, in this case, to love as opposed to a desire to talk about love as a substitute for the thing itself; such expression stands utterly at odds with both the self-conscious poses of a conventional Petrarchan and pastoral lover like Silvius or the early Orlando and the equally self-conscious detached observations of a Jaques.

Once Orlando and Rosalind have determined that the masquerade should cease, the play's main action is, in effect, completed. Before all the plot complications are resolved and the play's various lovers are paired off in appropriate manner, though, Shakespeare presents us with a picture of yet another pair of pastoral lovers, in a song which itself serves as a reprise for the wooing scenes in the forest. The song helps to enforce a final realistic vision of life in a pastoral world; for it tells of a country lover and his lass who live in a world in which time passes, and in its final two stanzas especially, it insists upon the consequent necessity of seizing the opportunity to love when one can:

> This carol they began that hour,
>   With a hey and a ho and a hey nonino,
> How that a life was but a flower,
>   In spring-time, the only pretty ring-time,
> When birds do sing, hey ding a ding, ding,
> Sweet lovers love the spring.
>
> And therefore take the present time,
>   With a hey and a ho and a hey nonino,
> For love is crowned with the prime,
>   In spring-time, the only pretty ring-time,
> When birds do sing, hey ding a ding, ding,
> Sweet lovers love the spring.
>   [V.iii.26–37][20]

Unlike Marvell's appeal to a coy mistress, this song is an uncompromisingly happy one. In that happiness, it reiterates much of the spirit of life in Arden as experienced by Rosalind and Orlando. Like Rosalind herself, the song recognizes time's passing and yet accepts that movement with joy and confidence. Touchstone claims that there is "no great matter in the ditty" and considers that it is "but time lost to hear such a foolish song" (V.iii.38–39, 43–44). The fool either misses the song's whole point or is merely guilty of indulging in his characteristic contentiousness. In either case, his response serves to remind us that mere criticism, which has been the mode of both Touchstone and Jaques, has not been Shakespeare's full or only purpose in the play. Shakespeare has sought to undermine romanticizing pastoralism, and Touchstone and Jaques have helped in that goal, but he has wished to build a fuller vision of life in its place. There has been more going on in *As You Like It* than those who set themselves up as critics within the play's world would have us believe.

ALL THE BRIEF minor debates in *As You Like It* give way finally to a single major debate, one whose opposing sides are expressed in their fullest form in the whole approach toward life of Rosalind and Jaques, respectively. When Jaques decides to stay on in the forest at the end of the play and join the convertite Duke Frederick, he is repeating the act of a former suitor that Ganymede claimed to have "cured" of love: Ganymede drove that lover "from his mad humour of love to a living humour of madness, which was, to forswear the full stream of the world and live in a nook merely monastic" (III.ii.406–9). Rosalind, for her part, in seeking love and marriage is submitting herself completely to the full stream of the world. The central conflict the two characters embody is at bottom one between an active life and a life of retreat, between a life of love in a world ruled by time and a life of escapist detachment from the world and from other human beings. It is in the particular terms of this conflict that we can perceive Shakespeare's unfairness to the pastoralist position. For that conflict is not the legitimate Renaissance debate between the claims for the active and contemplative life that a work in the pastoral mode might well have prompted, and Shakespeare is no more open to the arguments on behalf of the contemplative life than was Sidney before him. Shakespeare could conceivably have made his extreme pastoralist in the play a Platonic poet or a visionary—after the manner, let us say, of Spenser's Colin Clout of Book VI of *The Faerie Queene*. But in choosing instead to have Jaques betray escapist desires to be free of time's onward movement and of the social world's normal responsibilities, rather than be a true contemplative, the playwright banks his argument so that the pastoralist position is denied full intellectual and moral respectability.

In a debate with terms or sides such as we do have in *As You Like It,* there can be little doubt that Shakespeare's own sympathies lie with Rosalind rather than with the Jaques whose views romantic critics were apt to identify as some version of Shakespeare's own. If we wished, we could easily place not only Shakespeare but all of the play's various characters along a scale between Rosalind's and Jaques's positions. Corin, Celia, and the educated and reformed Orlando, for instance, would in their different ways stand close to Rosalind; Silvius seeks love, but seeks it in a timeless poetic realm and hence would be placed near Jaques. The Duke's position both early and late in the play, though, proves especially important in revealing the play's full stand on conventional pastoralism of, let us say, Lodge's sort. For the Duke (along with his alter ego, Amiens) is, as we have seen, the character most fully identified with Lodge's fictive assumptions; and in a debate with the terms as just defined, a character who indulges in dreams of an Arcadian land free from the usual worldly cares and difficulties would necessarily find himself in Jaques's camp. There are in fact a number of minor details in the play that connect the Duke and Jaques. The metaphor of the world as a stage which Jaques elaborates upon so that it becomes an expression of his own alienation was suggested to him by the Duke (II.vii.137–39); and the Duke confesses early on that it irks him that he and his courtiers are forced to hunt the "native burghers of this desert city" for food (II.i.22–23), a sentiment which the melancholy Jaques elsewhere in the forest carries to his characteristic extreme when he invectively pierces not only the usurping courtiers but even the natural "fat and greasy citizens" of the forest, who in his view have adopted some of mankind's more unattractive qualities (II.i.45–63). Given these metaphoric connections, Jaques takes on the appearance of being, like Amiens, an extension of the Duke himself, and he thereby points up for us the deeper implications of, and dangers in, the Duke's own thinking.

It is to the Duke's credit that he moves at the play's conclusion from Jaques's camp to that of Rosalind. His pastoral dream proves by the end to have been that of a basically good man on vacation. He was, after all, as Amiens has told us, making the best of bad fortune, his enforced banishment (II.i.18–20), and his essential moral health is affirmed at the play's end by his unhesitating willingness to return to court and take up responsible active life in the political world again. This final act of the Duke's is in turn a direct reflection of the whole play's anti-pastoral argument. For the Duke and the play both, the forest is initially a place of possible ease, idleness, and escape from normal cares and responsibilities, but that initial view provides the stimulus for Shakespeare's eventual insistence upon a more active stance. As Shakespeare proceeds to show that the forest is a realm in which time passes, in which man must make a living, and in which nature can be red in tooth and claw, it becomes increasingly clear that the proper response to this pastoral world is to view it for what it is and assume that life within it is not essentially different from life anywhere else. To a character with the sensibility Shakespeare wishes to endorse, a sensibility like Rosalind's, Arden becomes simply a place like any other where one can commit oneself to a life of responsible action and sympathetic involvement with others in a world constantly in motion.

EDEN AND BOHEMIA

Time in *The Winter's Tale* is not something merely talked or sung about but actually appears on stage—to announce a gap of sixteen years in the play's action. This Time is, to all appearances, a thoroughly benevolent and polite chap, anxious to please and careful not to offend: he wishes that the audience may never spend its time less agreeably than it does while watching the play. He speaks in slightly archaic rhymed verse and himself admits to being old-fashioned; but even in the course of this admission, he warns that he is not one to be snickered at or ignored. His admission comes in lines which show that he sees himself not merely as a chorus—the role assigned to him by the Folio's stage direction—but as the author of the play in which he appears:

> Let me pass
> The same I am, ere ancient'st order was,
> Or what is now receiv'd. I witness to
> The times that brought them in; so shall I do
> To th' freshest things now reigning, and make stale
> The glistering of this present, as my tale
> Now seems to it.
>
> [IV.i.9–15][21]

He is Shakespeare's agent in calling attention to the deliberate departure from realistic technique in the play, to the ways in which the play is like an old tale or romance. But at the same time he also asserts the play's ultimate realistic bias. For he notes the similarity between the world of his play and the world outside the play; he claims not only that he controls the lives of his characters but that his power extends over the audience as well; he can and will make just as stale and old-fashioned as this play the "glistering present" in which the audience finds itself. Benevolent and good-natured as he might appear to be, then, he reminds the audience of his very real power, of his ability to please some but try all, to make and unfold error, and to "o'erthrow law, and in one self-born hour / To plant and o'erwhelm custom" (IV.i.8–9).

Most modern critics of *The Winter's Tale* have been unwilling to grant Time the amount of power in the play's world that he claims for himself. The "triumph of time"—to borrow the subtitle from Shakespeare's source for the play—usually seen is one which amounts to a triumph *over* time. The play is most often read as a dramatic embodiment of a myth of renewal, perceived either in Christian terms of a fall and a redemption or in those of pagan fertility myths' cycle of death and rebirth.[22] There are indeed resonances both of vegetation myths and of the Christian drama of redemption in the play, and I am not about to deny their presence. A lost child is found again and is reconciled to her father in a scene which onlookers witness as if they were hearing of "a world ransomed, or one destroyed" (V.ii.15). The play begins in winter and ends in late spring or early summer; Perdita refers to Proserpina when she is handing out flowers; and she and Florizel are as welcome in Sicily "As is the spring to th' earth" (V.i.151). Leontes early in the play sins against Hermione by doubting her chastity and fidelity and commits blasphemy against heaven by denying that there is any truth in Apollo's oracle, acts for which he is evidently punished by the loss of his son and the apparent loss of his daughter and wife; he goes through a period of "saint-like sorrow" under the confessional guidance of a figure named Paulina; and when he wakens his faith (V.iii.95), he is rewarded with the miraculous return of his "gracious" wife, Hermione.

Yet Shakespeare points out that the Hermione who is redeemed is sixteen years older than the woman Leontes accused of infidelity. And no matter how much of a miracle Hermione's resurrection appears to be when it is played on stage, Shakespeare is careful to present us with a more prosaic explanation of how and why she has survived all these years: a gentleman of the court notes that Paulina has visited her removed house two or three times a day since Hermione's apparent death (V.ii.104–7), and Hermione herself tells us that she has remained alive so as to see the daughter whom the Oracle gave her reason to believe had survived (V.iii.125–28). The recognition by Leontes himself that Hermione has more wrinkles now than she did sixteen years earlier brings us to the realization that Time has not been routed after all. In his speech of IV.i, Time notes that he is the same as he was "ere ancient'st order was"; he is, then, beyond the control of his own ravaging power. But he is the only figure in the play who is. The final scene, despite its emphasis on the marvelous and the miraculous, does not bring its characters back to the point at which they began, and a full reading of *The Winter's Tale* must take into account the contradictory conceptions within the play of time being triumphed over and of time still triumphing and having its inevitable eroding effect on human life.

It is Shakespeare's particular use of a pastoral landscape and of the pastoral romance form in *The Winter's Tale* that brings that latter perception of time, as a destroyer, to our attention most forcefully. The play is less self-consciously grounded in the literary pastoral tradition than is *As You Like It* and contains relatively little direct criticism of the pastoral convention merely for being a convention and departing from normal perceived reality. But the play has an anti-pastoral dimension nonetheless, since it takes issue with what Shakespeare evidently saw as lying behind the use of the pastoral convention and pastoral romance form in the Renaissance period. *The Winter's Tale* drives the anti-pastoral argument of *As You Like It* harder and a step further toward a mythic or archetypal conclusion: it gives evidence of Shakespeare taking renewed notice of the merging of pastoral Arcadia with the Golden Age and prelapsarian Eden and objecting strongly to the nostalgic sentimentalism that follows upon the union of those originally quite separate landscapes. The play's action includes a sojourn in a pastoral setting that proves psychologically educative and therapeutic for its court characters, and in this respect, at least, *The Winter's Tale* adheres in relatively orthodox manner to pastoral romance form. But Shakespeare complicates that structure by introducing not the usual one, but two pastoral landscapes: the picture of Polixenes' and Leontes' youth evoked in pastoral terms by Polixenes in I.ii and the Bohemia of Acts III and IV, epitomized in the sheepshearing scene of IV.iv. The two versions of pastoral are significantly different, and in their difference lies much that the play has to tell its major characters and us. For while the first of the pictures of pastoral life is conceived in idealized, Edenic terms and is remembered with fondness by Polixenes (and presumably by Leontes as well), the details of his particular description and the play's subsequent action bring us to see that there is something basically wrong, even diseased, with Polixenes' picture of his youth, with his present nostalgic attitude toward that period in his life, and, by extension, with his whole attitude toward life and the world of time around him. Pastoral Bohemia is then used not simply to provide contrast with the court but to correct the version of pastoral that the court projects out of its tensions: a trip to the real countryside for a view of the country's actual conditions becomes a crucial step in the education or cure of Polixenes, Leontes, and, to the extent that he resembles his elders, Florizel. Through the use of these two versions of pastoral the play opposes, more strongly than *As You Like It* before it, any attempt to return to Edenic conditions in the present world: the yearning for prelapsarian conditions which is part of the discredited pastoral stand in *As You Like It,* but which appears only fleetingly in Jaques's look back to a time before there was strife between man and animal, is here the starting point for the play's central dramatic action.

WHEN IN THE second scene of the play Polixenes is asked by Hermione to describe his and Leontes' youth together, he draws upon imagery from the pastoral world to convey the particularly innocent quality of their experience:

> We were as twinn'd lambs that did frisk i' th' sun,
> And bleat the one at th' other: what we chang'd
> Was innocence for innocence.
> [I.ii.67–69]

It is not just any pastoral scene he is evoking but a specifically Edenic one; for the picture he presents denies the effects of time and the fall on the two young princes. The denial of time occurs in lines describing how he and Leontes felt when they were still young:

> We were, fair queen,
> Two lads that thought there was no more behind,
> But such a day to-morrow as to-day,
> And to be boy eternal.
> [62–65]

Such an attitude is typical of youth, perhaps, and is by no means objectionable. More troublesome, though, is the way Polixenes *now* looks upon that past experience. For as he continues his description he betrays a wish to be a child again and to live in what he considers to have been an unfallen state:

> we knew not
> The doctrine of ill-doing, nor dream'd
> That any did. Had we pursu'd that life,
> And our weak spirits ne'er been higher rear'd
> With stronger blood, we should have answer'd heaven
> Boldly "not guilty," the imposition clear'd
> Hereditary ours.
> [69–75]

These lines take us to the heart of Polixenes' version of pastoral and establish the initial grounds for a debate similar to that underlying *As You Like It*. In his rather futile and wishful "Had we pursu'd that life, / And our weak spirits ne'er been higher rear'd / With stronger blood," Polixenes is giving vent to escapist sentiments, which he expresses in dreams of a misconstrued Eden. He is to find immediate opposition to those sentiments from Hermione, who wittily tries to argue him out of such nostalgia and toward a more realistic and healthy view of his and Leontes' past (and present) state; in this play's court world, one under the control of a mentally disturbed and tyrannical Leontes, her words on this subject, as on virtually all others, are not heeded by the men to whom they are directed.

One of the ways Shakespeare has of distancing us from Polixenes and the sentiments he expresses in this conversation is to have him wander into theological error. The "hereditary imposition" Polixenes refers to is original sin, and he is suggesting that had he and Leontes remained in their childhood state, they would have escaped that taint.[23] With the reference to "stronger blood," he is implying further that it was sexual passion which brought about their fall from grace, an implication Hermione is quick to seize upon. She humorously challenges Polixenes with "By this we gather / You have tripp'd since" (75–76), thus inviting him to be more explicit; and he complies:

> O my most sacred lady,
> Temptations have since then been born to's: for
> In those unfledg'd days was my wife a girl;
> Your precious self had then not cross'd the eyes
> Of my young play-fellow
>
> [76–80]

But Polixenes is being slightly careless with his words and is still not completely aware of the theological implications of his own statements. In effect, he is accusing Hermione of being the cause of Leontes' fall from grace, while at the same time he uses courtly formulas and refers to her as "my most sacred lady." Hermione, for her part, shows that she is more aware of those implications, and she takes Polixenes to task for them. Her initial outburst to this explanation of Polixenes is the cryptic "Grace to boot," the spirit of which might best be expressed by a paraphrase like "Some thanks we get." A more literal translation would read "Grace in addition to the bargain," and by the remark Hermione could well be pointing to the discrepancy in being addressed as "sacred" while being called a Satanic or Eve-like temptress. But she does not stop here; apparently accepting for the moment Polixenes' definition of sexual love as sin, she announces that she is perfectly willing to assume responsibility for the "fall" Polixenes describes:

> Of this make no conclusion, lest you say
> Your queen and I are devils. Yet go on;
> Th' offences we have made you do, we'll answer,
> If you first sinn'd with us, and that with us

> You did continue fault, and that you slipp'd not
> With any but with us.
>
> [81–86]

Throughout this gay and lighthearted interchange, Polixenes has been unconsciously betraying a disapproval or even a fear of sexual love. It is a fear that Hermione plainly does not share. For in telling Polixenes to go on, she even welcomes the charge of being a devil or temptress, if it is only her participation in sexual love which makes her an offender. With such a definition of sin as that of Polixenes being applied by a prosecutor, she is confident of her ability to account for her actions before her judge. Her own implication here then is that she does not consider sexual love between marriage partners as itself a sin. Just as a moment earlier she questioned Polixenes when he suggested that he and Leontes might have escaped the taint of original sin, so here she has a surer hold on Christian doctrine than he does.

Hermione's manner since she began talking with Polixenes has been that of one who is confidently and wittily, yet warmly, cutting through the veneer of complex and courtly expression to the real meaning to be found beneath. Her remark "By this we gather / You have tripp'd since," for instance, reduces to a concise, explicit statement Polixenes' implication about his and Leontes' present moral state. At the end of the dialogue with Polixenes, she applies to her husband's words that same ability to examine speech closely. When she tells Leontes that Polixenes will stay on and is complimented with "Thou never spok'st / To better purpose" (88–89), she queries the remark, implying that it is overstated; she will not rest until she hears the full and explicit truth come from Leontes' mouth:

> LEON. Hermione, my dearest, thou never spok'st
> To better purpose.
> HER.   Never?
> LEON.   Never but once.
> HER. What! have I twice said well? when was't before?
> I prithee tell me: cram 's with praise, and make 's
> As fat as tame things: one good deed, dying tongueless,
> Slaughters a thousand, waiting upon that.
> Our praises are our wages. You may ride 's
> With one soft kiss a thousand furlongs ere
> With spur we heat an acre.
>
> [89–96]

Such a speech as this last gives evidence not only of Hermione's wit but also of her essential health. She is apparently belittling women, and when she says "cram 's with praise, and make 's / As fat as tame things," the primary level of her metaphor equates women with pets that one feeds. But she is eight months pregnant and plainly pleased with herself as she speaks these words, and the exuberance, bordering on harshness or even grossness, of the word "cram" here expresses the opposite of squeamishness. Unlike Polixenes, she is fully willing to accept the flesh and all that might, by some, be considered the gross part of human nature. Her demand to be made fat and her later suggestion of being ridden by a man are a far cry from the repressed mode of sexual innuendo: they are openly and enthusiastically sexual.

The fear of sexual love that Polixenes, on the other hand, reveals in this scene amounts to an inadvertent confession that he and Leontes simply could not deal with sexual passion without disastrous results. That confession is given immediate verification in the sudden outbreak of Leontes' perverted sexual passion, his jealousy. While there is no direct evidence from the text that Leontes overhears the interchange between Hermione and Polixenes, that interchange is in several ways closely connected with Leontes' sudden seizure. Leontes later objects to private conversations between Hermione and Polixenes, conversations which he claims involve paddling of palms, pinching of fingers, and practised smiles (I.ii.115–16), and this interchange between the two is the only one we see. And it is only after, and right after, this conversation between Hermione and Polixenes that we come upon the first definite sign of Leontes' jealousy—his aside of "Too hot, too hot!" (I.ii.108).[24] It seems reasonable to conclude that it is the conversation between Hermione and Polixenes about the princes' Edenic youth, whether Leontes overhears it or not, which provides the immediate stimulus for the outburst of his sexual jealousy, and especially reasonable when we note that the attitude toward sexual love that Polixenes expresses in that conversation is a more distant but deeper cause of that outburst and of Leontes' disease. With the definitions of innocence, sin, and the fall which Polixenes gives in that interchange, it is not surprising—in fact, it is almost inevitable—that one or the other of the princes should be subject to an uncontrollable outburst of misplaced sexual feeling. The sufferer in this case happens to be Leontes, though it was Polixenes who expressed the distrust of sexual experience; but the two princes are in many ways similar, and there is every reason to believe that Polixenes' feelings about his youth and loss of innocence represent those of Leontes as well.

In the opening scene of the play, we are told that the two princes were "trained together in their childhoods, and there rooted betwixt them then such an affection which cannot choose but branch now" (I.i.22–24).

1.1.22-24

Derek Traversi has pointed to the double and contradictory use of "branch" in this sentence, conveying the meaning both of "the unity of living growth" and "a spreading division within that growth."[25] But "affection" also has multiple meanings in this context, and throughout the play. Its principal use here is to indicate the strong emotional attachment the princes have for one another. Yet it can suggest also that the two princes have the same emotional makeup. A stronger suggestion of this similarity, and of their similar attitude toward their youth, is to be found later in I.ii, when Leontes himself brings up the subject of his childhood:

> Looking on the lines
> Of my boy's face, methoughts I did recoil
> Twenty-three years, and saw myself unbreech'd,
> In my green velvet coat; my dagger muzzl'd
> Lest it should bite its master, and so prove,
> As ornaments oft do, too dangerous.
>
> [153–58]

Leontes, like Polixenes, quite understandably looks back to his youth as a time of joy and safety, and he is quite consciously expressing a wish to be back in that happier period; he too wishes he could stop time's movement. But the lines betray something else as well. The reference to his muzzled dagger has sexual suggestions, and if we follow them out, we find the idea expressed that the male sexual organ was originally only an ornament, not designed to be used, but potentially very dangerous to its possessor. Leontes is no doubt largely or totally unaware of this meaning in his lines; he is, he thinks, talking about his dagger, although that in itself is evidence that at some level of his consciousness he is unwilling to confront the fact of his own sexuality. While he may not himself intend any comment on his early sexual experience or fear of it here, the lines, with their buried sexual meaning, do associate Leontes with the distrust of sexual love Polixenes voiced a moment earlier in his conversation with Hermione.

In addition, there is a general parallel in the actions of Polixenes and Leontes in the two halves of this sharply divided play. After a sixteen-year gap, Polixenes participates in much the same sequence of actions as Leontes did earlier. Polixenes' threat to scratch Perdita's beauty with briars (IV.iv.426) is, as Traversi has noted, the exact complement to Leontes' earlier violence against Hermione and Perdita. Outbursts of rage in both figures follow immediately upon the presentation of a picture of life in a pastoral setting, and the result of each outburst is that Perdita is put at the mercy of the sea.[26] The effect of such structural parallelism and of the similarity in the actions, sentiments, and temperaments of Polixenes and Leontes is to make the two characters virtually interchangeable. It is this similarity between the two princes that makes it safe to assume that Polixenes speaks for Leontes as well when he yearns for an existence unaffected by time's movement and provides that definition of primal innocence which implies that sexual love could be no part of man's experience in his unfallen condition. And the emphasized similarity makes it possible to say also that Polixenes is Leontes' stand-in on a trip to a pastoral landscape that is designed to cure them both of those misguided attitudes. The interchangeability of the two characters thus accommodates another of Shakespeare's variations upon pastoral romance form in *The Winter's Tale:* it allows for the pastoral education and regeneration of a character, Leontes, who himself never leaves the court.

THE ACTUAL COUNTRYSIDE in *The Winter's Tale* bears little resemblance to the idealized, innocent pastoral realm Polixenes yearns for and thinks he remembers. Bohemia, in fact, with its storm-ridden seacoast and its man-eating bears, provides one of Shakespeare's harsher pastoral landscapes. And Shakespeare is careful to show in this play also that living close to nature does not automatically or necessarily make a person intelligent, sensitive, attractive, or chaste. Autolycus at his first entrance sings of tumbling in the hay with country beggar women (IV.iii.12); and though Perdita says that her friends "wear upon your virgin branches yet / Your maidenheads growing" (IV.iv.115–16), her foster brother has evidently tripped with several and still has not retired from the field (IV.iv.239ff.). The rustic shepherds are like sheep themselves, unthinking easy prey for that wolf Autolycus, who enjoys his own kind of sheep-shearing feast. After Perdita, the country figure who possesses the most dignity is the Old Shepherd, her reputed father. He is differentiated from the rest by being given poetry rather than prose to speak (in the sheep-shearing scene, at least), and that poetry shows him to be hospitable, warm, and genial, with a firm love of the land and of tradition. Unaware of the true identity of either Perdita or Florizel, he at first warmly approves of their match. But at the moment Polixenes unmasks, the old man is selfishly concerned only for his own neck. And after his meteoric rise in social status, he becomes just as comic a butt for laughter as his mindless son. Perhaps more damaging yet is the fact that he is used to caricature Polixenes' response to the onset of sexual passion in youth. His solution of how to deal with that passion has simplicity to recommend it, but that is about all to be said on its behalf; he would merely eliminate the years between ten and twenty-three from young people's lives:

> I would there were no age between ten and three-and-twenty, or that youth would sleep out the rest; for there is nothing in the between but getting wenches with child, wronging the ancientry, stealing, fighting. [III.iii. 59–63]

With rustics such as these, Shakespeare is plainly not offering up the country merely as an escape from, or a blissful alternative to, life at court.

It is however not the rustics but a figure born at court, Perdita, who is most responsible in the play for demonstrating what country people and country life are like. Probably because of her royal birth she is idealized (a reflection of Shakespeare's adherence to social decorum), while the other shepherds are not; but she is nonetheless the one who speaks on behalf of nature in the debate with Polixenes on nature and art and who fully articulates the conditions under which country people live. In doing so, she also reasserts the vision that Hermione put forward in the play's opening acts. Whereas Hermione's views were in effect stifled and ignored at court, they flourish in the play's country scenes, and it is from Perdita, as representative of the country, that we and the play's court figures encounter an insistence upon time's movement and an endorsement of sexual love that provide definitive repudiation of Polixenes' conceptions of innocence, sin, the fall, and hence of the ideal human existence—those conceptions which were so closely connected with, and even the ultimate cause of, Leontes' diseased outburst of sexual jealousy.

Just as Leontes has his complement in Polixenes, so then does Hermione have a complement in the second half of the play, in her daughter Perdita. The word "grace," with its many meanings, appears frequently in the play, most often to denote a quality in Hermione; when Time reintroduces Perdita, sixteen years older than the newborn child we have just seen left on the coast of Bohemia, he uses the same term to describe the daughter: Perdita is "now grown in grace" (IV.i.24). Perdita has been raised in the country and is by no means as sophisticated as her mother: unlike Hermione, for instance, she is made uncomfortable by praise. But she shares her mother's distrust of courtly rhetoric and extravagant statement and possesses Hermione's ability to examine such expression critically. When Camillo very lamely flatters her with "I should leave grazing, were I of your flock / And only live by gazing" (IV.iv.109–10), she, after the manner of her mother, scolds him for his words by reducing them to their literal meaning, instead of accepting them merely as a vague compliment:

> Out, alas!
> You'd be so lean that blasts of January
> Would blow you through and through.
> [IV.iv.110–12]

And when in the same scene Polixenes attempts to defend art (and gillyvors) by arguing that grafting is an art "Which doth mend nature—change it rather" (IV.iv.96), Perdita is clever enough to see why he has made his last-second change in wording and wittily calls him to account for his near error. In her response she posits a hypothetical case in which she suggests that the young man standing next to her (Florizel) might desire to breed by her *only* because she were painted and he not so (IV.iv.101–3). Had Polixenes stayed with "mend," he would have been arguing that grafting is not simply a natural process but also an improvement upon what nature might produce on its own. Such logic, Perdita sees, would justify human couples' breeding merely because they happen to differ, a conclusion the class-conscious Polixenes would find distasteful on general principles—even if he had not come to this sheepshearing specifically to prevent a grafting or marriage between his son and what he assumes is a girl of low estate. Perdita has among other things, then, rather nicely reduced Polixenes' unstated belief in class distinctions to a mere matter of being painted or not, and far from being limited by a "peasant" mind she thus exercises her mother's critical sensibility even in the nature-and-art debate she is so often assumed to lose to the superior reasoning of Polixenes.[27]

The most important similarity between Perdita and Hermione, though, is in their attitude toward sexual love. Hermione's willingness to acknowledge being a devil in the definition of the fall that Polixenes provides in I.ii implies that she accepts sexual love as good and natural for man; Perdita brings back to the earth not only spring for Leontes but that attitude toward sexual love as well. While thoroughly chaste and modest, she is particularly frank and open about her sexual desires. And they are desires which exist not in a timeless world but in a time-governed one. It is the insistence on time passing and on the full acceptance of sexual love which most differentiates Perdita's pastoral vision from Polixenes' vision of his "Eden" earlier in the play. Whereas Polixenes sought to stop time and be free of sexual passion, Perdita fully accepts the first and rejoices in the second.

Her consciousness of time is shown to us initially in her words and actions as she distributes flowers to the various guests at the sheepshearing feast. She found herself engaged in the debate with Polixenes on nature and art as a result of her desire to find flowers appropriate to each recipient. She first gave Polixenes and Camillo the winter flowers of rosemary and rue, which were chosen, Polixenes assumes, as a gift suitable for aged men (IV.iv.78–79). Concluding from Polixenes' remark that he was insulted by this initial offering, Perdita goes on to explain why she gave them flowers betokening old age:

> Sir, the year growing ancient,
> Not yet on summer's death nor on the birth
> Of trembling winter, the fairest flowers o' th' season
> Are our carnations and streak'd gillyvors,
> Which some call nature's bastards: of that kind
> Our rustic garden's barren; and I care not
> To get slips of them.
>
> [79–85]

These lines are frequently misread as a reference to the present time of the scene as being not yet on summer's death nor on the birth of winter.[28] But the time of this scene is most likely late June, when sheepshearing feasts traditionally take place; and these lines instead are simply an explanation of why Perdita could not give Polixenes and Camillo the late summer flowers that would have been more appropriate for them: because the fairest late summer flowers suggest to her unchastity and work by an artist's hand, she does not have any of them in her garden. After the debate with Polixenes she proceeds to give Polixenes and Camillo midsummer flowers instead—hot lavender, mints, savory, marjoram, and marigolds—and in handing them over is consciously flattering her guests for a moment:

> these are flowers
> Of middle summer, and I think they are given
> To men of middle age. Y'are very welcome.
>
> [106–8][29]

Then she turns to Florizel and her younger friends and expresses a desire to give them flowers of spring. In her choice of and reference to flowers, Perdita has been moving gradually backward in time—from winter to late summer to middle summer to spring. In this backward movement, she is reenacting or recapitulating in small the redemptive scheme of the play as a whole. But at the very moment that time is symbolically redeemed by Perdita's actions and words, Perdita herself reasserts the concept of time as constantly moving forward. For she has to admit that she does not have those spring flowers she would like to hand out, and she points to a way, then, in which she is *unlike* Proserpina:

> Now, my fair'st friend, [*To Florizel*]
> I would I had some flowers o' th' spring, that might
> Become your time of day; and yours, and yours,
>   [*To Mopsa and the other girls*]
> That wear upon your virgin branches yet
> Your maidenheads growing: O Proserpina
> For the flowers now that, frighted, thou let'st fall
> From Dis's waggon!
>   [112–18]

There is a strong note of melancholy here and of regret that she cannot really bring spring back to the earth. In handing out her flowers, Perdita is very conscious of the limitations placed on human life by time's movement.

Perdita would appear, for the moment, to be like Polixenes in seeking a life in which one would not be limited by time's inevitable movement onward. But while Polixenes moved from a vision of a timeless world to a desire to retreat and avoid sexual involvement, Perdita quickly recovers from her melancholic mood and moves instead to a triumphant assertion of her dedication to active, living, sexual love:

> PER.   O, these I lack,
>   To make you garlands of; and my sweet friend,
>   To strew him o'er and o'er!
> FLO.   What, like a corpse?
> PER.   No, like a bank, for love to lie and play on:
>   Not like a corpse; or if—not to be buried,
>   But quick, and in mine arms.
>   [127–32]

She pauses on "or if" most likely because she has in her mind struck upon the root meaning of "corpse"; she would very plainly, then, be thinking about love which makes full use of the body.

There is, no doubt, a smile on Florizel's face as he teases Perdita with his question "What, like a corpse?" But the question points to a way in which Florizel has not yet reached Perdita's level of appreciation of the type of love she advocates. He is generally, next to her, a rather unsure figure. Like his father, when he wants to give the highest possible praise to something, he places it beyond time's control; in expressing his love for Perdita, he in his own way tries to deny time and make her action eternal:

> What you do,
> Still betters what is done. When you speak, sweet,
> I'd have you do it ever: when you sing,
> I'd have you buy and sell so, so give alms,
> Pray so, and, for the ord'ring your affairs,
> To sing them too: when you do dance, I wish you
> A wave o' th' sea, that you might ever do
> Nothing but that, move still, still so,
> And own no other function. Each your doing,
> So singular in each particular,
> Crowns what you are doing, in the present deeds,
> That all your acts are queens.
>
> [135–46]

G. Wilson Knight has commended this speech as a praiseworthy "striving after eternity," and F. David Hoeniger has called it "one of the most moving passages in the whole of Shakespeare."[30] But if Shakespeare had wanted us to accept these sentiments without qualification, he probably would not have had Perdita object to them. Perdita has earlier had to chide Florizel for his "extremes" in dressing her up as the goddess Flora for the feast (IV.iv.1–14), and here she finds his words too extravagant. His praise gives evidence of a verbal art which she distrusts and which disguises what she takes to be his true nature:

> O Doricles,
> Your praises are too large: but that your youth,
> And the true blood which peeps fairly through't,
> Do plainly give you out an unstain'd shepherd,
> With wisdom I might fear, my Doricles,
> You woo'd me the false way.
>
> [146–51]

Even in her mild rebuke, she retains her wit. For she knows very well that Doricles is a prince and not simply an unstained shepherd. But prince and representative of the court and its art that he may be, Florizel eventually justifies Perdita's confidence and trust in him. At the moment when he must choose between his succession and his love, he stands by Perdita; and in doing so he allies himself with all of nature as well:

> It cannot fail, but by
> The violation of my faith; and then

> Let nature crush the sides o' th' earth together,
> And mar the seeds within! Lift up thy looks:
> From my succession wipe me, father; I
> Am heir to my affection.
>
> [477–82]

It was Leontes' diseased "affection" (I.ii.138–46) which blinded him to the truth and caused him to commit the unnatural act of seeking the death of his own seed, Perdita. It is a mark of Florizel's health here that he can rely upon and dedicate himself fully to just those emotions which Polixenes and Leontes found so dangerous and disruptive. For Florizel *not* to follow the dictates of his "affection" would, in his view, be as bad as marring all the seeds germinating in the earth. He is speaking in overly exalted terms perhaps, but there is good reason to take his exclamation seriously. Perdita has by this time—as a result of her stand in favor of unadulterated nature in the nature-and-art debate, her distribution of flowers, and her identification with Flora—been fully associated with nature and natural life. On this level of association, Florizel in standing by her *is* helping to ensure nature's continuance from generation to generation. And in allying himself with nature and the country as opposed to the court, Florizel is assuming for his own the vision of human life in which time has a definite effect and in which sexual love plays a good and vital role.

The court's inhabitants can, and indeed do, learn from their country sojourn, then. One need not perhaps go to the country to find and develop a vision like that of Perdita; Hermione possessed that vision without ever having left the court. And the trip to the country is only one of two possible ways the play presents as a means of moving from the disease of Acts I–III to the health and happiness of the conclusion—the other way being the path of penance Leontes follows at court under the moral guidance of Paulina. But the action of the final scenes at court is thoroughly imbued with the specific lessons taught by the country and its representative, Perdita. The recognition that Hermione's statue has wrinkles which Hermione herself did not have sixteen years earlier reasserts the vision of time presented by Perdita when she confesses to her inability to bring back spring and to distribute spring flowers out of season. And the play ends with a rather stark insistence on time passing. When the statue first moves, Polixenes raises the question what exactly Hermione has been doing for these past sixteen years (V.iii.114–15). As Hermione begins to answer it and explain to her daughter why she kept herself alive, she is interrupted by Paulina with:

> There's time enough for that;
> Lest they desire (upon this push) to trouble
> Your joys with like relation.
>
> [V.iii.128–30]

Had the question been pursued further, it might have proved embarrassing for both Paulina and Shakespeare. But in having Paulina interrupt here, Shakespeare is not I think merely trying to hurry over a potential weakness in his play's construction. Rather, the effect of raising Polixenes' question and then cutting off its answer before a full explanation has been provided is to enforce upon our consciousness just how wide a gap of time sixteen years can be.

Finally, the concluding scene offers yet another of the instances in the play in which a character expresses a wish to halt time's and life's movement, only to be corrected or rebuked for that wish. Leontes and Perdita both, when they see Hermione's statue, desire simply to stand there and gaze at it for twenty years (V.iii.84–85). Polixenes proved to be misguided in desiring to return to a realm in which he could be "boy eternal," and Florizel was gently chided for desiring a Perdita constantly repeating the same action, like a wave of the sea. Here, time moving onward brings Leontes and Perdita greater joy than the single moment made eternal. For in the place of a statue, a work of art set in a timeless dimension, Leontes and Perdita are presented with a Hermione warm with life. Polixenes, in his description of his youth, expressed a distrust of his own "blood," by which he meant his passions and particularly sexual passion. In the sheepshearing scene, Perdita used the word "blood" to refer to a quality in Florizel that she could rely upon to express his true feelings when she could not trust his extravagant words (IV.iv.148); Florizel's "true blood," then, was cause for confidence and trust. For Leontes in this final scene, the fact that Hermione's statue appears to have veins which bear blood (V.iii.65) becomes cause first for wonder and then, when verified, for rejoicing. "Blood" at this point of course means not simply the passions but one's lifeblood, that which makes one a living being. The use of that particular word here helps to point out that Polixenes, in his distrust of his own blood and in his wistful look back toward the past and childhood, was denying life. The final scene of the play is a celebration of life. It is, in fact, life itself which Paulina calls Hermione's redeemer when she bids the apparent statue descend from its pedestal:

> Come!
> I'll fill your grave up: stir, nay, come away:

>   Bequeath to death your numbness; for from him
>   Dear life redeems you.
>   [V.iii.100–103]

"Life" in this final scene clearly means life as it exists in a moving world, a world governed by time. It is Shakespeare's considerable achievement in this play, no less than in *As You Like It,* that he can bring us to accept the view of time as constantly moving forward and hence eroding and destructive, and to accept it not merely with resignation but with equanimity and even enthusiasm. And it has been his picture of life in a realistically perceived pastoral setting, and the meeting with a pastoral figure whose approach toward life is the very opposite of the nostalgic, which has made us willing to grant that acceptance.

RETURNING HOME

As You Like It and *The Winter's Tale* in their different ways share the pastoral romance's three-step pattern of an expulsion or retreat, sojourn in a pastoral setting, and return to the normal world. What is perhaps most notable in Shakespeare's use of that structure in these plays is the relative emphasis he gives to the third of those steps. That which provides the generative impulse for the pastoral romance form and which we therefore might expect to be its most distinctive element—the sojourn in a pastoral setting—seems to have held comparatively little appeal for him in itself. He did keep returning to the form and its setting, and, admittedly, some greater health and freedom are to be found in the plays' green worlds: lovers get together in the Forest of Arden and Bohemia, and Perdita brings proper attitudes toward time and sexual love to the older generation of her play. But in one sense, the pastoral sojourn was not strictly necessary for the characters, since the love of Rosalind and Orlando was well under way even at the troubled court, Rosalind possessed the essentials of her philosophy before fleeing that court, and Perdita's views were also held by Hermione, a court figure. In any case, the main thrust of the pastoral sojourn in both plays is not back toward some ideal existence in the past, or even toward what one can do in Arcadia that one cannot do elsewhere, but rather toward the vision that one must have or develop in order to return to and live properly in the normal world. In this respect, the earlier pastoral plays aspire to the condition of *The Tempest,* the last of Shakespeare's plays to use the structure of pastoral romance. It is a play that is entirely a return.

The island upon which the action of *The Tempest* takes place *is* this time a realm of special conditions, where a human being can fulfill many of his fondest dreams and, through magic, assume a godlike control over both the natural elements and his fellowmen. But the action of the whole play is nonetheless one in which the main character seeks to earn his passage home so that he can immerse himself once again in the full stream of the world. And Shakespeare's distrust of idealized pastoral realms finds its most absolute expression in this play, since this time it is not simply thoughts of a misconstrued Eden (as was the case with Polixenes) but a true one that must be abandoned. What *The Tempest* adds to the earlier pastoral plays' mere assertions that man ought not to indulge in escapist dreams of ideal landscapes is insight into why he cannot afford such indulgence. That insight is provided, with a dramatic efficiency that is typical of the play as a whole, in a single critical incident in the play's action, the point at which Prospero interrupts the revels celebrating the betrothal of Ferdinand and Miranda. We can look at that crucial incident alone for a vivid and succinct summary statement of the dangers involved in giving oneself over to any kind of pastoral dream of better times and better places.

The interruption of the masque is an act that draws particular attention to itself in the play, for, as has been noted frequently, Prospero's anger when he bids his performing spirits vanish is out of all proportion to the cause of his interruption, Caliban's conspiracy.[31] Ferdinand observes that Prospero is "in some passion / That works him strongly" (IV.i.143–44), and Miranda remarks that she has never seen her father so distempered (144–45). The stage direction at the point Prospero begins speaking during the masque calls for a strange, hollow, and confused noise, which would, like Lear's storm on the heath, appear to be a representation of the protagonist's inner turmoil. Yet once Prospero directs his thoughts to Caliban's conspiracy again, he disposes of it with consummate ease. Given this disparity between Prospero's anger and the ostensible cause for it, what Frank Kermode has (I believe incorrectly) called the inadequate motivation for Prospero's anger, the scene in effect demands that we ask why Prospero is so angry.

The masque itself provides part of the answer. The masque is Prospero's gift to Ferdinand and Miranda and consists in part of various pagan deities in their turn blessing the lovers with the gifts at their disposal. Those blessings construct for the lovers a vision of an ideal pastoral realm even more rarefied than the island of the play's action. The lovers are presented with a foison or abundance similar to that which Gonzalo earlier claimed for the inhabitants of his Golden Age utopia (II.i.158–60);

the only difference is that here it is Ceres, the goddess of agriculture, an art that would not have been necessary in Gonzalo's ideal realm, who bestows the blessings of

> Earth's increase, foison plenty,
> Barns and garners never empty;
> Vines with clust'ring branches growing;
> Plants with goodly burthen bowing.
> [IV.i.110–13]

As part of her gift, Ceres would have the lovers flourish in a realm in which there is no winter:

> Spring come to you at the farthest
> In the very end of harvest.
> [114–15]

And such blessings are bestowed only after Ceres has been assured that Venus and Cupid, responsible with Pluto for the rape of Proserpina, are to be excluded from the celebration (IV.i.86–91). Venus and Cupid, in fact, having been unsuccessful in imposing some "wanton charm" on Ferdinand and Miranda, are already on their way back to Paphos, and the god of love has broken his arrows (91–101). The conditions of the visionary realm that Prospero's Juno and Ceres conjure up are, then, those of Spenser's Garden of Adonis, itself a source of fecundity and an ideal realm devoted to love, but love without the pain that ordinarily accompanies it in the rest of Book III of *The Faerie Queene* and in our world; in that garden, as here in Prospero's masque, Cupid has been deprived of his arrows and hence of his power both to raise unruly passions and to hurt.

The conditions of abundance, love, and innocence presented in the masque quite understandably make an onlooker think of Paradise, and Ferdinand, like Polixenes before him (and just as mistakenly), expresses the wish that such conditions might be made permanent:

> Let me live here ever;
> So rare and wonder'd father and a wise
> Makes this place Paradise.
> [122–24]

It is not completely clear whether in voicing the desire to "live here ever" Ferdinand refers to the visionary realm of the masque or to the island from which he views the masque and which is only a partial reflection of the masque's paradisal realm. The masque world, in any case, is plainly one that man cannot remain in forever: Prospero has been insisting all along on the tenuousness of his pageant and hence of the vision it projects. He refers to the masque initially as a "vanity" of his art (IV.i.41) and then as the enactment of his "present fancies" (121–22); here, at the point of Ferdinand's comment, he asks for silence, "or else our spell is marr'd" (127). Prospero's disturbed and violent interruption of the masque shortly afterward merely makes definite and final those assertions of the pageant's insubstantiality.

But the main reason why one cannot remain in the realm of the masque or even indulge in thoughts of such a realm very long is, of course, Caliban. In determining why Caliban should be so upsetting to Prospero, we should not lose sight of that savage and deformed slave's essential humanity. He is not a subhuman monster, half man, half fish: Trinculo and the drunken Stephano are hardly to be accepted as authorities on such a matter. And while Caliban's may be a nature upon which "Nurture can never stick" (IV.i.189), he is by no means simply a representation of that nature itself. The temptation to consider him an allegorical representation of man's flesh, untouched by spirit, arises no doubt from the inclusion of an "airy spirit" among the play's characters. But the figure in the play with whom Caliban stands in most direct contrast is not so much the spirit Ariel as another human being, Miranda. Miranda and Caliban have both grown up on the island and been subject to much the same education at Prospero's hand, with Miranda evidently on occasion called upon to act as teacher's aid for her slower fellow student.[32] Unfortunately, Caliban has not responded well to his lessons: with the language he has been taught, his profit is to know how to curse (I.ii.365–66), and Prospero's (and Miranda's) pains, humanely taken, have been in general "all, all lost, quite lost" on him (IV.i.190). Although Caliban is perhaps not as hopeless a case as Prospero would have us believe—he possesses several of the play's more beautiful lines, likes music, and can appreciate the island's beauty (see, for instance, III.ii.133–41)—he does epitomize all that is intractable and ineducable in human nature, and it is for those qualities that he serves in the play as a constant reminder of man's fallen state and is a threat to the particular vision that Prospero's masque presents.

In having Prospero break off the masque because of Caliban, then, Shakespeare is pointing to the incompatibility between the ideal Edenic world of the masque vision and the fact of man's fallen nature, as evidenced in Caliban. And Prospero's anger can be said to be in part attributable to his annoyance that man generally cannot be rid of the Caliban in himself, that human life refuses to correspond to man's dreams and aspirations, as projected in man's art and in this particular case by the masque and its vision of a paradisal realm. But we should note further how much Prospero, at the conclusion of his speech ending the revels, looks upon his mental disturbance as a personal weakness of his own rather than, let us say, a justified response to a sorry fact about the human condition generally:

> Sir, I am vex'd;
> Bear with my weakness; my old brain is troubled:
> Be not disturb'd with my infirmity.
> [IV.i.158–60]

This concentration on his own infirmity suggests that Prospero's distemper is directed as much toward himself as toward the recalcitrant and quite fallen slave who has been mounting a conspiracy against him.

This is a suggestion that gathers some force if we glance back at another instance of Prospero's vexation in the play—those repeated admonitions to Miranda in I.ii that she be more attentive to his account of past events. As with Prospero's anger when interrupting the masque, here too there appears to be little correlation between the immediate dramatic action before us and Prospero's response to it: there is no evidence that Miranda's attention is wavering and therefore that she needs to be reminded five times to listen more carefully to what Prospero says; on the contrary, Miranda herself observes that Prospero's account would cure deafness (I.ii.106). But there is good cause for Prospero's anger in the subject of his account, if not in its auditor. At the point in his narrative when he is most upset and when he bursts forth with the flurry of reminders to mark his words, Prospero is describing the treachery of his usurping brother:

> My brother, and thy uncle, call'd Antonio,—
> I pray thee, mark me, that a brother should
> Be so perfidious!—he whom next thyself
> Of all the world I lov'd, and to him put
> The manage of my state . . .
> [I.ii.66–70]

> The government I cast upon my brother,
> And to my state grew stranger, being transported
> And rapt in secret studies. Thy false uncle—
> Dost thou attend me?
> [75–78]

Although Prospero is willing to assume responsibility for having awakened the evil nature in his false brother (89–93), that willingness does not help him get past this particular point in his narrative any the quicker. Not only does he keep interrupting his account (ostensibly to make sure Miranda is listening), he is also given to repeating himself, to mulling over and again his own mistakes and the extent of his brother's falseness. Prospero's obvious distress here gives evidence of his still being unable to accept or comprehend his brother's action—"that a brother should / Be so perfidious!"; "Mark his condition, and th'event; then tell me / If this might be a brother"—and the admonitions he directs at Miranda would thus appear to be a means to focus himself as much as Miranda upon the full import of what he is saying. Since Prospero is delivering the whole account of past events as a preface to the acts he is to perform on the afternoon of the play's action, his reminders and repetition look very much like the efforts of someone forcing himself to concentrate upon his mistakes of twelve years back, lest he make the same mistake again.

And that is precisely what has happened during the betrothal masque of IV.i. Prospero's error in the past was to neglect worldly ends and dedicate himself solely to the liberal arts and to the bettering of his mind—in effect, to the contemplative life—at the expense of satisfying his assigned tasks in the political world (I.ii.89–93). Retired in his study, he lost cognizance of the true nature of the world around him and of the men in it (particularly of Antonio) and of the fact that men need to be ruled. Prospero designs the events of the present in *The Tempest* to rectify that mistake, to put himself back in the seat of power he held before he made only his library his dukedom. To achieve this end, he insists throughout the day's maneuvers upon the precision with which his instructions are to be followed by Ariel, how "exactly" and "to point" his orders are to be carried out (I.ii.194, 502; III.iii.83–86); and he has been showing, until the betrothal masque, a firm awareness of time passing and of the necessity of grasping "the very minute" to accomplish his goals (I.ii.37, 181–84, 240–41). The masque, as the creation of his art, with its picture of a life of pastoral bliss in a timeless Edenic setting, places the appeal of a retired, contemplative life before Prospero once again. It is an appeal to which he seems to have succumbed, despite his prior recognition of his pageant's insubstantiality; for in viewing the masque, Prospero momentarily loses his consciousness of the importance of each passing moment and forgets Caliban's conspiracy, the "minute" of which plot (IV.i.141) comes upon him unawares. And in losing that firm control over his own actions and the day's sequence of events, Prospero betrays that, as much as he might wish the contrary, he cannot after all separate himself from the Caliban he has so consistently berated in the course of the play. The ineducable Caliban is indeed, as Prospero is soon to acknowledge and only partly in a different sense, a thing of Prospero's own (V.i.275–76); Prospero himself reveals a failure to learn, an inability to profit from past mistakes.

It is this consciousness of having repeated a past error that can best account for the extent of Prospero's disturbance at the point when he interrupts the masque. His old fondness for a life of retirement and dedication to the liberal arts, of indulgence in timeless realms set off from life in the everyday political world, has once again made him vulnerable to men less controlled and worthy than himself. And the reason why one cannot afford to give one's imagination over to pastoral dreams of any sort of idealized realm is that so many such men, so much evidence of the fall, must be confronted and dealt with at all times. Prospero has of course been using his books during his twelve-year stay on the island; but as Leo Marx points out, he has not simply been living a life of retired contemplation there. He has brought the island from a savage state in which an Ariel is imprisoned and a Caliban allowed to run free to one in which the good spirit carries out an enlightened (if frequently angry) ruler's commands and a Caliban is controlled and put to work.[33] He has, then, been ruling the island in that twelve-year period, just as he has on the day of *The Tempest*'s action been carefully planning each event—until he is distracted by the betrothal masque and its offer of an ideal pastoral existence. Using his books and art for a social purpose, he has served his apprenticeship, in the limited sphere that a pastoral kingdom might provide, for the much more complex type of rule he will exercise in Milan.

And it is back toward Milan that the play's action takes us with increasing urgency, once the betrothal masque has been interrupted. One can no more stay forever on the island than in the Edenic realm of the masque. The disruption of the masque is merely one in a sequence of steps taking Prospero and everyone else in the play away from realms in which special conditions of any sort apply and back to life in the normal world as we all know it. Once the vision of an Edenic realm dissolves, Prospero announces his intention to abjure the rough magic that gave him control over the physical elements and to drown his book, thus relinquishing all his special magical powers over others. When his magic has brought all his enemies to the point at which they lie at his mercy, he decides not to exercise his avenging power, choosing instead a forgiveness based upon a recognition of his kinship with his enemies as fellow human beings (V.i.20–32). Miranda earlier referred to any figure able to control a storm such as the one opening *The Tempest* as a "god of power" (I.ii.10); later, the Folio's stage direction had Prospero during the performance of another of his theatrical shows, that of the vanishing banquet, assume a position "on the top (invisible)" (S.D., III.iii.17), and the figures fulfilling Prospero's wishes in that pageant claimed to be "ministers of Fate" (60–61). For Prospero, the movement in the last two acts is plainly one away from a status that gives him godlike attributes to one in which he fully embraces his humanity, acknowledging Caliban as his own and giving extended thought to his own death (V.i.311).

Such a move is not made without a struggle on Prospero's part and perhaps even on Shakespeare's. Prospero, like any artist, in the midst of his manipulating clearly enjoys the almost godlike power over others that his magic and art have given him; it is with a note of exultation that, immediately after the banquet vanishes, he can exclaim:

> My high charms work,
> And these mine enemies are all knit up
> In their distractions: they are now in my power.
> (III.iii.88–90)

And it is perhaps a reflection of the playwright's own pride in artistic achievement that the betrothal masque, that high point of Prospero's artistry, should be interrupted only in its second half, during the dance of the Nymphs and Reapers; the part of the masque most directly presenting the picture of a visionary realm of abundance and innocence, a paradise without winter or pain, is granted full expression and is played out intact.

But the movement back toward Milan and life in the everyday world is, nonetheless, reasserted strongly with Prospero's harsh interruption of his "insubstantial pageant." And the very harshness of that interruption, accompanied and underscored by that "strange, hollow, and confused noise" (S.D., IV.i.139), is of some significance in itself. When the revels are abruptly terminated, a sojourn in a pastoral landscape, this time in the extreme form of a fully idealized paradisal realm, has once again served Shakespeare as an occasion for asserting a commitment to the active over the contemplative life. The strength of Prospero's passion when he interrupts the masque creates a severe break in the play's action; it is a break which places Shakespeare at odds with those Renaissance contemporaries (like Castiglione and his Ottaviano Fregoso) who viewed the active and contemplative lives as complementary and who could envision a smooth transition from a contemplative life of study to active life in the political world.[34] For Shakespeare, the Renaissance debate between the active and contemplative lives remained exactly that, a debate, and his stand in it does not seem to have changed appreciably from the position implied in *As You Like It* when he rather unfairly chose to make a melancholy man the chief proponent of the contemplative life. The masque of *The Tempest* has Prospero moving off in a direction which the rest of the play denies, and the playwright's commitment to the active life is here revealed to be both a strong and a rather uncompromising one.

Given that commitment, made at the expense of not simply the pastoral setting of the island but the Edenic setting of the masque, it is only fitting that Shakespeare should turn next to a history play, *Henry VIII*—and that probably his last sole effort—and a history play presenting one of the playwright's harshest and most confusing political worlds. For it is toward just such a world of harsh, complex, day-to-day political fact that Shakespeare's anti-pastoral argument, extending through his most apparently carefree and unpolitical plays and culminating in *The Tempest*, had been propelling him all along.

CHAPTER V

Milton's Paradise

HE READING of Shakespeare's pastorals that I have proposed is a decidedly unmythic one. I would have Shakespeare in *As You Like It* and *The Winter's Tale* refusing to traffic in versions of pastoral that are either direct reflections of Eden or expressions of a collective dream of a happy, carefree, womblike place from which we have all been expelled and to which we should like to return. *The Tempest* does treat paradisal realms, both in the rarefied pastoral landscape of the island and in the fully idealized vision of the betrothal masque, only to insist upon the need, because of man's fallen nature, to abandon such landscapes and get on with the business of day-to-day living. *Paradise Lost,* however, presents us not simply with another pastoral landscape that may bear some slight or considerable resemblance to prelapsarian Eden in a fallen world but, of course, with the real thing, the true mythic place that is, for the Renaissance Christian, the ultimate source of all other necessarily less perfect idealized landscapes. Milton himself is continually pointing out both that this garden is superior to all others and that this one has the added advantage of having been historically real, while all other ideal landscapes are merely imitations:

> Thus was this place,
> A happy rural seat of various view:
> Groves whose rich Trees wept odorous Gums and Balm.
> Others whose fruit burnisht with Golden Rind

> Hung amiable, *Hesperian* Fables true,
> If true, here only, and of delicious taste.
> [IV.246–51][1]

For Hesperian fables here, we can substitute fables telling of Elysium, the Isles of the Blessed, the Garden of Adonis, the Golden Age, and even idealized versions of Arcadia. This is a garden, as I have already suggested, to which there ought to be no objection, and it would be this landscape, if any, that would offer that harmless ease and morally admissible relief from everyday cares that Pyrocles or any of our other pastoral sojourners mistakenly claimed to have found in Arcadia.

A good deal of modern criticism of Milton's epic has been based on just such an assumption, that Milton's Paradise is a landscape definitely and qualitatively different from our present postlapsarian world. Isabel Gamble MacCaffrey, perhaps the best advocate for this position, has provided a thoroughgoing reading of *Paradise Lost* as myth; in MacCaffrey's view, *Paradise Lost* is

> a direct rendering of certain stupendous realities now known only indirectly in the symbolic signatures of earthly life. Theology and popular opinion for generations had accustomed Christians to imagining life in Eden as unlike everyday life in certain distinct ways; human knowledge, and its objects as well, differed there from ordinary modes of seeing and being. The poet whose subject was Paradise set out, therefore, to reproduce forms of experience that no longer existed, and their peculiar conditions imposed upon his endeavors stylistic and technical limits.[2]

For evidence of the way Milton's contemporaries thought that human knowledge and perception were different before and after the fall, and hence that prelapsarian life was essentially different from our present life, MacCaffrey cites Du Bartas, Traherne, and Sir John Davies, all of whom argued that Adam's characteristic mode of apprehension before the fall was closer to the angels' intuitive and immediate understanding of phenomena than to fallen man's necessary reliance on discursive reason to gain knowledge; as Du Bartas expressed it:

> But our now-knowledge hath for tedious traine,
> A drooping life, an over racked braine,
> A face forlorne, a sad and sullen fashion
> A restles toyle, and cares selfe-pyning passion.
> Knowledge was then, even the soules soule for light,
> The spirits calme port; and lanthorne shining bright,

> To straight-stept feete, cleere knowledge; not confusd:
> Not sower, but sweet: not gotten, but infusd.³

Milton's own nod toward this distinction between knowledge "gotten" and "infusd" is to be found in Adam's account of how he named the animals, a favorite incident in the Genesis narrative for those medieval and Renaissance exegetes who wished to emphasize the difference between Adam's formidable mental capacity before the fall and our own incapacity since:

> I nam'd them, as they pass'd and understood
> Thir Nature, with such knowledge God endu'd
> My sudden apprehension.
> [VIII.352–54]

But an important passage in Book V suggests that Adam's account is in fact only a nod or gesture on Milton's part and that the poet does not wish to insist upon a precise distinction between fallen and unfallen modes of understanding. Raphael is explaining to Adam how it is that an angel eats earthly fruit, and that explanation in turn draws him into a description of the prelapsarian great chain of being. All things, whether of body or spirit, proceed from and return to God and are constituted of "one first matter" which merely becomes "more refin'd, more spiritous, and pure" (475) as it approaches God on the scale of being:

> So from the root
> Springs lighter the green stalk, from thence the leaves
> More aery, last the bright consummate flow'r
> Spirits odorous breathes: flow'rs and thir fruit
> Man's nourishment, by gradual scale sublim'd
> To vital spirits aspire, to animal,
> To intellectual, give both life and sense,
> Fancy and understanding, whence the Soul
> Reason receives, and reason is her being,
> Discursive, or Intuitive; discourse
> Is oftest yours, the latter most is ours,
> Differing but in degree, of kind the same.
> [V.479–90]

In these lines Raphael is playing down the difference between angelic and human modes of apprehension, an aim consistent with his later suggestion that things on earth may be similar to things in Heaven "more than on Earth is thought" (V.576); but the angel is making a distinction here nonetheless, and one that exists *before* man's fall from grace. Even before the fall, man was to rely primarily on discursive reason in order to gain understanding, and the need to do so was not one of the lamentable results of the fall that Du Bartas and others took it to be; rather, in Milton's view as in that of Aquinas and other theologians concerned with this issue, the discursive mode of intellection is simply a necessary concomitant of man's having been created human rather than angelic.[4]

There are, to be sure, some differences between our present existence and prelapsarian life as Milton conceived it. Adam and Eve live in a harmony with the natural world around them—the flowers at Eve's approach "sprung / And toucht by her fair tendance gladlier grew" (VIII.46–47)—a harmony we have since lost and can lay claim to only through the assertive fiction of pathetic fallacy. And in describing Paradise and Adam and Eve's life there, Milton has developed, as several critics have demonstrated, a type of "paradisal language," the effect of which is to remind us of the difference between our present life and conditions before the fall.[5] The stream that runs through Paradise can be described, for example, as rolling "With mazy error under pendant shades" (IV.239), and we understand that "error" in this instance carries its original Latin force of "wandering at random," without its customary modern suggestion of a mistake or trespass. The word in fact means not even simply "wandering" but, as Christopher Ricks puts it, "wandering (not error)."[6] Since the stream never misleads man or contributes to his fall in either the Genesis account or *Paradise Lost,* we must consciously exclude the tainted or "fallen" meaning of "error" from the context here. Milton plays in similar manner on a word like "wanton" when he uses it first, with its usual suggestion of lasciviousness, to describe the action of worshipers of the fallen angels (I.414, 454) and then, in a pure or innocent sense, to describe Eve's disheveled hair (IV.306) or the growth of the garden (V.295).

Perhaps the most startling instance of words meaning one thing for, and in, Paradise and suggesting quite another to us in our postlapsarian world occurs in Book V when Adam asks Raphael to join him and Eve for that noontime meal which is in no danger of cooling:

> voutsafe with us
> Two only, who yet by sovran gift possess
> This spacious ground, in yonder shady Bow'r
> To rest.
>   [V.365–68]

The disconcerting word here is "yet." Adam's meaning can only be that, even though he and Eve are only two beings, *nevertheless* they have been given this more than ample tract of land; but especially on a first reading, the temporal meaning of "yet" forces itself upon the reader's consciousness as well, and it is a meaning which, again, must be consciously put aside. For to allow it would have Adam ask Raphael to join them while they still remain in Paradise, and thus Adam would be showing knowledge of his own subsequent fall—a type of knowledge of specific future events that even the exegetes making the most exalted claims for Adam's prelapsarian mental capacity would be hesitant to claim for him. It is only the reader's awareness of Adam's fall that allows for the mistaken reading; and every time the reader must stop and correct himself or distinguish which of several meanings applies and which must be excluded, he is being forced to acknowledge that there has been a change from an ideal existence when words like "error" or "wanton" might have no pejorative connotations to a time when such words are inevitably associated with mistakes, transgression, and sin.

But despite these linguistic maneuvers whereby Milton points to differences between our present life and Adam and Eve's unfallen existence, there remain significant and striking ways in which prelapsarian life, as Milton conceived it, and our everyday lives are similar. There is much in the poem to suggest that just as Milton sought no precise distinction between human intellection before and after the fall, so he made no hard-and-fast distinction between pre- and postlapsarian man generally. Rather, in delineating man's existence in prelapsarian Eden, Milton seems to have conceived of it according to the formula employed by Sidney and Shakespeare when they wrote of Arcadia: Eden is a version of pastoral, an image of our normal, complex life in simplified form.[7] Even Eden, then, ceases to be a special, particularly sanctified place, and Milton, like Sidney and Shakespeare before him, is using his pastoral garden in order to speak about conditions of our present existence. And in doing so, he implies or assumes a reader who, while acknowledging that Adam and Eve are unfallen and hence not threatened by time or the weather or the animals, still recognizes the basic similarities he bears to Adam and Eve. This reader is of course fallen, but it is not that specific condition he necessarily holds uppermost in his mind at every point where he becomes self-consciously aware of himself as he reads the poem.[8] For unfallen Eve is just as liable to fall victim to Satan's logic in Book IX as we are to succumb to his rhetoric in Books I and II; and self-control is as necessary in prelapsarian Eden as it is in our postlapsarian life.

To say that Milton makes no definite and consistent distinction between human life before and after the fall is, I would emphasize, not the same as asserting (as one group of critics would have it) that Adam and Eve were "fallen before the fall." As that critical stand was first enunciated by Basil Willey, A. J. A. Waldock, and E. M. W. Tillyard, it provided a way of explaining how Milton dealt with the difficulties inherent in the particularly intractable narrative material he took over from Genesis: in order to make the fall from a perfect and sinless state humanly understandable and artistically plausible, it was necessary for Milton to resort to some (to use Tillyard's jaunty word) "faking," to ascribe to Adam and Eve feelings which though nominally felt in the state of innocence are actually incompatible with that state. Hence Eve's fascination with her own reflection in the pool, her dream of temptation in Books IV and V, and Adam's confession in Book VIII that he is subject to passion are all viewed simply as anticipations of the fall, designed to make the fall itself dramatically convincing.[9] It remained for Millicent Bell to carry this argument to its logical conclusion and to recognize its full implications. To consider Adam and Eve fallen before the fall is to make God, ultimately, responsible for man's fall, an implication Bell was fully willing to accept. For Bell, the "fortunate fall" was no paradox; she would have Milton giving the unfallen Adam and Eve fallen characteristics as an extension of his belief that the fall was a necessary and good act, the means whereby mankind could gain the requisite self-consciousness to direct itself toward redemption and the only paradises Milton thought relevant to man in his present condition, each Christian's "paradise within" (XII.587) and that "far happier place" into which Christ will welcome his elect at the world's dissolution (XII.464). The poem becomes in this reading a divine comedy in which there is no real fall and no meaningful Paradise lost but only one to be gained in the future.[10]

What Bell and the critics before her had observed was that Milton had imputed a good deal of complexity to Adam and Eve's prelapsarian existence, complexity that made his Eden look suspiciously like our own life. But this quite correct observation was in turn clouded by a vestige of mythic thinking, perhaps only partly acknowledged. No less than Mac-Caffrey's more overtly mythic reading of *Paradise Lost,* Bell's was based upon a preconception of what Paradise *ought* to be like, a preconception that arose from considering only the garden's otherness, that is, how its ideal conditions might be expected to differ from our present existence; Bell spoke of the Genesis fable's "donnée of inconceivable perfection" that Milton had to render in human terms he and his readers could understand. Since the Miltonic Eden that Bell and Tillyard saw did not correspond to that preconception, they merely jumped to the conclusion that

Milton wrote in anticipations of the fall in the Edenic portion of his poem, imputing those fallen qualities to Adam and Eve before the fall itself was actually committed.[11]

But there is no logical necessity for such a jump, and there remains possible a reading of *Paradise Lost* which does full justice to the complexity perceived in Milton's Eden and which is at the same time more orthodox in allowing for the existence of a very real and significant fall in the poem. Aided by Ruth Mohl's 1949 study of the different possible meanings of the term "perfection" as used by Milton and theologians before him, critics have come to see that any perfection Adam and Eve possessed in Eden was one relative to their particular species and creation, not the "absolute perfection" Bell postulated. Raphael's exposition of the prelapsarian great chain of being culminates with the suggestion that Adam and Eve might someday improve their state and become more like the angels:

> time may come when men
> With Angels may participate, and find
> No inconvenient Diet, nor too light Fare:
> And from these corporal nutriments perhaps
> Your bodies may at last turn all to spirit,
> Improv'd by tract of time, and wing'd ascend
> Ethereal.
> [V.493-99]

Accordingly, a host of critics in recent years has been insisting that Adam and Eve's prelapsarian existence, as portrayed by Milton, is by no means carefree, static, and easy (a view that is encouraged by considering Eden only in mythic terms); rather, Milton's Edenic life encompasses a good deal of moral activity, educative growth, even error and something bordering upon good old-fashioned hard work, in what are still specifically unfallen conditions.[12] This is a particularly fruitful approach to *Paradise Lost,* for there is evidence of Milton's having gone out of his way to complicate Adam and Eve's prelapsarian existence. In two important areas, he departed significantly from the large majority of hexameral writers before him—in the amount of physical labor he prescribed for Adam and Eve in Eden and in the specifically sexual nature of the relationship between them before the fall—and the effect of these particular points of relative originality is to add a good measure of complexity and difficulty to their prelapsarian life. As immersed in the hexameral tradition as *Paradise Lost* reveals Milton to have been, these determined and specific departures from earlier models provide grounds for considering his Paradise a version not simply of pastoral but of what I have been calling anti-pastoral: Milton's whole portrayal of Eden implicitly argues with earlier versions of that potentially most ideal of pastoral landscapes, with Edens that are distinctly less complicated and hence more likely to encourage regressive or escapist dreams of an easier existence for man. It is also the particular difficulties that Adam and Eve encounter in the garden that most enable the reader to see reflections of his own experience in Adam and Eve's Edenic life; the difficulties the unfallen Adam and Eve experience ally them with the fallen reader, and the prelapsarian education in their own nature that Adam and Eve undergo in Books IV through IX of the poem proves to be also the reader's own.

COUNSELING IGNOBLE EASE

The relative blank in any postlapsarian man's knowledge of the precise conditions of prelapsarian Eden allows for many individual emphases that might depend upon the particular purpose, prejudices, or even outright whims of the author who sets out to present a picture of Paradise. For many medieval and Renaissance commentators on Genesis, perhaps drawn toward monastic ideals or simply influenced by literary works (like Petrarch's *De Vita Solitaria*) which praised natural landscapes for the freedom they provide for the exercise of the mind, prelapsarian Eden could offer a most appropriate setting for the pursuit of the contemplative life. Adam's gardening labor in Eden was in fact often viewed as work only of the mind or spirit. This interpretation, as we might well expect from the reading of the Cain and Abel story cited in my first chapter, appealed to Francis Bacon, arguing for the unfettered use of human reason:

> After the creation was finished, it is set down unto us that man was placed in the garden to work therein; which work so appointed to him could be no other than work of contemplation; that is, when the end of work is but for exercise and experiment, not for necessity; for there being then no reluctation of the creature, nor sweat of the brow, man's employment must of consequence have been matter of delight in the experiment, and not matter of labour for the use.[13]

Such an interpretation of Adam's work, while by no means held by most who wrote on life in Eden, has a very long history. A number of Hebraic fathers interpreted Gen. 2:15's reference to dressing and keeping the garden as "being occupied in the words of the Torah and keeping all its commandments."[14] Within the specifically Christian tradition St. Ambrose, following up Philo's allegorizing bent, referred to Adam's tilling as the exercise of man's virtue.[15] And Augustine after him, even while attempting the most literal of his several extended expositions of Genesis, found himself attracted to a similar allegorical reading. He admitted the possibility of Adam's being a farmer in Eden but insisted upon the pleasantness and exhilaration of any work there, an honorable pleasure of the mind arising from admiration of God's administering power and a type of work to be distinguished sharply from the servile labor imposed upon man as a punishment for the fall. So effective was God's administering power behind nature's growth, in fact, that the main tending of the garden that Adam would be required to do was of the Paradise within himself, not any external garden: Adam was not to work or till Paradise itself, but rather *in* Paradise.[16]

What is behind such allegorical interpretations of Adam's Edenic work is the assumption that there really was no need for physical labor in Eden, that God in his bounty would have created conditions of "soft primitivism" in Eden. Any labor in Paradise would be, to use Bacon's terms, "for exercise and experiment, not for necessity," and this assumption gives rise to the view that any dressing or keeping of Paradise must therefore be something other than the gardening to which Gen. 2:15 apparently refers. As it happens, allegorical interpretations of Genesis as a whole, and of Adam's prelapsarian tasks in particular, fell into some disfavor in the Renaissance. Protestant and Catholic commentators alike, in their theoretical statements at least, insisted upon literal or historical rather than what they called "mystic" readings of Genesis.[17] And with an insistence upon literal readings of Genesis, we come over and again upon reaffirmations that Adam's work in Eden was, after all, gardening or farming. Milton, as we shall see, lodged with the majority of Renaissance commentators on this particular question. But the introduction of the minority view here is nonetheless instructive because it highlights the particular strength with which Milton put forth his view that Adam and Eve were engaged in specifically physical labor in Eden. The allegorical readings of Adam's work suggest, as well, the versions of Edenic life that Milton was arguing with in his own portrayal of Paradise. His commitment to the conception of an active Edenic life for Adam and Eve was in fact so strong that, as we might expect, it is also reflected in parts of the poem not directly concerned with Paradise; one such episode, the debate in Hell, with its rather striking treatment of Belial's speech, serves as a type of preface to the picture of paradisal life Milton later provides in Books IV through IX, and we might profitably look toward Eden from the perspective it provides.

MILTON'S WHOLE HANDLING of Belial's speech in Book II has proved troublesome for modern readers of *Paradise Lost,* particularly for the anti-Miltonists who have been quick to pounce upon the apparent clashes in the poem between the dramatic action itself and the author's or narrator's often heavy-handed comment upon that action. Belial's speech is, as is usually acknowledged, rather impressive, perhaps the most impressive, moving, and convincing of the speeches delivered in the infernal debate. His voice is apparently that of calm reason and common sense. He fully recognizes the real meaning of the word "Almighty," which is otherwise tossed about Hell as a meaningless adjective or an epic formula now devoid of its original force; he quite rightly sees that the fallen angels cannot possibly defeat or even surprise an omniscient God, and thus there is no point to continued opposition to him, either by open war or by covert guile. He rather neatly demolishes the preceding speaker's argument by taking up and providing an answer to Moloch's rhetorical question "what can be worse / Than to dwell here, driv'n out from bliss, condemn'd / In this abhorred deep to utter woe" (II.85–87). They were worse just a moment earlier when they lay chained on the burning lake instead of sitting and consulting in comparative comfort as they are now. And he looks beneath the call for open war and notes that Moloch's blustering is in fact based only upon despair of winning and the unreasonable hope that God in anger might destroy the continually rebellious angels completely, depriving them of any existence whatsoever and hence of any further consciousness of suffering.

It is in opposition to this misguided hope that Belial makes his most effective appeal, by means of a rhetorical question of his own:

> Thus repuls'd, our final hope
> Is flat despair: we must exasperate
> Th' Almighty Victor to spend all his rage,
> And that must end us, that must be our cure,
> To be no more; sad cure, for who would lose,
> Though full of pain, this intellectual being,
> Those thoughts that wander through Eternity,
> To perish rather, swallow'd up and lost
> In the wide womb of uncreated night,
> Devoid of sense and motion?
>
> [II.142–51]

This amounts to an intellectual's defense of the life of the mind. The lines gain resonance and force not simply because of the echo of Claudio's speech in III.i of *Measure for Measure* but because they reflect the sentiments of Plato and Seneca as well.[18] And they couch an appeal which would appear to have some power for Milton himself, since he used much the same terms in the *Areopagitica* in defending the free and full employment of the human mind from attempts at censorship:

> This justifies the high providence of God, who, though he command us temperance, justice, continence, yet pours out before us, even to a profuseness, all desirable things, and *gives us minds that can wander beyond all limit and satiety.*[19]

In addition, Belial favors a course of conduct which might have been best not only for the fallen angels but for ourselves as well: it is the devils' decision to go against Belial's plea for peace which leads directly to man's fall.

And yet Milton or his narrator in *Paradise Lost* does not seem to like the speech at all; or, at least, he does his best to predispose us against anything Belial might say. The speech is preceded by a stern warning to the effect that although his words are likely to please the ear (which they certainly do), Belial's is not a voice one can trust:

> On th' other side up rose
> *Belial,* in act more graceful and humane;
> A fairer person lost not Heav'n; he seem'd
> For dignity compos'd and high exploit:
> But all was false and hollow; though his Tongue
> Dropt Manna, and could make the worse appear
> The better reason, to perplex and dash
> Maturest Counsels: for his thoughts were low;
> To vice industrious, but to Nobler deeds
> Timorous and slothful: yet he pleas'd the ear,
> And with persuasive accent thus began.
>   [108–18]

And at the end of the speech, the attack on Belial continues:

> Thus *Belial* with words cloth'd in reason's garb
> Counsell'd ignoble ease, and peaceful sloth,
> Not peace.
>   [226–28]

Belial's is the only speech in the debate which is given both a prefatory warning and a summary denunciation, and it is this particular meddling with the narrative that has roused the ire of Waldock, John Peter, and R. J.

Werblowski.[20] What would appear to give some substance to their charges of unfairness and literary cheating is the fact that Beelzebub, the final speaker in the debate and the one who proposes the "easier enterprise" of gaining revenge upon God by seducing man, is introduced with apparent approval:

> with grave
> Aspect he rose, and in his rising seem'd
> A Pillar of State; deep on his Front engraven
> Deliberation sat and public care;
> And Princely counsel in his face yet shone,
> Majestic though in ruin: sage he stood
> With *Atlantean* shoulders fit to bear
> The weight of mightiest Monarchies; his look
> Drew audience and attention still as Night
> Or Summer's Noon-tide air, while thus he spake.
> [300–309]

The approval implied here is of course only apparent: in describing Beelzebub, the narrator is merely assuming for a moment the point of view of the fallen angels witnessing the debate. But the change in point of view prevents the narrator from making any direct statement that might match the strength of his disapproval of Belial's speech; and we are left with the apparent anomaly of a narrator (claiming to be, even if inspired, a fallen human being like the rest of us) who first delivers an all-out attack on the speaker who proposes a plan which might have spared mankind from death and "all our woe" and who then turns around and, by his very absence of comment, expresses no distress at all over a speech that leads eventually to man's seduction and fall.

Such carrying on by a narrator who from the opening lines of the poem has been lamenting his own fallen condition would appear to be very odd conduct indeed. That conduct has prompted the most convincing defender of Milton's poetic practice at this particular point in the poem to look past the noble-sounding rhetoric of Belial's speech and examine the logic of the speech more closely. And what Stanley Fish has found is that the warnings against the speech are merited, that Belial in effect answers his own stirring rhetorical question of who would be willing to "lose . . . this intellectual being": Belial himself would. At the very end of his speech, Belial suggests that in time the fallen angels may become so accustomed to their surroundings that they will either lose all feeling or simply become indistinguishable from, in effect subsumed into, their environment:

> Our purer essence then will overcome
> Thir noxious vapor, or enur'd not feel,
> Or chang'd at length, and to the place conform'd
> In temper and in nature, will receive
> Familiar the fierce heat, and void of pain.
> [215–19]

Belial has thus belied his own claim to be interested in intellectual activity; his ultimate hope is not after all so different from Moloch's.[21]

But what both Fish and the anti-Miltonists have assumed is at issue here is simply whether there is a discrepancy between the content of Belial's speech and what Milton or the narrator of the poem has to say about it. The concluding comment on the speech states that Belial spoke "with words cloth'd in reason's garb," and both Fish and his (and Milton's) opposition have taken that phrase to mean merely that Belial's words may sound reasonable but in fact are not so. The phrase, however, has another meaning as well and one which might better suggest why Milton himself was so concerned with the speech that he felt obliged to provide two different warnings against it: "words cloth'd in reason's garb" can mean that Belial is placing a very different interest or concern under the respectable cloak of "reason." Belial may not, then, have been saying precisely what he meant. The final comment on the speech adds also that Belial "counsell'd ignoble ease, and peaceful sloth, / Not peace." Now nowhere in Belial's speech does he specifically suggest that ease is what he desires; his speech in fact is the only one in the debate in which the word "ease" or one of its adjectival derivatives does not appear. Belial may well be desiring ignoble ease and peaceful sloth, but that is not what he has counseled aloud.

What ought to make us aware of the possibility that Belial is not telling his cohorts and ourselves what he really means, and aware of it even before we get to the explicit summary statement, is, of course, that it is a figure named Belial who has been arguing in favor of intellectual pursuits or the contemplative life. Milton could easily have given this speech to any other fallen angel, but instead he chose this particular one, "than whom a Spirit more lewd / Fell not from Heaven, or more gross to love / Vice for itself" (I.490–92). A figure bearing a name that has strong and long-standing associations with lasciviousness is not likely to be sincerely interested in nourishing "this intellectual being, / Those thoughts that wander through Eternity."[22] And what, in sum, the reader of Sidney especially can see in Belial's speech in the debate is that it is merely an infernal version of Pyrocles' argument for remaining in Arcadia. Just as Pyrocles masked his true desires with a false argument on behalf of the contemplative as opposed to the active life, so here Belial, as the combination of his own words and the narrator's comments upon them shows us, is using the traditional appeal to the contemplative life to mask his true wish to indulge himself in idleness and whatever lascivious pleasures are still possible for fallen angels in Hell.

By putting an argument on behalf of the contemplative life in the mouth of Belial, Milton presents us with another instance of an English Renaissance poet refusing to allow the question whether the active or contemplative life is superior to develop into the legitimate debate it might in the hands of an Augustine, an Aquinas, an Italian Humanist like Coluccio Salutati or Leonardo Bruni, or a Neoplatonist of the Florentine Academy. Rather, like both Sidney and Shakespeare before him, Milton casts the apparent debate between the claims of action and contemplation in the form of a debate between the active and the merely idle life, the outcome of which debate could never be in doubt for a serious Renaissance writer or reader.[23] Like his anti-pastoral predecessors, Milton is simply not giving the argument for the contemplative life a fair hearing, and his unfairness here suggests very strongly that he will not be likely to favor such a life elsewhere in the poem either. It is in this way that Belial's speech in the infernal debate can be said to foreshadow Milton's treatment of Paradise. For Milton in books IV through IX has provided us with a particularly uncontemplative Paradise.

There are, admittedly, some suggestions of the propriety of contemplation in Milton's Paradise. As part of the poem's insistence upon hierarchy and hence upon Adam's superiority to Eve, we are told,

> For contemplation hee and valor form'd
> For softness shee and sweet attractive Grace.
> [IV. 297–98]

Accordingly, at Adam's first moment of life he turned his wandering eyes toward Heaven

> And gaz'd a while the ample Sky, till rais'd
> By quick instinctive motion up I sprung,
> As thitherward endeavoring.
> [VIII. 258–60]

Adam says that he seems in Heaven when he discourses with Raphael (VIII. 211), and he recognizes that it is in contemplation of created things that "By steps we may ascend to God" (V.511–12). Those particularly Protestant morning and evening prayers that Adam and Eve deliver without outward rite, "unmeditated," and "in various style" might in themselves qualify as a mode of contemplation, since they contain a good measure of praise of God and of his creations (IV.720–35; V.153–208; IX.197–99). But all in all, it is remarkable how little contemplating Adam and Eve actually do.

We can, I believe, perceive some of Milton's bias or emphasis in this respect by noting what happens at the conclusion of each of Adam and Eve's prayers. The first prayer we hear moves from praise of God to gratitude for their mutual love, "the Crown of all our bliss," and after the prayer Adam and Eve proceed to their nuptial bed (IV.736–39). Immediately following their second prayer, the next morning, Milton has them *haste* to their rural work in the garden (V.211). And at their third prayer, the one which they offer on the morning of the fall and which is merely reported, not presented, they proceed from their vocal worship to, once again, consideration of how they might accomplish their "growing work" (IX.201–3). The closest we come in the poem to the type of contemplation suggested by Belial's call for "thoughts that wander through Eternity" is in Hell, where some of the fallen angels "reason'd high / Of Providence, Foreknowledge, Will, and Fate" (II.558–59); and that mental exercise arises as a direct result of the fallen angels' not having enough to occupy their time. When Satan is off attempting to seduce man, the other fallen angels are left until that leader's return to pursue each his several way

> as inclination or sad choice
> Leads him perplext, where he may likeliest find
> Truce to his restless thoughts, and entertain
> The irksome hours.
>   [II.523–27]

Contemplation of any sort tends to be deemphasized in Paradise simply because there proves to be too much else for Adam and Eve to do. J. M. Evans has referred to the amount of physical labor Milton prescribes for Adam and Eve as "the most strikingly original feature" of his treatment of prelapsarian life.[24] That distinction should, I think, be saved for Milton's treatment of Adam and Eve's prelapsarian lovemaking. But it remains true that Milton's garden provides a good deal more work for Adam and Eve than we might expect from earlier exegetical statements about life in Eden, even those insisting that it was in fact physical labor that was to be performed.

EDENIC WORK IN A WILDERNESS OF SWEETS

The first time that the subject of Adam and Eve's work in the garden arises in *Paradise Lost*, we are told that their labor was designed by God simply to add to the many pleasures already heaped upon them in Eden:

> They sat them down, and after no more toil
> Of thir sweet Gard'ning labor than suffic'd
> To recommend cool *Zephyr,* and made ease
> More easy, wholesome thirst and appetite
> More grateful, to their Supper Fruits they fell.
> [IV.327–31]

Adam's own first mention of their labor similarly attests to its basically easy quality:

> But let us ever praise him, and extol
> His bounty, following our delightful task
> To prune these growing Plants, and tend these Flow'rs,
> Which were it toilsome, yet with thee were sweet.
> [IV.436–39]

Such statements are in full accord with the comments of the medieval and Renaissance exegetes who (like Augustine) distinguished sharply between our labor since the fall and that "plesant exercise" assigned to Adam and Eve in Eden.[25] A little later Adam speaks of their work in somewhat more significant and symbolic terms:

> other Creatures all day long
> Rove idle unimploy'd, and less need rest;
> Man hath his daily work of body or mind
> Appointed, which declares his Dignity,
> And the regard of Heav'n on all his ways;
> While other Animals unactive range,
> And of thir doings God takes no account.
> [IV.616–22]

Although there is some suggestion here that they have enough work to make them tired, their labor would appear to be primarily a token of man's central position on earth and of God's continuing concern for man.

But Adam continues speaking and quickly moves into descriptive terms which suggest that their work is more substantial and toilsome than such a symbolic interpretation of it might imply:

> Tomorrow ere fresh Morning streak the East
> With first approach of light, we must be ris'n,
> And at our pleasant labor, to reform
> Yon flow'ry Arbors, yonder Alleys green,
> Our walk at noon, with branches overgrown,
> That mock our scant manuring, and require
> More hands than ours to lop thir wanton growth:
> Those Blossoms also, and those dropping Gums,
> That lie bestrown unsightly and unsmooth,
> Ask riddance, if we mean to tread with ease.
> [IV.623–32]

Eden has for Adam and Eve not simply what they need but a good deal more than they need. And the strength of the verbs Adam uses to describe Nature's actions here—"mock" and "require"—suggests that Nature's richness can be viewed as a threat to our first parents. In this passage the "ease" referred to has been placed within a conditional clause; it is not merely something to be relished at will but rather is contingent upon getting some specific work done. The emphasis here is thus a good deal different from the initial assertions that their work was not toilsome or was designed simply to make their ease more easy.

This later emphasis is consistent with descriptions of Paradise which since the beginning of Book IV have suggested that Nature has been rather excessive in her generosity; for these descriptions imply in turn that Adam and Eve have a considerable task on their hands if they wish to bring Nature's bounty under control. We have been told that "Nature boon" poured forth her flowers "profuse on Hill and Dale and Plain" (IV.242–43) and that "the mantling Vine / Lays forth her purple Grape, and gently creeps / Luxuriant" (IV.258–60). And in Book V, after Adam and Eve awaken, we see them hasten forth to their labor:

> On to thir morning's rural work they haste
> Among sweet dews and flow'rs; where any row
> Of Fruit-trees overwoody reach'd too far
> Thir pamper'd boughs, and needed hands to check
> Fruitless imbraces.
> [V.211–15]

These early descriptions of Nature's exuberance culminate in the description of the garden as Raphael, bearing a warning from God lest man swerve "too secure," approaches Adam and Eve:

> Thir [the angels'] glittering Tents he pass'd, and now is come
> Into the blissful field, through Groves of Myrrh,
> And flow'ring Odors, Cassia, Nard, and Balm;
> A Wilderness of sweets; for Nature here
> Wanton'd as in her prime, and play'd at will
> Her Virgin Fancies, pouring forth more sweet,
> Wild above Rule or Art, enormous bliss.
>
> [V.291–97]

There is nothing strong enough to suggest outright evil in these descriptions of Nature's luxuriance, profuseness, and wantonness or in the reference to the garden as "a Wilderness of sweets." Rather, such terms could well be part of the attempt to construct a "paradisal language": Milton could be saying that Eden is different from our postlapsarian existence in that wantonness and luxuriance are possible there without the fallen world's implication of evil or danger. But still, these terms do consistently point to the need for Adam and Eve to work in the garden and to control Nature's luxuriance. Those fruit trees which threaten to reach too far need hands to "*check* Fruitless embraces" (V.214–15); and Adam and Eve need more help to "*lop*" overgrown branches' "wanton growth" (IV.629). The very statement that the overgrown branches "mock" their "scant manuring" suggests that Adam and Eve are fighting a losing battle in their attempt to control the garden's bounty. The more we, or Adam and Eve, see of this garden, the less inclined any of us might be to turn our backs upon it. Adam and Eve's work would appear to be, to use Bacon's terms once again, more for "necessity" than for "exercise and experiment."

As I have already suggested, Milton was by no means the first writer to focus upon the importance of Adam and Eve's prelapsarian work. The Geneva Bible provides a gloss upon Gen. 2:15 to the effect that "God would not have man idle, though as yet there was no neede to labour"; and numerous Renaissance (and some earlier) exegetes used discussion of Gen. 2:15 as an occasion to deliver a brief homily on the evils of idleness. Even while they continued to make the distinction between pre- and postlapsarian labor and hence to insist that Adam's Edenic tasks would not have been difficult, Protestant exegetes particularly were fond of noting that Adam had a "calling" assigned to him by God even in Eden, that of dressing and keeping the garden.[26] What appears to be Milton's personal contribution on this question is his emphasis not so much on the mere *fact* of Adam and Eve's labor as upon the extensive *need* for it. "In no previous Eden," J. M. Evans tells us, "had there been anything 'overgrown' or 'wanton,' 'unsightly' or 'unsmooth,' to demand Adam's urgent attention."[27] The closest we come to Milton's own emphasis is the suggestion by the early Puritans John Dod and Robert Cleaver that "God saw it needfull for *Adam* to have a Sabbath" even in his innocence, because of the danger that "his calling (though followed without tediousnesse) would yet partly have withdrawne his heart . . . [from the] praising of God, and considering of his [God's] power, wisdome, and mercie."[28] Dod and Cleaver are arguing here that the Sabbath was instituted at creation and hence that its observance is not a ceremony that could have been abrogated by the coming of Christ; they are not focusing directly upon the significance of Adam's work or upon life in Eden, but they could in passing envision the possibility of that work's becoming so extensive as to demand full attention in itself, extensive enough perhaps to confuse and distract Eden's inhabitants in their efforts to satisfy God's wishes. What Dod and Cleaver posited merely as a possibility, Milton fully dramatized.

It is fair, I think, to call Milton's portrayal of Edenic work one of his particularly Protestant, even Puritan, emphases in his poem. Protestantism's reaffirmation of the value of manual labor (in opposition to Aquinas's and much of Catholicism's view of the superiority of mental over manual labor) and its insistence that all Christians and not merely the clergy had "callings" were tenets likely to prompt an adherent to fasten upon the physical labor mentioned in Gen. 2:15.[29] But more important for our immediate reading of *Paradise Lost* is the fact that the emphasis upon the extent of Adam and Eve's Edenic work has a significant effect upon the way we understand subsequent events in the poem itself. For on the morning of the fall, Eve suggests that she and Adam work apart so that they may be less distracted by one another's presence and thus more efficient in their work. While, as the narrator tells us, both Adam and Eve are thinking about the work to be done that day, Eve especially seems concerned that "much thir work outgrew / The hands' dispatch of two Gard'ning so wide" (IX.202–3). She assumes that God in requiring them to dress and keep the garden is exacting day labor from them, that a given amount of work must be completed by the close of each day; she is worried lest "th' hour of Supper come unearn'd" (IX.225). She is of course wrong in this assumption, and she is immediately corrected by Adam, who reminds her that

> not so strictly hath our Lord impos'd
> Labor, as to debar us when we need
> Refreshment, whether food, or talk between,
> Food of the mind, or this sweet intercourse
> Of looks and smiles.
> [IX.235–39]

He reasserts the view that their work was designed by God as one of their pleasures; and in any case, she need not fear that the garden will outstrip their efforts, for help will come by the time it is needed:

> For not to irksome toil, but to delight
> He made us, and delight to Reason join'd.
> These paths and Bowers doubt not but our joint hands
> Will keep from Wilderness with ease, as wide
> As we need walk, till younger hands ere long
> Assist us.
> [IX.242–47]

And yet it is difficult for us to accept Adam's words here simply as the full expression of Milton's own view or to conclude that Eve is merely or flagrantly wrong in her assumptions about their work. For Eve's suggestion that they work apart has been expressed in a speech reiterating many of the very phrases that have been used earlier, often by Adam himself, to describe the garden and to convey the idea that its growth provides very real work for them:

> *Adam,* well may we labor still to dress
> This Garden, still to tend Plant, Herb and Flow'r,
> Our pleasant task enjoin'd, but till more hands
> Aid us, the work under our labor grows,
> Luxurious by restraint; what we by day
> Lop overgrown, or prune, or prop, or bind,
> One night or two with wanton growth derides
> Tending to wild. Thou therefore now advise
> Or hear what to my mind first thoughts present,
> Let us divide our labors. . . .
> [IX.205–12]

Because we have already seen phrases like "luxurious" and "wanton growth" used to describe the garden and have heard earlier of the need to "lop" the garden's overgrown branches and of Nature's tendency to mock or deride Adam and Eve's efforts, we tend to view this speech neither as an insincere feminine ploy for attention (as Tillyard would have it) nor as merely "proud self-presumption" on Eve's part, but rather as a sincere and troubled response to the specific garden Eve sees before her.[30] Eve may well be piqued by Adam's subsequent speech, which she feels slights her firmness and ability to withstand trial. But here in this speech at least she is responding to the garden around her in a way which, in view of Milton's earlier emphasis, we can only see as perfectly understandable if not even absolutely correct.

The emphasis upon work in Eden, quite apart from what it might tell us of Milton's Protestant inclinations, can in fact be seen as preparation for this particular moment in the poem. Either that, or poor Eve has been victimized by a personal emphasis of her author. For if Milton wanted us to view Eve simply as wrong in her concern over the garden's wantonness and in her suggestion to Adam that they work apart, and wanted us to censure her for her mistake, we might well wonder why the poet went out of his way to portray his garden as more difficult to dress and keep than previous Edens. What the emphasis in fact does is give us a type of double perspective on an important moment in the poem's action: we have two very different and even contradictory simultaneous responses to Eve's suggestion. We recognize immediately that she is wrong in assuming that she and Adam must earn each night's supper, that she is viewing their work too literally as necessary and effective in itself; and yet we fully understand and appreciate what prompted her to make the suggestion that they divide their labors. This moment in the poem marks only one of several significant instances in which we view the action with this double vision; these occasions in the poem are important because it is when they occur that we participate most fully in the poem's action and best comprehend the particular conditions of Adam and Eve's prelapsarian existence. And it is at such moments especially that we are prompted to view Adam and Eve's Edenic life as a reflection of our own experience since the fall.

Milton's emphasis upon work in the garden, then, tends to make any talk about an easy or effortless Edenic existence, either from Adam or from modern critics of the poem, inappropriate for this particular Eden. But the insistence upon the garden's growth, and hence upon the need for work by our first parents, has significance beyond itself. For the garden is, of course, a reflection of the human beings who inhabit it.[31] The flowers Eve tends are closely identified with Eve herself: as she gardens alone in Book IX, "oft stooping to support / Each Flow'r of slender stalk, whose head . . . / . . . Hung drooping unsustain'd," she is herself described as the garden's "fairest unsupported Flow'r," far from her "best prop" (IX.427–33). And just as the overwoody fruit-tree boughs "needed hands to check / Fruitless imbraces" (V.214–15), Eve at her first moments of consciousness needed to be warned and guided to prefer Adam and his embraces over the image of herself reflected in the smooth lake (IX.449–91). Adam, for his part, must have his desires and fancies restrained just as the overgrown branches in the garden must be checked and lopped. The wantoning Nature that Raphael meets in Book V has "Virgin Fancies" that play at will "Wild above Rule or Art" (V.296–97), and Adam confesses to this same Raphael that he too has a mind or "Fancy" that is apt "to rove / Uncheckt, and of her roving is no end; / Till warn'd, or by experience taught" (VIII.188–90).

Man and Nature in Milton's garden are thoroughly intertwined. The same actions and needs are imputed to both and in the same terms. There is a tendency toward disorder both in the garden and in its inhabitants, and the control that Adam and Eve must exercise over the garden is clearly a reflection of the control they must exercise over themselves as well. As original and as significant as the emphasis on the garden's bounty is, in fact, one cannot help but think that the emphasis is primarily a means of bringing us to focus upon that second type of control, that which Adam and Eve must exercise over themselves and their own feelings. It is Eve more than Adam who is concerned about the garden's threat to outstrip their efforts. This is fitting, since it is Eve generally who is seen to be in closer touch with the garden: it is at her approach that the fruits and flowers "sprung / And toucht by her fair tendance gladlier grew" (VIII.46–47); Adam is at no time greeted with the same enthusiasm by the garden. And Eve demonstrates a more precise knowledge of the garden's capacities: she corrects her husband's suggestion that she clear her larder to prepare a meal for Raphael, pointing out that the garden's continuous growth makes storage of fruits and vegetables unnecessary (V.313–25). But as the hierarchical formula "Hee for God only, shee for God in him" (IV.299) tells us, Adam is the more important human figure in the poem; and it is what most concerns or disturbs Adam, not Eve—what makes Edenic life particularly difficult or complicated for him, not for his wife—that will tell us most about man and his interests in the poem. And what Adam sees as the most disturbing and hence the most complicating feature of his prelapsarian existence is simply Eve and the feelings she arouses in him. It would appear to be no mere coincidence that those feelings arise as a direct result of Milton's other distinguishing feature or original emphasis in his treatment of Edenic life—the specifically sexual nature of the love relationship between Adam and Eve before the fall.

"THE CROWN OF ALL OUR BLISS"

Just as, strictly speaking, Milton was not the first interpreter of Genesis to envision a significant amount of physical labor for Adam and Eve in Eden, so too he was not the first to assume sexual intercourse between the unfallen Adam and Eve. Many medieval and earlier Jewish exegetes had imputed sexual union to Adam and Eve in their innocent state. Even those rabbis who used their reading of Ps. 49:13, "Man tarrieth not overnight in his glory," as a gloss of Chapters 2 and 3 of Genesis, and who thus agreed with many Christian commentators that Adam and Eve fell on the first day of their creation, often made sexual intercourse one of our first parents' activities in an hour-by-hour timetable of the events of their first day.[32] And Jacob Cats, a Dutch diplomat and poet, whose poem in praise of marriage, *Trou-ringh,* Milton may have read in the original Dutch or its Latin translation, celebrated at great length and with considerable vehemence the sexual joys experienced by Adam and Eve while in Paradise (though these joys seem to have been more appreciated by Cats's Adam than by his rather reluctant Eve).[33] And then there were also Grotius's *Adamus Exul* and Vondel's *Adam in Ballingschap,* both of which plays deal with Milton's main subject, the fall of man, and both of which postulate, even if they do not emphasize, sexual consummation before the fall.[34] But such a stand presented rather severe difficulties for most Christian exegetes. Committed as they were (unlike the Hebraic fathers) to the doctrine of original sin and hence to the belief that Cain, Adam's first born, was evil because Adam before him was already sinful, Christian interpreters were virtually forced to conclude that Adam and Eve's first act of intercourse must have occurred after the fall. As Andrew Willet put it, "so ungracious a sonne, as Caine was" could not have been begotten by Adam while still in a state of innocence. If, Willet argued a few pages earlier, Adam and Eve had remained in Paradise more than a brief period, "it is not other like but the man should have knowne his wife in Paradise . . . and so they should have gotten children without sinne."[35] Either, then, there was no sexual intercourse before the fall or God was guilty of inefficiency when he commanded Adam and Eve to increase and multiply and then failed to have them conceive a child upon any prelapsarian intercourse. The implications attendant upon this latter option no doubt helped push the vast majority of Christian theologians and scriptural exegetes before Milton to the position that there in fact was no act of prelapsarian coition.

Thus, even if Milton's stand on prelapsarian sexual love was not completely original with him, it was certainly that of a small minority. And both his willingness to risk running afoul of the Christian doctrine of inherited sin (and inherited at conception) and the very prominence and emphasis he gave to Adam and Eve's Edenic lovemaking in *Paradise Lost* suggest that Milton's stand reflects some particularly personal interest and belief and is not something he borrowed casually while reading earlier works in the hexameral tradition.[36] In *Paradise Lost* he was in fact very self-consciously assuming an extreme position in what he quite rightly understood to be a long-standing exegetical debate on this question of the possible existence and nature of our first parents' sexual activity in Eden. To appreciate fully the distinctiveness of his stand and its importance for *Paradise Lost*, it should be of help to have the main outlines of this debate also before us.

THE DEBATE WAS from its earliest stages clearly connected with attitudes toward sexual intercourse and marriage generally. At perhaps the opposite extreme from Milton was the fourth-century church father St. Gregory of Nyssa, who expressed the early Christian disapproval of conjugal union. Gregory put forward the argument that had Adam and Eve not fallen, they would have reproduced in a manner similar to that of the angels. In Gregory's view, as in that of such other fathers as St. John Chrysostom and St. John Damascene, prelapsarian life was a kind of angelic existence, and "whatever the mode of increase in the angelic nature is (unspeakable and inconceivable by human conjectures, except that it assuredly exists), it would have operated also in the case of men." While Gregory thus admitted that he no more than anyone else had any specific idea how angels or unfallen man might propagate, he was sure that it would be by a method very different from "that animal and irrational mode" fallen man is forced to use.[37]

If Gregory of Nyssa could not even imagine the sexual act without its fallen manifestations of libidinousness and animal passion, Augustine could, and in Book XIV of *The City of God* he objected strongly to a view expressed by Gregory, among others, that God had created two sexes before the fall with his eye on the manner of procreation to be used only after man first sinned. Such a view was plainly unacceptable to Augustine, since it rendered God dependent upon man's sin to accomplish his ultimate plan for man and complete the requisite number of saints to fill the heavenly city.[38] Augustine thus directly opposed the argument that unfallen man would have reproduced the way angels do and asserted that God created two different sexes so that Adam and Eve might procreate specifically by means of sexual union, even without a fall from grace. Indeed, he argued elsewhere (and was followed by Thomas Aquinas in this), were it not procreation that God had in mind when he created Eve, he might more wisely have created a male companion as a helpmeet for Adam.[39] In Augustine's judgment, there *could* have been sexual union in the manner of fallen human beings even before the fall, but with the important difference that in prelapsarian sexual love the generative organs would have been moved by the will, not excited by lust:

> In such happy circumstances and general human well-being we should be far from suspecting that offspring could not have been begotten without the disease of lust, but those parts, like all the rest, would be set in motion at the command of the will; and without the seductive stimulus of passion, with calmness of mind and with no corrupting of the integrity of the body, the husband would lie upon the bosom of his wife.[40]

Contrary to what Gregory and others had implied, then, the sexual act was not in itself bad; what defiled it was fallen man's inability to procreate without being subject to immoderate passion. Yet for all his defense of the original purity of the sexual act itself, Augustine was quick to add that there was in fact no sexual intercourse before the fall; his whole discussion was perforce being carried on in hypothetical terms. For, as he suggested in the *De Genesi ad Litteram,* either because Adam and Eve sinned soon after Eve's creation and were forthwith expelled from Eden or because they awaited God's precise command about the time of their first act of intercourse, our first parents did not have the opportunity to participate in that tranquil generation proper to their unfallen state.[41]

Augustine's argument had a great deal to recommend it, since it not only avoided the possible blasphemy of viewing God as dependent upon man's sin to accomplish his ends but also neatly sidestepped the similar difficulties implicit in the idea of an unfruitful act of intercourse commanded by a God who wished to see man increase and multiply. It enabled Christians to hold to the doctrine of original sin, and thus account for Cain's evil nature, and at the same time to accept even carnal sexuality with a gratefulness proper to man when approaching any of God's gifts. Augustine's logic proved in fact to be the most important and influential of the various patristic attempts to solve our question of prelapsarian sexual union. It was taken over outright by later theologians and commentators such as Aquinas, Peter Lombard, Peter Comestor, and the Renaissance Jesuit Benedictus Pererius,[42] and it not only became what amounted to accepted doctrine of the Catholic church but was readily adopted by many Protestants also. Echoes of it are to be found, for instance, in Luther's assertion that Adam and Eve were virgin at their fall, even though unfallen procreation would have been very pure and honorable work, and in the attack of the seventeenth-century Protestant convert John Salkeld on Gregory of Nyssa's and St. John Damascene's view of an angelic prelapsarian Adam and Eve.[43]

Augustine can be said, then, to have effected a partial redemption of man's sexual organs—but only a partial one. Despite the argument that pure and unsinful sexual relations could have taken place in prelapsarian Eden (but did not), orthodox Catholicism continued in the main to hold to what it understood to be St. Paul's, and indeed Augustine's own, distrust of postlapsarian conjugal love and thus to prefer celibacy over the married state.[44] The opposition to celibacy as a necessarily better state, and particularly to a celibate clergy, was of course one of the main issues whereby early Protestant reformers differentiated themselves from the Catholicism they were attacking. Luther referred to those who deny there is any chastity in marriage and who prefer a celibate clergy as "the tools of Satan and the enemies of Christ." Calvin, in a similar polemical vein, looked upon the defamation of marriage and preference for celibacy as the particular "artifice of Satan" designed to confuse man and bring about his destruction.[45] Following their masters' lead, score upon score of sixteenth- and seventeenth-century Protestant preachers (many of them of distinctly Puritan leanings) were to accord marriage a dignity and respect in large part new to it in the Christian tradition. St. Paul, whom no Protestant (and least of all a Puritan) would be likely to slight, may indeed have said that it was better to remain celibate as he was (1 Cor. 7:7), and he may have deprecated marriage in his "It is better to marry than to burn" (1 Cor. 7:9); still, the influential Cambridge Puritan William Perkins could easily find other passages from Paul to justify the conclusion that though "marriage is of itselfe a thing indifferent, and the kingdome of God stands no more in it, than in meats and drinks . . . yet it is a state in it selfe, farre more excellent, then the condition of single life."[46]

But the many Protestant preachers who spoke and wrote on the subject of marriage were most concerned with presenting a practical code of conduct for life in a fallen world, and while they might pause to note that God ordained marriage in Paradise, they did not occupy themselves greatly with the theoretical question whether there was sexual union before the fall. And even when a poet who shares many of Milton's and the more adamant Protestants' beliefs does have time and cause to examine prelapsarian life in detail, he does not necessarily carry the Protestant enthusiasm over the joys and comforts of married life to the logical conclusion Milton did. The French Huguenot Du Bartas, in fact, though he did stop to present a delighted epithalamium at the point that Eve is presented to Adam, nonetheless backed away from the questions whether and how Adam and Eve made love in Paradise. Proceeding much in the manner of St. Augustine, Du Bartas assumed that it was likely that God intended Adam and Eve to procreate in the way that fallen men do, though without the "tickling flames" that now surprise our "fond soule":

> Or whether else as men ingender now,
> Sith spouse-bed spot-les lawes of God allow,
> If no excesse commaund: sith else againe
> The Lord had made the double sex in vaine.[47]

Du Bartas would venture such a statement, however, only in the form of a question, and he even prefaced the question (along with the questions how long Adam and Eve remained in Paradise and whether they were virgin at their fall) with a warning to his muse that she should not attempt to deal with such unprofitable and unanswerable matters lest she prove "too busie-idle" and "over bold" in treading such "too-curious" paths.[48]

Distrust of sexual relations had led to the early Catholic disapproval of marriage generally and to the banning of sexual love from Paradise; the obverse of the early Catholic attitude involves not only praising marriage but reinstituting its sexual consummation in Eden. That is what Milton did, and his particular contribution to this debate on prelapsarian sexual love was to bring the Protestant preachers' enthusiasm for marriage fully to bear on Adam and Eve's prelapsarian state. Far from considering speculation over our first parents' conjugal relations "busie-idleness," in *Paradise Lost* Milton portrayed prelapsarian sexual love with an explicitness approached by only one figure (Jacob Cats) in the Christian tradition before him.

BELIEVING THAT there in fact was prelapsarian sexual love, Milton quite understandably made it an important part of Adam and Eve's Edenic life. In Du Bartas's view, Adam's "best and supreme delectation" in Eden was the frequent and direct "holy conversation" both his body and soul had there with God.[49] Milton's Adam would himself seem to hold to the same opinion after his fall, when he laments that what most afflicts him in leaving Paradise is being deprived of God's countenance (XI.315–17); but before the fall, while still experiencing all his joys, "the sum of earthly bliss" for him is the enjoyment, and particularly the sexual enjoyment, of Eve (VIII.522). Adam and Eve together, in their evening prayer, refer to their "mutual help and mutual love" as "the Crown of all our bliss" (IV.728). And Satan even considers an embrace between Adam and Eve to be Paradise in itself:

> Sight hateful, sight tormenting! thus these two
> Imparadis't in one another's arms
> The happier *Eden,* shall enjoy thir fill
> Of bliss on bliss, while I to Hell am thrust.
>   [IV. 505–8]

While such sentiments are probably to be expected from an Adam and Eve who are enjoying their mutual love and a Satan who is jealous of it, we cannot conclude from such evidence alone that the poet himself shared his characters' estimate of sexual love as the greatest of prelapsarian pleasures. Satan is hardly a figure whose words or opinions we can accept without careful examination, and one might well argue that it is precisely because Adam puts too high an estimate on Eve and on his relationship with her that he falls—an act which Milton could not but condemn. But we ought to be able to rely upon the poem's narrator with some confidence, and when our guide through the poem also expresses abounding enthusiasm over the gift of prelapsarian sexual love, we have good cause to consider both that Milton himself thought this gift the crown of Eden's blessings and that he wanted us to think so too.

The first time in the poem that we see Adam and Eve retire for the night, the narrator breaks in with his famous and impassioned eulogy on wedded love. It is at this point that Milton comments most directly upon the earlier exegetical debate on prelapsarian sexual love and works that debate fully into the fabric of his poem.[50] I present the passage in full, because it is important that we be aware, among other things, of its length:

>   into thir inmost bower
> Handed they went; and eas'd the putting off
> These troublesome disguises which wee wear,
> Straight side by side were laid, nor turn'd I ween
> *Adam* from his fair Spouse, nor *Eve* the Rites
> Mysterious of connubial Love refus'd:
> Whatever Hypocrites austerely talk
> Of purity and place and innocence,
> Defaming as impure what God declares
> Pure, and commands to some, leaves free to all.
> Our Maker bids increase, who bids abstain
> But our Destroyer, foe to God and Man?
> Hail wedded Love, mysterious Law, true source
> Of Human offspring, sole propriety
> In Paradise of all things common else.

> By thee adulterous lust was driv'n from men
> Among the bestial herds to range, by thee
> Founded in Reason, Loyal, Just, and Pure,
> Relations dear, and all the Charities
> Of Father, Son, and Brother first were known.
> Far be it, that I should write thee sin or blame,
> Or think thee unbefitting holiest place,
> Perpetual Fountain of Domestic sweets,
> Whose bed is undefil'd and chaste pronounc't,
> Present, or past, as Saints and Patriarchs us'd.
> Here Love his golden shafts imploys, here lights
> His constant Lamp, and waves his purple wings,
> Reigns here and revels; not in the bought smile
> Of Harlots, loveless, joyless, unindear'd,
> Casual fruition, nor in Court Amours,
> Mixt Dance, or wanton Mask, or Midnight Ball,
> Or Serenate, which the starv'd Lover sings
> To his proud fair, best quitted with disdain.
> These lull'd by Nightingales imbracing slept,
> And on their naked limbs the flow'ry roof
> Show'r'd Roses, which the Morn repair'd. Sleep on,
> Blest pair; and O yet happiest if ye seek
> No happier state, and know to know no more.
> [IV.738–75]

Milton was no mean polemicist himself, and the attack on the "hypocrites" who defame sexual union echoes both the vehemence and the words of Paul and, perhaps, Calvin or Luther. Paul's hypocrites of 1 Tim. 4 were those ascetics who forbade marriage in a fallen world, whereas the whole context of Milton's use of the word and specifically his reference to "purity and place and innocence" plainly show that he also had in mind those who had ruled out even the possibility of sexual love in Paradise. Milton is clearly lumping together all opponents of sexual union, be it pre- or postlapsarian, and his "hypocrites" then would include Gregory of Nyssa as well as the Catholics of his own time who might still favor celibacy over married life. While to Milton and his Protestant audience, no term of abuse for a contemporary Catholic might seem too strong, that mantle of "hypocrite" does fall a bit heavily on Gregory and the other early church fathers, who, while betraying an ascetic streak, were after all merely following what they understood to be the implications of the Gospels and St. Paul. Harsh as the term may be, and particularly when joined with that sarcastic "austerely," it points up sharply the obvious strength of its speaker's feelings on an issue of evident importance to him.

The length of the outburst is of course another indication of the strong feeling behind it. Everything from the reference to hypocrites up to the description of the nightingales is, as eighteenth-century critics and editors such as Addison and Bishop Thomas Newton were wont to observe, very strictly speaking a digression from the straight narrative progress of the poem—though ultimately no more of a digression from the whole of the poem than the so-called digressions in "Lycidas." In a voice that seems indistinguishable from Milton's own (in view of Milton's distinctive stand on the very existence of prelapsarian sexual love), the narrator moves from a description of specifically prelapsarian wedded love to praise of wedded love in general. Because Adam and Eve's marriage, instituted by God in Paradise, was in the eyes of Milton and the Protestant apologists for marriage the example and prototype for all subsequent Christian marriages, this move or jump is not hard to understand. But by the time he is distinguishing postlapsarian wedded love from prostitution, "Court Amours," and Petrarchan love, this narrator has wandered well away from the ostensible main subject of this part of Book IV— Adam and Eve in Paradise.[51] We seem to have come, in this extended and rhetorically heightened passage, upon a speaker who has struck upon a subject dear to his own heart and who cannot resist the temptation to rhapsodize on it for a while. The whole passage is in fact only one of several emotionally charged outbursts from the narrator which have a significant effect upon our reading experience and interpretation of events in the latter part of the poem. For whether or not we remember the outbursts specifically by the time we reach Adam's fall, they help to predispose us toward appreciating Adam's motives when he decides to fall along with Eve. While we never lose consciousness that Adam's acceptance of the apple was a mistake which had disastrous effects for him and for all of us, these outbursts are greatly responsible for bringing us to see that Adam did nonetheless have a difficult and meaningful decision to make, that he had something valuable to lose in refusing the apple.

Another such outburst, much briefer but similarly interrupting the poem's narrative action and attesting to the importance of prelapsarian wedded love to the narrator, comes near the beginning of Book VIII. Adam has just asked his question about celestial motions, implying in effect that God has been inefficient in constructing a geocentric universe. Milton has two different ways of telling us that Adam ought not have asked the question: one, of course, is Raphael's long answer telling Adam that it is not for him, a mere human, to doubt the wisdom of God's ways or logic; the other is having Eve wander off when Adam enters on such "studious thoughts abstruse" (VIII.40). Milton implies that in asking the question Adam is not paying enough attention to what ought to interest him most—Eve and her beauty. Both right before and after Eve moves off, we are told that she has such majesty, grace, and beauty that those who saw her ought to wish her to stay (VIII.43, 63). Yet Adam and Raphael continue to talk on their abstruse intellectual plane. Eve, for her part, prefers to have the discussion of such matters mixed in with a certain amount of immediate, less rarefied and intellectualized, pleasure:

> Her Husband the Relater she preferr'd
> Before the Angel, and of him to ask
> Chose rather: hee, she knew, would intermix
> Grateful digressions, and solve high dispute
> With conjugal Caresses, from his Lip
> Not words alone pleas'd her.
>
> [VIII. 52–57]

Milton might at this point be having Eve adhere, insofar as her prelapsarian state allows for such a parallel, to St. Paul's instruction of 1 Cor. 14:35, that women should ask their husbands questions at home rather than in church, where it is shameful for a woman to speak. Paul, however, says nothing about interspersed kisses and conjugal caresses, and from these lines alone we might be tempted to doubt that Eve really cares how the universe is organized. But the narrator of the poem has no such doubts. He has a moment before informed us that Eve is not uninterested in such matters—"Yet went she not, as not with such discourse / Delighted" (48–49)—and right after these lines he intervenes with a rhetorical question which implies total approval of her desire to learn from Adam alone:

> O when meet now
> Such pairs, in Love and mutual Honor join'd?
>
> [57–58]

The full force of this question runs somewhat counter to the earlier eulogy on wedded love, for it implies that one of the unfortunate results of the fall has been the loss of true or ideal wedded love. But it does, in any case, direct our attention once again to a narrator for whom wedded love is very important.

Perhaps the most striking and revealing of the narrator's emotional outbursts—revealing in that it shows us a figure very susceptible to Eve's charms and laboring under a great deal of stress as he speaks to us—occurs in the middle of Book V. When Eve is serving dinner to Adam and Raphael, the narrator stops to consider her naked beauty and breaks in with:

> O innocence
> Deserving Paradise! If ever, then,
> Then had the Sons of God excuse to have been
> Enamour'd at that sight; but in those hearts
> Love unlibidinous reign'd, nor jealousy
> Was understood, the injur'd Lover's Hell.
> [V.445–50]

A general distinction is being made in these lines between the love of Adam and Eve (and that of Raphael also) and the libidinous love of the Sons of God for the Daughters of Cain, this latter love to be described for us in disparaging fullness much later in the poem (XI. 573–92). The scene here in Eden has to do, though, not with the glittering enticements of women anxious to catch men in an "amorous Net" (XI. 586), but with Eve and with love that is pure, so pure that a third figure, the angel Raphael, can look upon the naked Eve without either arousing Adam's jealousy or becoming jealous of Adam himself. This scene in Eden, in fact, presents such a special case that the narrator appears well on his way toward assuring us, and evidently himself also, that it is all right to become enthralled by feminine beauty, if that beauty belongs to someone as innocent and good as Eve. The rhetorical power of the repeated and heavily stressed "then" in the clause "if ever, then, / Then had the Sons of God excuse to have been / Enamour'd at that sight" builds to the point of expressing outright the wish that one could allow oneself to become enamored. But still, that clause carries within it its own contradiction: the word "excuse" implies that becoming enamored at all, even of unfallen Eve, is a weakness or a mistake, some lapse that must be pardoned. And "if ever," suggesting a situation contrary to fact, implies by its very presence here its opposite "never," and hence the idea that not even in Paradise and with the sinless Eve does one have an excuse for becoming enamored. Although the narrator goes on and tries to make the qualitative distinction between the pure and good love of Adam and Eve and the love of the Sons of God, the implication remains that becoming enamored at all, whether the lover is Adam or the libidinous Sons of God, is inexcusable and hence wrong.

When we recall that the narrator moved into this brief but excited outburst as a result of his enthusiasm for the innocent Eve's naked beauty, the main impression that we are left with is that of a momentarily troubled and confused narrator, one who is confused specifically by Eve. By this time in the poem, we can well sympathize with and understand this confusion. We too have witnessed, for instance, that moment when Eve

> with eyes
> Of conjugal attraction unreprov'd
> And meek surrender, half imbracing lean'd
> On our first Father, half her swelling Breast
> Naked met his under the flowing Gold
> Of her loose tresses hid.
> [IV.492–97]

Eve is indeed beautiful, and much of Milton's most effective and affecting writing has gone into the descriptions of her. We can understand, then, why the narrator himself might feel pulled in two different directions, toward, let us say, recognizing that passion must always be kept under the control of reason and toward the recognition that Eve is, after all, very beautiful and ought to be cherished. And in the outburst in Book V, we find a narrator who betrays an intense personal awareness of just the feelings that Adam had to deal with when he had to choose between taking the apple from Eve and living on in Eden without this particular Eve.

What is most remarkable about these outbursts, what in effect draws our attention to them so strongly, is that the narrator's voice in them is so different from his voice elsewhere in the poem, that voice which has angered the anti-Miltonists of this century. At other points in the poem, this narrator apparently shows no awareness at all either of Eve's beauty or of the effect that her beauty and love might have upon Adam. When Adam takes the apple from Eve and receives death for his act, for instance, this same narrator sums up the action taking place in the vindictive and legalistic terms "for such compliance bad / Such recompense best merits" (IX.994–95) and four lines later describes Adam merely as "fondly overcome with Female charm" (IX.999). With such a deprecatory formula as this last, the narrator would seem to be forgetting his own earlier excitement over that "Female charm." The fact that the narrator's voice is inconsistent is not in itself very important or damaging to the poem's coherence: the narrator is not a character as in a novel or a play. Rather, he is in the poem primarily to direct and mold *our* consciousness as we read. And what becomes most significant about an outburst such as the one in Book V over Eve's naked beauty is simply that the feeling of confusion, the tension between what one feels one ought to do and what one would like to do, has been presented to us and has become part of our own experience as we proceed through the poem.

Were we to judge these emotional outbursts simply on the basis of the number of lines devoted to them in the poem, they might not appear of major importance. But their effect on a reader is considerable, especially if he has any awareness at all of the relative originality or distinctiveness of Milton's position in the debate concerning the existence of prelapsarian sexual love (and the argumentative nature of the first of the outbursts, the eulogy on wedded love, suggests that Milton envisioned his readers as having some awareness of it). For not only are these passages a departure from the narrator's usual calm, they are also of course a reflection and extension of Milton's initial decision to endow Adam and Eve with the gift of prelapsarian sexual love. They underline that original decision and provide what is evidently authorial endorsement of Adam's enthusiasm for Eve and for marriage to her. These passages in effect tell us directly that marriage to Eve is something to be excited about, and it is in large part because of the emphasis they provide that even readers who are not Waldocks are likely to bristle at reductive summaries such as "fondly overcome with Female charm." While back in Book IV Adam himself referred to God's restriction against tasting the fruit of the Tree of Knowledge as "one easy prohibition" (IV.433), these passages serve to show us how that prohibition could have become hard—hard enough to make Adam incline to disobey it when forced to choose between his love of God and his love of Eve.

BOTH MILTON'S OWN position on the very existence of prelapsarian sexual love and the emphasis given that subject by the narrator's excitement over it would appear to be preparing us for the particular moment in the poem when Adam must decide whether to accept the apple from Eve and fall with her. It is at this point that the force of the emphasis on conjugal love as valuable and to be cherished comes into direct conflict with God's prohibition of the fruit of the Tree of Knowledge, and we would ordinarily expect a scene of considerable dramatic tension and excitement to do justice to a decision and moment of such significance. But, perhaps in order to prevent his audience's too easy identification with Adam when he makes his disastrous mistake and falls, Milton does two things which put some distance between Adam and ourselves at this important point: he has the lying Eve who offers the apple appear far less attractive than anywhere else in the poem (she thus becomes someone whose offer *we* at least might resist accepting); and he reduces the dramatic tension and impact of the scene by having Adam quickly and incorrectly treat his decision as a foregone conclusion, a direct logical consequence of Eve's fall. Adam conceives of himself at his fall as the mere object of verbs, without an independent will ("And mee with thee hath ruin'd," "I feel / The link of Nature draw me" [IX.906, 913–14]), and at no point in the inward speech following Eve's offer of the fruit does he pause to consider seriously not falling with her. Adam's decision is, in effect, made before we have a chance to argue it out for ourselves and hence place ourselves fully in his position.[52] While Adam's fall may be, then, the point in the poem at which he himself reacts most strongly to the feelings created in him by the gift of prelapsarian sexual love, it is not the point in the poem at which we feel the effect of the poem's emphasis on that love most forcefully. That particular point comes earlier, at the end of Book VIII and the culmination of Adam's prelapsarian education by Raphael. It is at this earlier point that Adam most explicitly articulates, and hence lets us share, the feelings that Eve and his relationship with her arouse in him, and it is there that the whole treatment of prelapsarian sexual love is most likely to influence our understanding of the poem's overall action and argument.

After Adam is "clear'd of doubt" on the organization of the universe, he agrees to descend to matters more "at hand" (VIII.199) and to talk of his life in Eden. The term "at hand" is perhaps a slight joke at Adam's expense, for by this time in the poem, it is likely to suggest mainly one subject to the reader: it is Eve who goes "handed" with Adam into the bower and is several times pictured walking "hand in hand" with him. Not surprisingly, then, Adam's account of his own life narrows down quickly to the importance of Eve to him. And having been told by Raphael that he ought to joy in his fair Eve (VIII.170–72), Adam proceeds to let slip the fact that the sum of his earthly bliss, the joy he experiences in Eve, is in fact passion:

> but here
> Far otherwise, transported I behold,
> Transported touch; here passion first I felt,
> Commotion strange, in all enjoyments else
> Superior and unmov'd, here only weak
> Against the charm of Beauty's powerful glance.
> [VIII.528–33]

Adam himself recognizes that there is something wrong in the strength of this feeling and at first he incorrectly tries to blame Nature for it:

> Or Nature fail'd in mee, and left some part
> Not proof enough such Object to sustain,
> Or from my side subducting, took perhaps
> More than enough; at least on her bestow'd
> Too much of Ornament, in outward show
> Elaborate, of inward less exact.
> [VIII. 534–39]

In the last two and one-half lines here Adam is committing much the same error as in his earlier question about the organization of the universe: he is implicitly accusing God (through his handmaiden, Nature) of inefficiency, of putting more ornament or beauty than was strictly necessary on the less important exterior of Eve while not giving proportionate care to her more important inner faculties. Such a charge would rightly bring down upon Adam a rebuke similar to that following his earlier question about the heavens. But Adam goes on to a more complete and less irreverent statement of the difficulty he experiences when dealing with Eve. He fully grants that he is the superior being, yet this understanding does not help him much when he listens to what Eve has to say:

> For well I understand in the prime end
> Of Nature her th' inferior, in the mind
> And inward Faculties, which most excel,
> In outward also her resembling less
> His Image who made both, and less expressing
> The character of that Dominion giv'n
> O'er other Creatures; yet when I approach
> Her loveliness, so absolute she seems
> And in herself complete, so well to know
> Her own, that what she wills to do or say,
> Seems wisest, virtuousest, discreetest, best;
> All higher knowledge in her presence falls
> Degraded, Wisdom in discourse with her
> Loses discount'nanc't, and like folly shows;
> Authority and Reason on her wait
> As one intended first, not after made
> Occasionally; and to consummate all,
> Greatness of mind and nobleness thir seat
> Build in her loveliest, and create an awe
> About her, as a guard Angelic plac't.
> [VIII. 540–59]

The number of harsh sibilants in a line like "Seems wisest, virtuousest, discreetest, best" may be expressing Milton's own disapproval of what Adam is saying here. But Adam himself is being very honest, and he is confessing to something which he too knows should not in theory be true. He knows he ought to be able to separate the value of what is being said from the person saying it, yet Eve's loveliness confuses him and makes it difficult for him to distinguish true wisdom from the mere show of it. What exactly Adam means by "loveliness" may not be totally clear, but it is evident from the last four lines of his account that he does not mean simply what Raphael is about to call her fair "outside." Her loveliness, for Adam, would appear to reside in the harmony of her whole being ("so absolute she seems / And in herself complete") and in the *combination* of her external beauty with inner virtues of nobility and greatness of mind.

Raphael's response to this troubled confession is, as Waldock noted in outrage, not completely to the point.[53] The angel directs himself mainly to the first part of what Adam has said—his confession of passion and the accusation against Nature—and berates Adam for hearkening only to Eve's outer appearance:

> Accuse not Nature, she hath done her part;
> Do thou but thine, and be not diffident
> Of Wisdom, she deserts thee not, if thou
> Dismiss not her, when most thou need'st her nigh,
> By attribúting overmuch to things
> Less excellent, as thou thyself perceiv'st.
> For what admir'st thou, what transports thee so,
> An outside? fair no doubt, and worthy well
> Thy cherishing, thy honoring, and thy love,
> Not thy subjection.
> [VIII. 561–70]

Raphael insists, then, on accepting "loveliness" as only physical beauty. He goes on to tell Adam to have more self-esteem, to weigh Eve with himself and then "value" or judge (VIII. 570–73), advice which in view of Milton's own opinion on man's clear superiority to woman is certainly sound enough. But Adam has said in his speech that he *has* weighed Eve with himself, and still he finds it difficult to determine whether what Eve says is wise or only seems so because it is she who is saying it; Raphael is thus reasserting doctrine which Adam has already acknowledged to be true. And without providing any concrete help toward relieving the difficulty that persists even after Adam acknowledges Eve his intellectual inferior, Raphael reverts to an earlier part of Adam's speech, to that description of his sexual love as the "sum of earthly bliss" (VIII. 522). The angel proceeds into an attack which is particularly striking because it runs directly counter in spirit both to Milton's own unusual decision to grant Adam and Eve sexual love before the fall and to the narrator's vehement defense of sexual love, back in Book IV, as proper and good for man even in Paradise:

> But if the sense of touch whereby mankind
> Is propagated seem such dear delight
> Beyond all other, think the same voutsaf't
> To Cattle and each Beast: which would not be
> To them made common and divulg'd, if aught
> Therein enjoy'd were worthy to subdue
> The Soul of Man, or passion in him move.
> [VIII. 579–85]

Raphael does urge Adam to love what is higher and rational in Eve and in the process makes a Neoplatonic distinction between sacred and profane love, or rational love and merely carnal passion:

> What higher in her society thou find'st
> Attractive, human, rational, love still;
> In loving thou dost well, in passion not,
> Wherein true Love consists not; Love refines
> The thoughts, and heart enlarges, hath his seat
> In Reason, and is judicious, is the scale
> By which to heav'nly Love thou may'st ascend,
> Not sunk in carnal pleasure, for which cause
> Among the Beasts no Mate for thee was found.
> [VIII. 586–94]

This may be all very well and good in Neoplatonic theory, but Raphael is making sharp distinctions where Adam has just confessed he cannot make them. His love for Eve simply cannot be separated so easily into its rational and carnal aspects.

Adam has some cause to believe, then, that Raphael has oversimplified both what he has just said and his prelapsarian difficulties, and this is one of the reasons, I take it, why Milton has Adam only "half abash't" (VIII. 595) by Raphael's rebuke. The other possible reason would be that Adam is not sufficiently acknowledging the justice in Raphael's rebuke and the applicability of Raphael's remarks to him—that is, that he ought to be more abashed than he is. It would be very difficult and probably misguided to attempt to determine which of these interpretations is correct; most likely, both are. For this is another of those moments in the poem that we view with a double perspective. Raphael has not actually been contradicting the rest of the poem. Though the point of the narrator's eulogy to wedded love was to establish the body and that "sense of touch whereby mankind / Is propagated" as good and pure in themselves, in that eulogy the narrator referred to love, as Raphael in effect does here, as "Founded in Reason" (IV.755). And no one has ever told Adam that there is no need for control in Paradise. Adam in fact implicitly accepts part of Raphael's rebuke as justified when he goes on to claim that he is only telling the angel what he feels inwardly as a result of Eve's loving words, actions, and compliance and is not therefore foiled (VIII.600–608). Yet from the analysis of the conversation in Book VIII provided thus far, it should be clear that, as legitimate as Raphael's theories about the makeup of human nature might be, we cannot very easily accept Raphael simply as Milton's authoritative spokesman in the discussion.

What we have here in Book VIII is the kind of discussion or debate found frequently in Milton between two different kinds of beings, or even two human figures, who are arguing from different assumptions—the kind of debate we witness, for instance, between Comus and the Lady. The two figures are putting forth arguments not completely related and are not successful in making themselves fully understood to one another. If Adam does not sufficiently apply Raphael's words to his own case, Raphael, for his part, does not comprehend and speak to the type of difficulty Adam is talking about. As far as the angel is concerned, man has reason and passions, and he must always keep reason uppermost and remain in firm control over the passions. Adam has learned what it means actually to *be* human, and his point is that ordinary human experience is not as simple as Raphael implies that it should be, that even in prelapsarian Paradise it is not easy to determine when the senses and passions are affecting reason and when they are not.

The turn that the discussion takes immediately after Raphael's rebuke of Adam helps to explain why the angel cannot fully comprehend Adam's very human difficulties in distinguishing between what his reason and what his senses tell him. Through the course of the poem there have been several suggestions, one of them rather sly, that Eve's particular attractiveness presents no great appeal to Raphael. The sly hint came at the angel's first entrance into Paradise, when the "undeckt" Eve was described as "Virtue-proof, no thought infirm / Alter'd her cheek" (V.384–85); this description occurs just thirteen lines after Raphael himself has been called by the narrator an "Angelic Virtue" (V.371). The phrase "virtue-proof" on its primary level undoubtedly means that, as Merritt Hughes says in his note to the line, Eve is proof against evil because of her virtue; but there remains also the implication that Eve has little to fear from the "Angelic Virtue," Raphael, either because the angel is not interested in her nakedness or because she does not feel any attraction toward him.[54] Both of these possibilities prove subsequently to be true: as we have seen, Eve wishes to receive her information from Adam's lips rather than the angel's; and at the moment early in Book VIII when Eve wanders off to tend her garden and the narrator twice remarks that Eve has grace and beauty "that won who saw to wish her stay" (VIII.43; see also 63), both Raphael and Adam fail either to notice that she is leaving or to beg her (as the narrator implies that *he* at least would) to stay on with them as they talk. Raphael's deprecatory references to Eve's fair "outside" and to that "sense of touch whereby mankind / Is propagated" here at the end of Book VIII merely make more explicit an attitude of his which has only been suggested thus far. Raphael's rebuke, then, betrays little appreciation of Eve's physical being and of human sexuality; and Adam responds with two final questions for his teacher which, given Adam's own feelings on those subjects, follow quite logically upon that rebuke: do angels love, and if so, how?

Raphael's answer is illuminating in several different ways:

> Let it suffice thee that thou know'st
> Us happy, and without Love no happiness.
> Whatever pure thou in the body enjoy'st
> (And pure thou wert created) we enjoy
> In eminence, and obstacle find none
> Of membrane, joint, or limb, exclusive bars:
> Easier than Air with Air, if Spirits embrace,
> Total they mix, Union of Pure with Pure
> Desiring; nor restrain'd conveyance need
> As Flesh to mix with Flesh, or Soul with Soul.
> [VIII.620–29]

The tone of these lines may well be difficult to grasp at first; it looks as if Raphael may be embarrassed or annoyed by the question, especially so since the answer is accompanied by "a smile that glow'd / Celestial rosy red" (VIII.618–19). But, tempting as it may be to interpret that blush as a token of Raphael's embarrassment (or even repressed adult society's embarrassment at childhood's innocent and unrestricted interest and delight in sexuality), the narrator refers to the blush or glow as "Love's proper hue" (VIII.619). Presumably then, the glow results from some fitting warmth or enthusiasm rather than shame, and Raphael is to be seen as basically pleased (though not without some hauteur) with the opportunity to talk about angelic love. The answer itself proves to be part of Milton's own overall emphasis on love in the poem: that even angels have some way of uniting to express their love, and a way that plainly has been modeled on human sexual embraces, reflects upon the goodness and propriety of sexual union for humans as well. But at the very moment when Milton is having Raphael suggest a type of similarity between angels and humans, that very similarity highlights the differences that remain between the two types of beings. Raphael's description of angelic love implies a nature for angels which is simpler than man's, because more uniform; angels can express their love through total union without having to rely upon or be distracted by limbs, flesh, or that sense of touch which Raphael has spoken of so harshly. Spirits, we have been told much earlier in the poem, are "uncompounded . . . thir Essence pure, / Not ti'd or manacl'd with joint or limb" (I.425–26). It is because Adam, even as an unfallen human being, has senses and a tangible, physical body that love presents more difficulties and dangers for him than for an unfallen angel. Because Raphael has no fleshly body, it is considerably easier for him to make that sharp distinction he insists upon between love that has its seat in reason and *carnal* pleasure. And the difficulty unfallen Adam experiences, both in distinguishing between what reason and what his senses and passion tell him and in trying to vindicate himself to Raphael, arises directly from his having been created by God as human, as a being of both spirit and flesh, with reason, passions, and a sense of touch.

Raphael has been sent by God to Adam to "advise him of his happy state" (V.234) and to warn him of his danger; the angel's stay in Eden might have proved to be an education for him as well as Adam, had he been able to comprehend fully what Adam has tried to tell him in their discussion. But Raphael has proved unable, in part simply because he is an angel, to grasp completely what Adam has to say about his human nature and the importance of Eve to him; and because of this inability, even though Raphael is a God-appointed teacher, we do not necessarily share the angel's point of view. If anything, we are by this point in the poem more likely to appreciate and hearken to Adam's words than to Raphael's. And we are so disposed, not simply because we are fallen human beings with a natural penchant for sin, or merely because we too as human beings have been subject to the conflict between reason and the passions that Adam speaks of (though undoubtedly such causes do contribute to our response); rather, our response is in large part the result of all the previous emphasis Milton himself has given to the subject of prelapsarian sexual love: first in his decision to endow our first parents with that love and then in his strategy of having his narrator stress the importance of that gift through rhetorically heightened passages of enthusiasm over it. Our sympathy with Adam at this important point in the poem is a reaction that Milton has gone out of his way to cultivate.

JUSTIFYING GOD'S AND MILTON'S WAYS

The stated purpose of *Paradise Lost* is to justify the ways of God to men, and that justification hinges completely on Milton's ability to convince us that man alone is responsible for his fall from grace, and God not at all so. Insofar as Milton's emphasis on prelapsarian sexual love brings us to appreciate Adam's reasons for accepting the apple from Eve, it may well bring us also to object to the conditions God set upon Adam's life as unfair and could easily work counter to Milton's overall purpose in the poem. Further, for Milton to choose the minority position of providing Adam and Eve with prelapsarian sexual love, to insist upon that love as good, important, and the crown of their prelapsarian bliss, and then to condemn Adam for succumbing to what in effect is the poet's own emphasis in the poem might also appear patently unfair of Milton, as well as of his God. The same unfairness might be charged against Milton if he expected us to reject out of hand Eve's suggestion that she and Adam work apart, after the poet has given his residents of Eden more gardening to do than was required of any previous Adam and Eve in the hexameral tradition. While I have assumed throughout the preceding discussion that the emphases on prelapsarian sexual love and on Edenic work in *Paradise Lost* are a consciously controlled and intended part of the poem's total meaning, the possibility does I suppose still exist that, as Waldock claimed, Milton was not at all times in full control of his material,[55] that these particular emphases represent personal and isolated interests that Milton could not resist indulging to the extent that they interfered with the meaning and intent of the poem as a whole.

Several arguments, however, militate against such a critical position: just as the emphasis on the garden's exuberance does not lead us to overlook the mistake in Eve's thinking when she makes her suggestion to work apart, so the emphasis on prelapsarian sexual love does not necessarily bring us to condone Adam's decision to fall; rather, in the latter case, we simply see Adam's decision at the point of his fall as complex and difficult. And second, there is the fact that there are two such emphases in the poem, not merely a single instance, and both have precisely the same effect of pointing to the relatively complicated and difficult conditions of Adam and Eve's prelapsarian life. The quandary in which Adam finds himself at the moment Eve offers him the fruit can, in fact, be seen as a paradigm of his whole prelapsarian experience. For the sexual love that Milton granted our first parents in Eden represents the culmination of all their prelapsarian difficulties as well as of their joys; and nowhere, as the discussion on love in Book VIII tells us, is control in Paradise more necessary, important, or difficult for Adam than over those passions that arise as a result of his love for Eve.

It is the whole emphasis on a difficult Eden, on the amount of physical work required of Adam and Eve and particularly on the sexual love which epitomizes Eden's difficulties, that undermines any hard-and-fast distinction one might seek to make between pre- and postlapsarian life in Milton's poem. There remain, of course, differences between our present existence and Adam and Eve's life before the fall; the use of that "paradisal language" mentioned earlier reminds us most quickly of the changes. Milton's Paradise is both like our present life and not like it, and the advantage of Milton's having portrayed it in such a way is that he can enforce upon our consciousness that there was a fall which was important and disastrous for all mankind and at the same time can use the Edenic portions of his poem to teach us about our present existence, and by very direct means. And when he does the latter, he is plainly not using his Eden to indulge in dreams of what might have been or even to point to the wretchedness of man's present life by contrasting it with a better time. This Eden is not so much a version of Paradise (that is, a mythic place to be sharply distinguished from all other landscapes) as a version of Empsonian pastoral: Milton is "putting the complex into the simple," presenting our complex life in small without establishing a qualitative difference between our present life and the simplified image epitomizing it.[56] We need not conclude as darkly as Empson does that Milton intends by this method to convey the idea that "the human creature is essentially out of place in the world and needed no fall in time to make him so."[57] Milton, wayfaring and warfaring Christian that he was, no doubt exulted in the prospect of a human life that from the very beginning demanded control, concentration, and full moral engagement: such demands, like Edenic work, can be viewed as tokens of man's dignity rather than his misery.

But Milton's choosing to portray a difficult Eden does mean that in the Edenic portions of his poem particularly, he is doing something in addition to justifying God's ways; and he is not simply writing an "official" poem, one that merely projects the point of view of God and his party in the poem. Rather, Milton is providing a definition of man, and it is a definition drawn from man's, not just God's, point of view. He is distinguishing man from other types of beings, as becomes most evident perhaps when he has Adam's most notable difficulty arise out of a tension to which Adam as a human being is subject and Raphael as an angel is not; and as the narrator's and our own response to Eve's beauty might suggest to us, this definition of human nature applies not simply to unfallen man but to man after the fall as well. Milton is engaged, then, in providing a statement of the human condition, and that in turn has a liberating effect upon *Paradise Lost*. For it is as a statement of what it means to be human that Milton's thoroughly Christian epic can continue to speak directly and forcefully to readers who themselves may have ceased to believe actively in the myth of the fall and the Christian doctrine Milton espoused. The poem neither presumes upon nor is limited by its audience's adherence to that Christian doctrine for its power and effectiveness.

CHAPTER VI

English Anti-Pastoralism:
Sources and Analogues

HREE ANTI-PASTORAL authors do not in themselves make a literary tradition. There was a formidable amount of pastoral writing in Renaissance England and many different motives for undertaking it. At the time when Sidney, Shakespeare, and Milton were expressing their opposition to what they understood as pastoral assumptions and an Arcadian (or Edenic) life of uncomplicated ease, others were writing pastoral of a very different sort. As we have seen, in his *Rosalynde* Lodge fully utilized the convention that places courtier next to shepherd on equal terms and accepted the view that pastoral life represented an improvement upon court life. Drayton throughout his career kept returning to the pastoral mode and reworking his own earlier eclogues in an attempt to express in Theocritean manner the detachment, simplicity, and charm of a pastoral existence. And Marvell, with his own characteristic detachment, can be said to have taken up and examined all sides of any version of the debate between pastoral and anti-pastoral that we might wish to formulate. Yet even admitting such variation, there is nonetheless a considerable amount of criticism of the pastoral mode and its assumptions in English Renaissance pastoral works, and, more intriguing, this criticism is on the whole confined to England.

This is not to say that it is only in England that we find criticism of pastoral and its assumptions and implied ideals. We do on occasion find it in Continental literature as well. One of the dogs in Cervantes' *Dialogue of the Dogs,* for instance, objects that the shepherd life his master's lady reads about in her idealizing pastoral romances bears little resemblance to the actual country life he witnessed in his own experience as a guard of a shepherd's flock. The shepherds he saw "spent most of the day picking fleas off themselves, or mending their leather sandals; and not one of them ever mentioned Amaryllis, Phyllis, Galatea, or Diana."[1] And there is Cervantes' outright burlesque of pastoral motifs in the final two chapters of Part I of *Don Quixote,* in which Anselmo and Eugenio, in the manner of Montemayor's Sireno and Sylvano, take to the woods and pastoral garb and together lament the loss of their beloved Leandra. But this Leandra has been lost to them first because she has previously run off with a swaggerer and gallant who robbed and abandoned her (and no doubt worse yet) and then because she has been confined to a convent by her father. And not only have Anselmo and Eugenio resorted to these woods, but many others of her suitors have accompanied them as well, so many in fact that it seems that the place has been "converted into the Pastorall Arcadia"; here the brooks murmur "Leandra" and the woods ring with her name, not because the pathetic fallacy happens to apply but because there are simply so many suitors lolling about, many of whom have only the slightest acquaintance with Leandra.[2] The whole episode containing Eugenio's account ends, appropriately enough, not with any new understanding or mutual respect between courtly figures and country ones (howsoever new the latter might be to their country outfits) but with Don Quixote, the representative of the court, or at least of its romances, rolling in the dust with the goatherd, having previously flattened his opponent's nose with a loaf of bread.

France too has a full-scale attack, in Cervantes' manner, on previous pastoral literature's assumptions and preciosity, in Charles Sorel's *Le Berger extravagant* (1627), the merchant-turned-shepherd in question having given himself over to too much reading of earlier pastoral romances like D'Urfé's *L'Astrée*. But such criticism is largely of pastoral's artificial conventions and not of the possible ideals implied by the pastoral mode. And even this much criticism occurs only infrequently on the Continent. Much more common is an uncritical acceptance, in the manner of Sannazaro and Montemayor, of both the pastoral convention and the idealized picture of country life pastoral writing tends to portray.

The pattern we find more in English Renaissance literature, on the other hand, is one of a movement away from specific foreign pastoral sources and the general tenor of the prior pastoral tradition toward greater moralization and distrust of the life typically pictured in pastoral works.[3] We find this pattern even in as unexpected a place as Barnabe Googe's handling of material taken over from Mantuan—unexpected because Mantuan himself, of course, was no easygoing figure but rather an anti-pastoralist in his own right, strongly opposed both to pastoral love and to pastoral *otium*. Mantuan's Amyntas, whose thoroughly ill-conceived and unsuccessful love affair and then lamentable death were described in that poet's Second and Third eclogues, is at least allowed the consolation of a happier afterlife in the Elysian Fields; Googe's parallel figure is denied even that much consolation. While Dametas's fellow shepherds initially assume that their dead friend too is now in heaven or the Elysian Fields, his unhappy spirit returns in Googe's Fourth Eclogue to reveal what really happened to him: his unrestrained passion drove him to suicide, and instead of finding the release from pain and woe he expected, he has been subject to even greater suffering in Hell, where he now resides. Googe's heavy-handed moralism has thus led him to darken even what he borrowed from so redoubtable a source as Mantuan, lest anyone miss the earlier poet's overall point.[4]

There is an instance of this movement toward greater moralism also in Spenser's treatment of Calidore's stay among the shepherds in Book VI of *The Faerie Queene,* an episode which seems most directly indebted to the pastoral episode in Canto VII of Tasso's *Gerusalemme liberata*. There are many occasions in Renaissance literature in which a figure from the heroic or courtly world takes up pastoral garb either to pursue love or to recover from a love conceived elsewhere, but it is only in these two poems that the figure explaining the advantages of pastoral life has spent some of his life in the city employed as gardener to the chief of state (the caliph and prince, respectively).[5] Even if Tasso's pastoral episode is not the chief source for Calidore's whole sojourn among the shepherds, comparison with Tasso's poem is illuminating because it presents us with the difference between what begins to emerge as a characteristic Italian and a more English treatment of a stay in Arcadia.

In the Italian poem it is a female figure who, driven to desperation by her love, leaves Jerusalem and eventually comes upon a pastoral community; here she learns from an old shepherd both why the shepherds' poor estate is safe while every tower and town in the land has been destroyed and how superior life in the peaceful country is to life in the vice-ridden court. Erminia, like Sannazaro's Sincero before her, never does find total relief for her troubled soul in the Arcadian woods and eventually leaves; but the pastoral community lives on after her departure, unharmed by the outside world because of its very insignificance; and pastoral life is allowed to stand as a legitimate alternative to life in the heroic world. That part of Spenser's episode which corresponds most directly to Tasso's, the conversation between an old shepherd and a figure from the outside world on the advantages of pastoral life, is complicated several times over in the English poem.[6] For one thing, it is a knight on an assigned quest who commits himself to the shepherd life. Second, it is not simply pastoral life that attracts Calidore but also the young woman he looks at while he listens to the shepherd life being praised; it is "twixt" Meliboe's "pleasing tongue" and Pastorella's "faire hew" that Calidore loses himself and "like one halfe entraunced grew" (VI.ix.26.8–9).

Further, Spenser's Meliboe is not quite the conventional old shepherd Tasso's was. After Calidore has heard Meliboe commend the shepherd life (and has seen Pastorella), the knight expresses the wish that "the heauens so much had graced mee, / As graunt me liue in like condition" (VI.ix.28.6–7). Meliboe's response is not the gracious welcome we might expect in such a context; rather, he rebukes Calidore by informing him that it is "in vain" that men "the heauens of their fortunes fault accuse," since the heavens know what is best for each man (VI.ix.29.1–3). A man becomes fortunate or happy simply by considering himself so:

> It is the mynd, that maketh good or ill,
>   That maketh wretch or happie, rich or poore:
>   For some, that hath abundance at his will,
>   Hath not enough, but wants in greatest store;
>   And other, that hath litle, askes no more,
>   But in that litle is both rich and wise.
>   For wisedome is most riches; fooles therefore
>   They are, which fortunes doe by vowes deuize,
> Sith each vnto himselfe his life may fortunize.
>   [VI.ix.30]

Calidore's response, in turn, reveals a serious misunderstanding of what Meliboe has said. The happiness that Meliboe presently enjoys and describes depends simply upon accepting the place in life assigned by the gods and remaining content with it. It does not follow, then, that Calidore should beg leave to *change* his life and stay on awhile in Arcadia, on the grounds that "Since then in each mans self . . . / It is, to fashion his own lyfes estate" (VI.ix.31.1–2). Meliboe's happiness is part of an attitude that can be assumed anywhere, in court or the country; like Shakespeare's Corin, he does not insist that a shepherd's life is necessarily better than life at court for all men. It is the heroic figure and courtier, Calidore, who makes the more conventional assumption that Meliboe's kind of happiness can be achieved only under pastoral conditions.[7]

That Calidore and Meliboe are talking at cross purposes here does not answer the question that has long concerned critics of Spenser, that of whether Calidore is being truant in assuming a shepherd's garb. But it does mean that once again in an English work we have a figure from the heroic or courtly world entering into Arcadia while laboring under misguided assumptions about the land and type of life to be found there. In Canto x, a band of brigands attacks Meliboe's pastoral community and eventually kills all the shepherds except Pastorella and the cowardly and bungling Coridon. Spenser multiplies the meanings of his Arcadia so that it also encompasses the realm of contemplative vision in which a poet intuits directly the source of the virtue which the active figure must struggle to achieve without benefit of such clarity of vision. But Spenser also maintains a rather strict distinction between Meliboe's Arcadia, which Calidore can enter (even if under false assumptions), and Colin Clout's, which he cannot. Colin's vision of the graces disappears upon Calidore's approach, and in a book devoted to the exposition of courtesy, Colin is no more pleased to have to take up conversation with Calidore than was Contemplation to talk with the active "man of earth," Red Cross Knight, in Book I. Calidore must ultimately recognize that, for him at least, the same conditions reign in Arcadia as in the outside world. As in Sidney's *Arcadia,* no possibility of escape from the conditions and responsibilities of normal life exists for a figure who rightly belongs in the heroic or court world.

I have suggested that Spenser's treatment of Calidore's sojourn in Arcadia has a particularly English look about it. Spenser's movement away from Tasso parallels Sidney's from Sannazaro and Montemayor, and even Googe's from Mantuan. Once again an English author has stopped to think twice about the prospect of life in an idealized pastoral setting and has found it necessary to point out that man's condition must be examined with greater moral seriousness than the inherited pastoral material implies.[8] The questions that remain to be considered at greater length are why there should be so much hesitation and distrust expressed over the pastoral ideal in English literature of the Renaissance, and why primarily there rather than in the literature of other countries; that is, what was so conducive to the expression of anti-pastoral sentiment in that particular country?

THE ANTI-PASTORAL expression examined in this study represents instances of writers' personal beliefs interfering with their ability or willingness to adhere to the conventions and assumptions they associated with the given type of writing they had undertaken. In Sidney and Shakespeare, this uneasiness with the generic agreements that have to be made between author and reader before either can proceed initially took the form of objecting to pastoral's conventions merely as conventions, artificial departures from a realistic presentation of country life and country people. But in both cases this criticism quickly became much more than an argument over what constitutes realistic treatment of a given subject or how realistic such treatment must be. It became instead a statement of adherence to an ethical code that demanded holding to the active life of well doing and engagement with others in a fallen world. What is odd is that these statements should appear in pastoral writing, a mode that theoretically would seem to accommodate better, and in fact had historically favored, the opposite type of life, that of contemplative retirement. One might well argue that writers feeling as strongly as they did on this issue of the active versus the contemplative life had no business undertaking pastoral writing to begin with. But they did write pastoral and kept returning to that mode in order to reassert the same views. The result, as we have seen, is that the contemplative life took a rather bad beating at their hands. It is an attack that Milton joined when he pictured his Paradise as a particularly difficult and uncontemplative Arcadia. In all three writers we have seen little of the customary or polite way of presenting the active-contemplative debate. Arguments for the contemplative life have not received a fair hearing, and opposition to that life has taken the form of outright rejection rather than mere preference for activity over a slightly less worthy, but still respectable, alternative.

The attack on contemplation has been carried out in two different ways. One I would call the flippant (even cheap) level, in which the contemplative life is over-easily identified with the merely idle life; Sidney's Musidorus makes that rather unfair connection on Sidney's behalf as a response to Pyrocles' suspect claim to be indulging in contemplation in Arcadia. It is reflected as well in Shakespeare's having a melancholy escapist, one who wishes only to observe life and do nothing, represent the contemplative position. And Milton's version of it was to put the argument for contemplation in the mouth of a figure named Belial, whose true desire was idleness and that lasciviousness which many a Renaissance Englishman assumed would follow, as if automatically, upon idleness. Much of this kind of attack is related to those constant gibes Elizabethans were apt to hurl at monks and the monastic life, a phenomenon of some interest, since the attacks on monasticism continued so long after the dissolution of the monasteries in the 1530s and 1540s: Spenser pictured his vice of Idleness as a monk, and William Perkins equated monks with vagabonds and idle gentlemen; "abbie lubber" seems to have been a favorite Elizabethan term of abuse; and the early English Puritan John Gough revealed both his love of alliteration and his dislike of Catholic practice when he praised the anonymous *Godly Boke* he found among his father's papers for showing "the lyfe of a very Christian . . . to exceade and far passe, the counterfayte lyves of cloyning cloysterars, of mummynge monkes, fonde fryers, or of hypochrytical heremytes."[9] Such gibes are perhaps only ways of announcing that one is an ardent Protestant and a true-blue Englishman to boot and are hence not to be taken as considered or very profound criticism of the monastic life and the contemplation it was presumed to foster.

Amid such gibes, though, are more thoughtful objections to the monastic ideal, and these correspond to the more serious objections of Sidney, Shakespeare, and Milton to what they understood as pastoral assumptions. There were several doctrinal grounds on which Protestants, following Luther's example, opposed monasticism: it was, for instance, a violation of their belief in justification by faith rather than works and an affront to their sense of Christian liberty, since it required prescribed duties or works; it ran counter to their belief in the priesthood of all believers, and hence in the equality of all the elect before God, because it set one group of believers apart from and above others. But most relevant for my argument here is the kind of objection recorded by Andrew Willet, who, citing Calvin, observed that monasticism assumed too perfect a life for fallen man; Milton's version of this objection involved placing monks and friars in his Paradise of Fools for trying to vault to heaven by too sudden means.[10] The contemplative ideal, as envisioned by the Christian mystic or by a Neoplatonist, involves a separation from the affairs of this world in order to apprehend or converse with God while still on earth. And this ideal, in the view of its detractors, was both inhumane and inhuman, in that it ignored the plight of one's fellowmen and did not take into proper account the true extent and meaning of man's fallen nature; because of man's fall, direct communion with God is no longer possible for man. Insofar as pastoralism also postulates a separation from the affairs of most men, isolation in an ideal setting, and following from that, devotion to the contemplative life in an attempt to rise above man's everyday concerns, anti-pastoralism can be said to constitute another, a literary, closing of the monasteries.

For an anti-pastoralist, then, the pastoral mode or a sojourn in a pastoral setting provides an occasion for asserting one's adherence to the active life over the contemplative, the latter being seen as the ideal exercise of both the Christian mystic and the Renaissance Platonist. And as I have suggested at the end of Chapter I, in the cases of Sidney and Milton at least, it is relatively easy to establish the source for this preference. The Sidney we have seen comes to his activist stand primarily by virtue of his training in the English Humanist tradition. This was a training embodied at home in his father's service to the Elizabethan state and continued at Shrewsbury School, an institution modeled on St. Paul's and like that creation of John Colet and Erasmus having a strong dose of Cicero at the core of its curriculum; it was a training later explicitly reinforced by the friendship and guidance of the French Huguenot diplomat and statesman Hubert Languet, whose exhortations to activity I have cited in Chapter II. This tradition or training is England's equivalent to what Hans Baron, primarily, has identified for us as the "Civic Humanism" of early fifteenth-century Florence, a movement headed by figures devoted to classical scholarship and marked by a strong commitment to active engagement in the social life of the community and to political service in the Florentine Republic, after the manner of the philosopher-statesman of Republican Rome, Cicero.[11] Baron's conception of Civic Humanism has been criticized for postulating too direct a relation between immediate historical events and cultural change: he believes that a change in intellectual orientation, a general cultural phenomenon, necessarily arises from a specific and readily identifiable political crisis, in this case the threat to the Florentine Republic in 1402 from Milan's Giangaleazzo Visconti.[12] And his notion of Civic Humanism may not appear to travel very easily from a republic like that of early fifteenth-century Florence (which would have good reason to look back to the hero of Republican Rome for a model) to a monarchy like that of Tudor England, whose rulers were not particularly interested in full political participation by all citizens of the state. But we do know that several generations of English aristocrats and gentlemen, under the influence of the new schools and such figures as Erasmus, Elyot, and Ascham, were educated in the classics and particularly Cicero with the specific goal in mind of providing service to the Tudor state.[13] The mid-sixteenth-century English version of this brand of Humanism appears more closely related to religious concerns than Baron's Italian version: it is, for instance, Euarchus's and Sidney's vision of man's limitations, his fallen nature, and not simply the threat of a hostile political state (like Viscontean Milan) which accounts for the requirement that a political leader be forever active and on guard. And the links with Protestantism in Sidney's particular case are strong. The headmaster of

Shrewsbury School, Thomas Ashton, whom Sidney's parents chose as the first teacher of their young son, was a Protestant of the advanced, even Puritan, sort (it was Calvin's Catechism that Sidney purchased under Ashton's tutelage);[14] and the Huguenot Languet's goal for Sidney was that he assume a leading role in a specifically Protestant alliance of powers in Europe. But we still need something like an "English Civic Humanism" and not simply Protestantism to explain completely Sidney's activist stance. There is no reference to religious training in the description of Pyrocles' and Musidorus's education; and the amount of legitimate and meaningful human achievement (even if subject to erosion) that Sidney grants Euarchus and the princes in the *New Arcadia* particularly would seem to exclude him from the ranks of the staunch Calvinists and more adamant Protestants of his time.

Milton's anti-pastoralism and activism have their source in more exclusively religious beliefs. The major expression of his anti-pastoralism is his portrayal of a particularly difficult paradisal life, one that is decidedly uncontemplative and a closer reflection of our present existence than any previous literary portrayal of Eden. The two features that make his Paradise a more difficult place in which to live than any previous Eden, prelapsarian lovemaking and the amount of physical labor, are, I have said, mainly personal emphases that Milton brought to his material; they represent relatively original features in a narrative subject treated many times before. But these two distinctive features of his Paradise are also extensions of Protestant and, more specifically, English Puritan thought and teaching. It was the Puritans in England who were most zealous in defense of married life and in the claim that such a state was the equal of—in fact, superior to—the older and for them particularly Catholic ideal of celibacy. And the emphasis on labor in the garden can be seen as a reflection of the Calvinist or Puritan insistence upon the need for constant work and discipline in one's life in this world. Such labor is of course not to be confused with good works that might help one toward salvation; as Eve has to be reminded when she assumes that she and Adam have to earn each night's supper, efficacy or the amount of work accomplished is not the concern of such labor. The Puritan love of work might best be seen as a way of ordering one's existence, of giving man a feeling of control in a world otherwise seen as beyond human control.[15] The emphasis on work, and Milton's picture of a particularly difficult Paradise reflecting it, are thus closely connected with, even part of, the Calvinist and English Puritan perception of life as a constant struggle, a view expressed in those recurrent metaphors of life as warfare and a pilgrimage which William Haller has taught us to see as constituting the central appeal of Puritan sermons to several generations of worshipers in prerevolutionary England.[16]

But as the example of Sidney might suggest, it is difficult and, finally, artificial to separate the two influences of Protestantism and England's version of Civic Humanism in trying to account for the strength and degree of adherence to the active life in Renaissance England. Milton himself went to St. Paul's School; he was as deeply immersed in the classics as anyone in his own or the preceding generation in England; and his whole career as poet and secretary to the Council of State was a fulfillment of the Civic Humanist ideal. One conclusion that a focus on English anti-pastoralism prompts is that it is a mistake to pit Humanist and Reformation interests against one another in the English Renaissance. Opposition to Arcadian *otium* and to the contemplative life it was taken to foster and to symbolize was at once a Ciceronian commitment to active service to the state and opposition to a specifically Catholic, ascetic withdrawal from life in the everyday world; it was a statement of belief that responsible leadership could lead to the improvement of man's lot in this world, that one should therefore not turn one's back on this world, and a recognition that man's fallen nature ruled out any relaxation from the pursuit of such improvement. The image of human life as perpetual warfare was a recurrent one in Calvin's writing and in the Puritan preachers of prerevolutionary England; but it was also an informing metaphor in the works of Erasmus, one of the founding fathers of sixteenth-century English pedagogy and a frequent and strong critic of monastic asceticism, yet a figure who remained Catholic. That *Godly Boke* which the early Puritan John Gough found among his father's papers and which he translated and published without knowing its author was in fact an abridgment of Erasmus's *Enchiridion;* and that extremely popular and frequently reprinted "handbook" or "dagger" for the Christian soldier takes for its main theme, as Gough duly informs us, the reminder from the seventh chapter of the Book of Job that "the lyfe of man in this worlde is nothing but continuall battell and conflyct."[17]

Given the several and varied sources prompting adherence to the active life, it should not come as a surprise to find Shakespeare standing alongside the more obviously political and religious figures, Sidney and Milton, in explicit opposition to a life of retirement and ease. I do not mean to suggest by such a statement that Shakespeare's anti-pastoralism was determined or conditioned by his culture, that he had no choice in the matter. For there were figures, like an Andrew Marvell, who might at times resist the stream and use pastoral for their own very self-conscious purpose of examining the appeal of a life devoted to contemplation. But there does seem to have been a clear cultural bias in Renaissance England against any prospect of ease and anything that might have been thought to resemble, encourage, or endorse it. There remained sharp differences of opinion and attitude among those who shared that bias. A Sidney would continue to insist that some human achievement is possible and meaningful, even if performed against a background of human recalcitrance. And he might well be appalled at the sometimes thumping heaviness of Milton's sense of humor. Milton, for his part, while he did emphasize strongly man's free will and presented man's plight from both man's and God's point of view, would tend to agree with his fellow Puritans in discounting human achievement and giving glory to God instead. Yet all three shared a vision of man in conflict, beleaguered by forces from without and by confusion from within; and all three saw a pressing need for man to join with his fellowmen and insist on his common humanity in an attempt to fend off those forces and that confusion. And they saw this need as so pressing that they were willing, or felt themselves compelled, to put their expression of it in a type of writing which, if anything, historically tended to favor a relaxation of a sense of responsibility to one's fellowmen. Yeats's happy shepherd, opening that much later poet's work, may have been no more correct than Sidney before him in accusing the whole pastoral mode of mere antique dreaming. But in first accusing pastoral of having its major appeal there and then opposing it for that very reason, Sidney and the anti-pastoral poets after him helped to bring about the eventual withering of Arcadia's woods which Yeats in his turn celebrated. At what was perhaps the high point of its long history, the pastoral mode was being undermined from within by its own questioning, argumentative practitioners.

NOTES

CHAPTER I. PASTORAL AND ANTI-PASTORAL

1 · The disagreement is specifically with pastoral literature and its presumed attitudes; it does not arise only as a result of an author's adhering to values and ideals associated with another mode of writing, for instance, the heroic. In writing an epic, a poet does not necessarily have to state his antipathy to pastoral attitudes: if Sidney wished simply to provide examples of heroic and honorable conduct and thereby to instill in his readers the desire to be worthy, he was by no means obligated to entitle a work with this purpose "Arcadia" and to place his action in a land of that name.

2 · Thomas G. Rosenmeyer, *The Green Cabinet: Theocritus and the European Pastoral Lyric* (Berkeley, 1969), p. 281.

3 · In establishing the Renaissance "pastoral context" in the opening chapter of his study *Spenser, Marvell, and Renaissance Pastoral* (Cambridge, Mass., 1970), Patrick Cullen uses the terms "Arcadian" and "Mantuanesque" pastoral, which correspond roughly to my "pastoral" and "anti-pastoral," respectively. The Arcadian pastoral, best seen in Virgil and Sannazaro, takes as its pastoral ideal the soft life of *otium;* the Mantuanesque, like my anti-pastoral, views the Arcadian pastoral as a temptation to be avoided. Cullen's terms have the advantage of reminding us that strong opposition to pastoral *otium* was fully part of the Renaissance pastoral tradition (even if, as Cullen admits, it was a minor strand in the whole history of pastoral writing) before that sentiment's appearance in sixteenth-century England. I have, however, kept my terms "pastoral" and "anti-pastoral," because Sidney's, Shakespeare's, and Milton's objections to an Arcadian sojourn or to Arcadian idealizing owe little to Mantuan's particular type of moralism. Mantuan's strong opposition to love and his antifeminism are certainly not shared by Shakespeare and Milton; and the anti-pastoralism I deal with expresses not Mantuan's *contemptus mundi* and yearning for the "golden age" of early Christianity, but rather a very different program of actively embracing life in the world of the present.

4 · Hallett Smith, *Elizabethan Poetry: A Study in Conventions, Meaning, and Expression* (Cambridge, Mass., 1952), pp. 9–10.

5 · Francis Bacon, *The Advancement of Learning,* in *Works,* ed. James Spedding, Robert Leslie Ellis, and Douglas Denon Heath, 15 vols. (Boston, 1860–64), VI, 138; cited in Smith, *Elizabethan Poetry,* p. 3.

6 · Latin text is from Vergil, *Eclogues,* ed. Robert Coleman (Cambridge, 1977); translations, designed to be literal, are my own. Line numbers are given in parentheses in the text.

7 · Rosenmeyer, *The Green Cabinet,* pp. 51–64; Rosenmeyer might well not appreciate my imputing what he calls Theocritus's "simplicity" to Virgil's eclogue as well, since in these same pages he points out that on the whole Virgil's syntax and overall poetic structures are a good deal tighter than those of Theocritus.

8 · For much fuller and excellent discussion of the First Eclogue, one might best go to Paul Alpers, *The Singer of the Eclogues: A Study of Virgilian Pastoral* (Berkeley, 1979), pp. 65–95; and Charles Paul Segal, "*Tamen Cantabitis, Arcades:* Exile and Arcadia in *Eclogues One* and *Nine,*" *Arion,* 4 (1965), 237–66. Alpers, incidentally, views the First Eclogue as suspended between the lyric and dramatic modes (I have emphasized only its nondramatic qualities) and sees its two speakers as moving closer to one another than I do at the poem's end. He considers the poem to be concerned not so much with contrasting Tityrus's pastoral bliss with Meliboeus's woe as with comparing two experiences of unhappiness and the way that unhappiness is resolved and accepted. But Tityrus's unhappiness is well in the past and does not affect us with the same immediacy as does that of Meliboeus.

9 · Renato Poggioli, "The Oaten Flute," *Harvard Library Bulletin,* 11 (1957), 147, 148, 159; this essay is reprinted in Poggioli's *The Oaten Flute: Essays in Pastoral Poetry and the Pastoral Ideal* (Cambridge, Mass., 1975), pp. 1–41.

10 · See Walter W. Greg, *Pastoral Poetry and Pastoral Drama* (London, 1906), p. 6: "The keynote of what is most intimately associated with the name of pastoral in literature" is "the reaction against the world that is too much with us." See also Bruno Snell, *The Discovery of Mind,* trans. T. G. Rosenmeyer (1953; rpt. New York and Evanston, 1960), p. 293: "Virgil [in the *Eclogues*] . . . turns away from this harsh and evil world, he leaves it far behind, and sets out for Arcadia. . . . A nostalgic refugee from sombre realities, he places his hopes, not upon a just state, but upon an idyllic peace in which all beings will live together in friendship and fraternity." The view of pastoral as escapist literature has received new and unabashed expression in Laurence Lerner's *The Uses of Nostalgia* (London, 1972).

For criticism of this escapist view and, in the latter three cases, of Poggioli especially, see Smith, *Elizabethan Poetry,* pp. 2–12; Rosenmeyer, *The Green Cabinet,* pp. 68, 77–78, 108–9, and 65–129 passim; and Paul J. Alpers, "The Eclogue Tradition and the Nature of Pastoral," *College English,* 34 (1972), 352–71, and *The Singer of the Eclogues,* pp. 1–8 et passim.

11 · For the most thorough examination of the Neoplatonic use of pastoral,

see Richard Cody, *The Landscape of the Mind: Pastoralism and Platonic Theory in Tasso's "Aminta" and Shakespeare's Early Comedies* (Oxford, 1969).

12 · Sannazaro's *Arcadia* enjoyed an extraordinary success in the Renaissance. It went through seventy-one editions in Italy before 1600: five in the unauthorized 1502 (Venetian) edition, which ended with the Tenth Eclogue, and sixty-six in the longer (Neapolitan) edition, which added the Eleventh and Twelfth Prose and Eclogue sections and the Epilogue, "A la sampogna." It was translated into French in 1544 and into Spanish in 1547. For bibliographical information, see "Nota sul testo," in Alfredo Mauro's edition of Sannazaro's *Opere volgari* (Bari, 1961), pp. 427–28.

13 · Iacopo Sannazaro, *Opere*, ed. Enrico Carrara (Turin, 1952), pp. 50, 111: "Che certo egli è migliore il poco terreno ben coltivare, che 'l molto lasciare per mal governo miseramente imboschire"; "tra queste solitudini di Arcadia, ove . . . non che i giovani ne le nobili città nodriti, ma appena mi si lascia credere che le selvatiche bestie vi possano con diletto dimorare." My translations. Subsequent quotations and page references will be taken from this edition. Cullen (*Spenser, Marvell, and Renaissance Pastoral*, pp. 13–16) provides a more extended discussion of Sannazaro's ambivalent attitude toward Arcadia and of his failure to reconcile idealization of the pastoral stance with the desire to pass on to higher verse forms and action.

14 · Ovid, *Metamorphoses*, X, 86ff.; Sannazaro, *Opere*, pp. 51–52.

15 · The notes to Michele Scherillo's edition of the *Arcadia* (Turin, 1888) show nicely the extent of Sannazaro's debts to earlier, usually (but not always) pastoral, works.

16 · David Kalstone, *Sidney's Poetry: Contexts and Interpretations* (Cambridge, Mass., 1965), p. 13.

17 · Virgil's Tenth Eclogue deals with love as an all-absorbing passion, but as both Kalstone (*Sidney's Poetry*, p. 13) and Rosenmeyer (*The Green Cabinet*, p. 83) point out, the figure so afflicted, Gallus, is neither a shepherd nor an inhabitant of Arcadia, and Gallus himself assumes that his love would be simpler and more benign in Arcadia (lines 41–43); Gallus's suffering cannot be accepted as typical of Virgil's Arcadia, in the way that it might well be of Sannazaro's. On Theocritus's treatment of love, see Rosenmeyer, *The Green Cabinet*, p. 85: "Love, in Theocritus, is the animating force that enlivens *otium,* without however spelling the end of *otium.* If the love were successful, either spiritually or physically, it would establish itself as a higher value than *hasychia.* If it were profoundly unhappy, it would disrupt the equilibrium without which *otium* cannot flourish."

18 · See Kalstone's first chapter, "The Transformation of Arcadia" (*Sidney's Poetry,* pp. 9–39), for an extended demonstration of Sannazaro's joining of Petrarchan sentiments, motifs, and cadences with the material of classical pastoral.

19 · Erwin Panofsky, "*Et in Arcadia Ego*: Poussin and the Elegiac Tradition," in Panofsky, *Meaning in the Visual Arts* (Garden City, N.Y., 1955), p. 301.

20 · It is not unusual to see modern critical comments referring to the Golden

Age as "the most important of all pastoral myths" (Poggioli, "The Oaten Flute," p. 163) or to Arcadia as "the literary expression of the Golden Age" (Edward William Tayler, *Nature and Art in Renaissance Literature* [New York, 1964], p. 89). See also the opening sentence of J. E. Congleton's entry "Pastoral" in *Encyclopedia of Poetry and Poetics,* ed. Alex Preminger, Frank J. Warnke, and O. B. Hardison, Jr. (Princeton, 1965), p. 603: "The pastoral imitates rural life, usually the life of an imaginary Golden Age, in which the loves of shepherds and shepherdesses play a prominent part."

21 · Arthur O. Lovejoy and George Boas, *Primitivism and Related Ideas in Antiquity: A Documentary History of Primitivism and Related Ideas* (Baltimore, 1935), pp. 9–11. "Hard primitivism," which insists upon the harsh conditions of life in the state of nature and views such conditions as conducive to the development of moral virtue and self-discipline, has relatively little to do with the pastoral tradition as I understand it, at least until the time when poets themselves begin to protest that pastoral writing has not portrayed life in the country in a realistic manner.

22 · See Rosenmeyer, *The Green Cabinet,* p. 221.

23 · On the widespread Renaissance reference to the Golden Age in complimentary pastoral, see W. Leonard Grant, *Neo-Latin Literature and the Pastoral* (Chapel Hill, N.C., 1965), pp. 291–305, 330–50; Elizabeth Armstrong, *Ronsard and the Age of Gold* (Cambridge, 1968); and Patrick Cullen, "Imitation and Metamorphosis: The Golden-Age Eclogue in Spenser, Milton, and Marvell," *PMLA,* 84 (1969), 1559–70.

24 · This is Harry Levin's reminder in *The Myth of the Golden Age in the Renaissance* (Bloomington, Ind., 1969), p. 43.

25 · Virgil, *The Whole XII Bookes of the Aeneidos,* trans. Thomas Phaer and Thomas Twyne (London, 1573), sig. ⏼; I have emended the text's plainly incorrect last word, "wordle," to "worlde." The translation of Donatus's life of Virgil appears as the Preface or Introduction to the volume. The 1573 edition of Phaer's translation was the first to include the life by Donatus (presumably translated by Twyne, since this edition was also the first to include Twyne's Bks. X–XII, left undone by Phaer at his death in 1560). The full, joint translation, with the prefatory life and Twyne's subsequently added translation of Mapheus Vegius's "Thirteenth Book," was reprinted in 1584, 1596, 1600, 1607, and 1620; in this form alone Donatus's views can be said to have had fairly widespread exposure in the Elizabethan period. In addition, Latin versions of the life could be found in any number of well-annotated Renaissance editions of Virgil's works, for instance, those of Lyon, 1499, or Venice, 1555.

26 · Julius Caesar Scaliger, *Poetices,* I, iii–iv, in *Select Translations from Scaliger's Poetics,* trans. Frederick Morgan Padelford (New York, 1905), pp. 20–23.

27 · George Puttenham, *The Arte of English Poesie,* ed. Gladys Doidge Willcock and Alice Walker (Cambridge, 1936), pp. 37–39.

28 · For surveys of the merging of the two myths in the medieval and Renais-

sance periods, see Tayler, *Nature and Art*, pp. 72–101; A. Bartlett Giamatti, *The Earthly Paradise and the Renaissance Epic* (Princeton, 1966), pp. 48–86; and Levin, *The Myth of the Golden Age*, pp. 32–57. In reading the various texts presented in George Boas's *Essays on Primitivism and Related Ideas in the Middle Ages* (Baltimore, 1948), one can see the two myths impinging upon one another, although syncretism is not the main focus of Boas's book. Of these works, Giamatti's is the most thorough in tracing the process of syncretism, and Tayler's the most relevant to my purpose here, since he deals extensively with the merging of the Golden Age and Eden myths in specifically pastoral works. While Tayler rather too easily assumes that Arcadia from antiquity on was an unattainable ideal, he shows nicely how an idealized pastoral landscape could become a "trope" or "metaphor" for Paradise, a way of talking about and referring to prelapsarian Eden (*Nature and Art*, pp. 98–101).

29 · *Natalis Comitis Mythologiae Sive, Explicationis Fabularum . . . Accessit . . . Anonymi Observationum in totam de Diis Gentium narrationem Libellus* (Geneva, 1596), sig. Xxx.i; my translation. The anonymous author's observations were reprinted in many but not all subsequent editions of the *Mythologiae*. For Douglas Bush's comment, see his *Mythology and the Renaissance Tradition in English Poetry*, rev. ed. (New York, 1963), p. 29.

30 · Henry Reynolds, *Mythomystes* [1632], in *Critical Essays of the Seventeenth Century*, ed. J. E. Spingarn (Bloomington, Ind., 1957), I, 175–76. The Latin quotation is from *The Georgics*, Bk. I, lines 125ff.: "No tillers subdued the land . . . and Earth yielded all, of herself more freely, when none begged for her gifts."

31 · *Shakespeare's Ovid, Being Arthur Golding's Translation of the Metamorphoses*, ed. W. H. D. Rouse (Carbondale, Ill., 1961), "The Epistle," line 334. Line numbers are given in parentheses in the text.

32 · I refer here of course to Milton's ill-tempered attack in the *Eikonoklastes* on the *Arcadia* as "no serious book, but [a] vain amatorious poem . . . a book in that kind full of worth and wit, but among religious thoughts and duties not worthy to be named, nor to be read at any time without good caution, much less in time of trouble and affliction to be a Christian's prayer-book." The source of Milton's anger was his discovery upon reading the *Eikon Basilike* that one of the prayers Charles I was purported to have uttered the night before his execution was one "stolen" (Milton's word) from the mouth of Pamela in Bk. III of the *New Arcadia* ("a heathen fiction praying to a heathen God"); see John Milton, *Complete Poems and Major Prose*, ed. Merritt Y. Hughes (New York, 1957), p. 793. But two entries in Milton's Commonplace Book reveal that when not engaged in public debate, Milton like many of his contemporaries viewed Sidney's *Arcadia* as a sourcebook for ethical and political observations; see *The Works of John Milton*, ed. Frank Allen Patterson et al., XVIII (New York, 1938), 133, 189.

33 · See Harold E. Toliver, *Marvell's Ironic Vision* (New Haven, 1965), pp. 88–90 and the whole chapter "Pastoral and Reconciliation with History," pp. 88–151,

which builds upon those introductory definitions. See too the examination of the tension between "Arcadian" and "Christian" pastoral perspectives in both Spenser and Marvell, in Cullen's *Spenser, Marvell, and Renaissance Pastoral.* Both Spenser's and Marvell's explorations of the pastoral mode have received their fair share of critical attention; in addition to the works of Toliver, Cullen, and Tayler already cited, see Donald Cheney, *Spenser's Image of Nature: Wild Man and Shepherd in "The Faerie Queene"* (New Haven, 1966); Humphrey Tonkin, *Spenser's Courteous Pastoral: Book Six of the "Faerie Queene"* (Oxford, 1972); and Donald M. Friedman, *Marvell's Pastoral Vision* (Berkeley, 1970).

CHAPTER II. SIDNEY'S *Old Arcadia*

1 · R. W. Zandvoort, *Sidney's Arcadia: A Comparison between the Two Versions* (Amsterdam, 1929), p. 197.

2 · For a similar view see Richard Helgerson (*The Elizabethan Prodigals* [Berkeley, 1976], pp. 150–51), who considers the structure of the *Old Arcadia* to be that of a Prodigal Son story: "As inevitable as sin or death, the pattern of the Old *Arcadia,* which is also the pattern of education drama and of Euphuistic fiction, is built into the New. The scene of admonition is dislocated, fragmented, and dispersed, but it is there and it sets up an expectation of eventual judgment."

It should be noted as well that the *Old Arcadia* gives us the only version of the Eclogues fully authorized by Sidney himself. The text of the *New Arcadia* makes clear that Sidney envisioned eclogue sections for that version, but, a prefatory note by the 1590 editors tells us, he did not get around to reshaping those sections before leaving off work on the revision. If we are to consider the poetry of these sections at all, we ought rightly to discuss them in the context of the *Old Arcadia*.

3 · *The Poems of Sir Philip Sidney,* ed. William A. Ringler, Jr., (Oxford, 1962), pp. 375–79; hereafter cited as Ringler.

4 · That evidence must of course be used with a great deal of care. Although it appears that at the time he revised the passages in question Sidney *intended* them for his completed *New Arcadia,* we cannot assume that they would necessarily have been inserted later in the *New Arcadia* narrative. Bk. III of the *New Arcadia* not only makes the last three books of the *Old Arcadia* an incongruous continuation but would also necessitate yet more alteration in the revised version of the scene in Philoclea's bedchamber; see below, Chap. III, n. 8.

5 · See, for instance, the recent studies of Sidney by A. C. Hamilton (*Sir Philip Sidney: A Study of His Life and Works* [Cambridge, 1977], especially pp. 1–16 and 27–35) and Helgerson (*The Elizabethan Prodigals,* pp. 124–55) and the earlier brief study by F. J. Levy, "Philip Sidney Reconsidered," *ELR,* 2 (1972), 5–18, all of which are helpful in suggesting the expectations that Sidney's Christian Humanist training were likely to have aroused within Sidney himself.

6 · See Ringler, pp. 366–70; and Sir Philip Sidney, *The Countess of Pembroke's Arcadia (The Old Arcadia),* ed. Jean Robertson (Oxford, 1973), pp. lii–lvii. Quotations from the *Old Arcadia* will be from Robertson's edition and cited as *OA* in

my text; when the citation is to poetry, page and line number of the page will be given.

The reference to "a trifle, and that triflingly handled" is in Sidney's Dedicatory Letter to his sister, prefacing the 1590 edition of the *Arcadia*. Although this letter appears in none of the extant manuscripts of the *Old Arcadia,* it was evidently designed for that version (it refers to a completed work) and probably given to the editors of the 1590 edition by the Countess of Pembroke; see Ringler, pp. 382–83, and *OA,* 418.

7 · Polybius, *The Histories,* trans. W. R. Paton, 6 vols. (Cambridge, Mass., 1922), II, 349–53, Bk. IV, secs. 20–21. Elizabeth Dipple tends to overstress the relation between Sidney's opening description of Arcadia and Polybius's account, first claiming that Sidney's description was taken "almost verbatim" from Polybius ("The 'Fore Conceit' of Sidney's Eclogues," in *Literary Monographs, I,* ed. Eric Rothstein and Thomas K. Dunseath [Madison, Wis., 1967], n. 27) and then, in a subsequent article, referring somewhat more accurately to Sidney's account as an "eclectic, ironic copying of Polybius" ("Harmony and Pastoral in the *Old Arcadia,*" *ELH,* 35 [1968], 311). She does note Sidney's more substantial debt (for ironic effect) to the literary pastoral tradition in his initial description of Arcadia, observing that "we can very early clear the *Old Arcadia* of any imputation that it is generically in the mainstream of pastoral" ("Harmony and Pastoral," p. 313).

8 · Sannazaro, *Opere,* p. 50: "le rozze Ecloghe da naturale vena uscite; così di ornamento ignude esprimendole, come . . . da' pastori d'Arcadia le udii cantare."

9 · For a helpful survey of the ways in which medieval and Renaissance pastoral poets sought to reconcile their efforts to write in a highly artistic (Virgilian) poetic tradition with a theory of decorum that demanded that the shepherd of literature should mirror the shepherd of real life, see Helen Cooper, *Pastoral: Mediaeval into Renaissance* (Ipswich, England, 1977), pp. 127–43.

10 · William Empson, *Some Versions of Pastoral* (1935; rpt. New York, 1960), pp. 11–12; Empson places this breakdown in English pastoral literature (and the society behind it) some time after the Restoration. That Sidney was of course ultimately interested in keeping the Elizabethan social order as it was we know from other passages in his work as well, most notably perhaps from his particularly harsh, even savage, treatment of the clownish rebels at the end of Bk. II of the *New Arcadia* (Chap. 25); on this passage, see the stimulating article of Stephen Greenblatt, "Murdering Peasants: Status, Genre, and the Representation of Rebellion," *Representations,* 1, no. 1 (February 1983), especially pp. 14–19.

11 · Ringler, pp. 385–86. Neil L. Rudenstine (*Sidney's Poetic Development* [Cambridge, Mass., 1967], pp. 82–85) offers some adjustments to Ringler's reading but does not, I think, alter the basic conception of the poem as a victory for Dorus. Cf. also Kalstone's discussion of the poem in *Sidney's Poetry,* pp. 65–68; Kalstone views Lalus as intended by Sidney primarily as a figure of fun. Rudenstine tends to grant the Arcadian shepherd a good deal more and would have his lines (particularly lines 123–30 in Ringler's edition; p. 62, lines 4–11, in *OA*) articulate "beautifully the rhythms of freedom and control underlying Arcadia's

life of pastoral love and pastime" (*Sidney's Poetic Development,* p. 84); such wording makes Sidney grant more credence than I think is warranted to the possibility of an achieved pastoral ideal.

12 · See Rudenstine, *Sidney's Poetic Development,* pp. 84–85; and Kalstone, *Sidney's Poetry,* pp. 67–68.

13 · Sidney appears, in fact, to have been willing to grant his native Arcadians less emotional range and poetic sophistication the longer he stayed with them and the *Old Arcadia.* In the earliest *Old Arcadia* manuscripts (what Ringler and Robertson call the Group I manuscripts), the First Eclogue section concluded with two of those Arcadians, Dicus and Lalus, conversing on the relative merits of quantitative and rhymed verse; this rather learned debate was canceled in subsequent manuscripts and its substance dealt with instead in the *Defence of Poetry.* And in the Fourth Eclogue section, consisting of stately poems lamenting the loss of the apparently dead Basilius, the "very born Arcadians" were in early manuscripts given opportunity to express their grief in verse alongside some distinguished visiting poets (for instance, Strephon and Klaius). By the time of the final (Group IV) manuscripts, Dicus's poem has been transferred to Agelastus and Agelastus himself transformed from a mere shepherd to a former Athenian senator now become an Arcadian shepherd. In the final manuscripts, then, only foreign-born shepherds are given leave to express themselves in verse in what is plainly intended to be a moving and dignified series of poems, and Sidney by his changes reveals himself not quite able to overlook the gap separating the upper courtly class from more humble sorts.

14 · See Katherine Duncan-Jones, "Sidney in Samothea: A Forgotten National Myth," *RES,* ns 25 (1974), 174–77.

15 · Like a number of critics before me (for instance, Zandvoort [*Sidney's Arcadia,* p. 193] and Robertson [*OA,* xx], I envision Sidney rereading the *Diana,* or at least consulting it anew, in the process of composing the *New Arcadia;* that is, he was already familiar with the Spanish work at an earlier stage in his life, and its opening provided the germ that was to grow into the Strephon and Klaius of the *Old Arcadia* as well as the opening chapter of the *New Arcadia,* which, with its poignant remembrance of a past time when the speakers last looked upon their beloved, is plainly taken over from Montemayor's opening scene.

16 · See Kalstone, *Sidney's Poetry,* pp. 13–39, 71–83.

17 · Walter R. Davis's first chapter of *A Map of Arcadia: Sidney's Romance in Its Tradition,* in Davis and Richard A. Lanham, *Sidney's Arcadia* (New Haven, 1965), outlines the psychological development that corresponds to these changes in setting; the "standard" pastoral romance action subjects its main character to a movement from disintegration in a turbulent outer circle, through education in the pastoral circle (by means of observing other figures with similar afflictions), to reintegration or rebirth at the sacred center (see pp. 38–39). In that chapter Davis also shows nicely, by focusing upon the function and implications of the pastoral setting and its appeal, how the pastoral romance form evolved out of the earlier collections of only slightly connected lyric poems.

18 · For the text of Sidney's letter, a fine expression of the spirit of English Humanism handed down to Sidney by his elders, see Albert Feuillerat's edition of Sidney's *Prose Works* (1912–26; rpt. Cambridge, 1962), III, 124–27. Robert Sidney is urged to "furnish yourself with the knowledge of such things as may be serviceable to your country and fit for your calling, which certainly stands not in the change of air, . . . no more in learning languages, although they be of good serviceable use, . . . but in the right informing your mind with those things which are most notable in those places you come to" (p. 125). Among those latter things are the knowledge of all alliances between prince and prince, the topographical features of each country visited, and the *mores* of each nation, by which Sidney means not merely behavior ("although truly behaviour is not to be despised") but "their religions, policies, laws, bringing up of their children, discipline both for war and peace, and such like" (p. 126). I have modernized spelling and punctuation.

19 · Pyrocles' bow metaphor here is borrowed from Sidney's own letter of February 11, 1574, to Hubert Languet: "For in your letters I fancy I see a picture of the age in which we live: an age that resembles a bow too long bent, it must be unstrung or it will break" (*The Correspondence of Sir Philip Sidney and Hubert Languet,* trans. Steuart A. Pears [London, 1845], p. 36). In a fine discussion Rudenstine (*Sidney's Poetic Development,* pp. 3–45) shows how much of Pyrocles' argument in favor of pursuits other than the active life—be those pursuits the necessary health-reviving relaxation suggested here, or dedication to the contemplative life (to be brought up by Pyrocles next), or what Rudenstine calls the "poetic" apprehension of experience—reflects sentiments Sidney himself voiced in his correspondence with his Christian Humanist friend and mentor, in whose creed there was no time for retirement and idleness. Rudenstine is certainly right in suggesting that the correspondence reveals an impulse in Sidney in the direction of relaxation of tensions and withdrawal from action and that there is more than a little of Sidney's own self in Pyrocles. But the correspondence with Languet still lies outside the structure of the *Old Arcadia,* and there remains some danger in relying overmuch on the correspondence as a gloss upon Sidney's pastoral work. Coming to the *Old Arcadia* from the correspondence, Rudenstine sees the debate between Pyrocles and Musidorus as expressing a conflict within Sidney that is never fully resolved, and he finds a "quality of irresolution" in the letters to Languet and in the *Old Arcadia,* which sets both off from the "more assertive" revised *Arcadia* (p. 25). If anything, I find that it is the *Old Arcadia* which can be faulted for being too assertive.

My differences from Rudenstine may well be determined by our different points of entry into the *Old Arcadia*. If one starts from the Sidney-Languet correspondence, the Sidney perceived behind the *Old Arcadia* looks much like Pyrocles in the early debate, certainly lighter of touch and possessing more wit than the sturdy and sober Huguenot statesman, thirty-six years Sidney's elder. If, on the other hand, one approaches the *Old Arcadia* by way of Sidney's most immediate pastoral sources, the works of Sannazaro and Montemayor, the Sidney behind the

Old Arcadia looks much like Musidorus in the early debate or like Languet, figures a good deal more morally serious and openly committed to responsible action in the public sphere than one is accustomed to finding in pastoral literature.

20 · Ernst Robert Curtius, in *European Literature and the Latin Middle Ages,* trans. Willard R. Trask (1953; rpt. New York and Evanston, 1963), was the first to argue that the *locus amoenus,* or pleasance, deserves to be considered an independent *topos* of landscape description (parallel to, for instance, the standardized catalogue of trees); he observes that the pleasance is invariably "a beautiful, shaded natural site. Its minimum ingredients comprise a tree (or several trees), a meadow, and a spring or brook. Birdsong and flowers may be added. The most elaborate examples also add a breeze" (p. 195). If we can consider Arcadia's "air" that "breathe[s] health" as equivalent to a breeze, Sidney's description qualifies as one of those most elaborate examples.

21 · Walter R. Davis's Neoplatonic reading of the 1593 *Arcadia* is founded upon the assumption that the final justification for staying in Arcadia, for the resemblance it bears to a paradisal setting, follows directly and logically upon the preceding defense of Arcadia as a place conducive to the practice of contemplation. It was in the Terrestrial Paradise that Dante-the-pilgrim in the *Divine Comedy* was led by Matelda (who corresponds to Leah and the active life) to Beatrice, who was to be his guide to contemplative vision; Davis claims that, like Dante's Terrestrial Paradise, this Arcadian image of Eden draws the mind to contemplation of the Celestial Paradise, and thus the structure of the 1593 *Arcadia* as a whole is designed to exalt the contemplative over the active life (see Davis, *A Map of Arcadia,* pp. 59–69 et passim).

But Davis fails to note Pyrocles' sudden stop ("like a man unsatisfied in himself") between the arguments for contemplation and for Arcadia's paradisal qualities, which stop suggests a logical break rather than any continuity between the two defenses; and he fails to take into account that Pyrocles' arguments in any case are being used (for humorous effect by Sidney) to hide his true motive for wishing to remain in Arcadia. This distance from the immediate context makes Davis's reading of this particular debate—and his interpretation of the whole 1593 *Arcadia* arising from that reading—extremely doubtful. And then there is the difficulty in his use of the 1593 text to talk about Sidney's beliefs. For a convincing, full-scale refutation of Davis's view of Sidney as a Neoplatonist, see Nancy R. Lindheim, "Vision, Revision, and the 1593 Text of the *Arcadia,*" *ELR,* 2 (1972), 136–47, an article which is included in altered form in her *The Structures of Sidney's "Arcadia"* (Toronto, 1982), pp. 133–39.

22 · Curtius, *European Literature,* p. 199.

23 · Pears, *Correspondence of Sidney and Languet,* p. 185 [letter of September 24, 1580]; cited in Rudenstine, *Sidney's Poetic Development,* p. 19.

24 · See Richard A. Lanham, *The Old "Arcadia,"* in Davis and Lanham, *Sidney's Arcadia,* p. 254 and his analysis of this whole debate (pp. 244–56), emphasizing particularly its humor and its rhetorical posing.

25 · Ringler, p. 404.

26 · A number of critics have found fault with Euarchus's judgment, prompted I think by attitudes toward justice that are their own rather than any view suggested by Sidney within the work. Kenneth Orne Myrick (*Sir Philip Sidney as a Literary Craftsman* [Cambridge, Mass., 1935], p. 247), for instance, has objected that the laws of Arcadia are too harsh, and hence Euarchus in applying them relies on a limited and defective kind of justice; and Jon S. Lawry (*Sidney's Two "Arcadias": Pattern and Proceeding* [Ithaca, N.Y., 1972], p. 149) claims that "more than a suspicion of over-righteousness" invades even the careful judgment of Euarchus. Rudenstine sees the supposed murder of Basilius as placing the princes' rather minor faults in a serious perspective and thus making the "strictest possible conduct of justice seem necessary" (*Sidney's Poetic Development*, p. 42); but he views Euarchus's continued insistence upon justice after he learns of the princes' true identity as verging on a "ridiculous adherence to law for the sake of law" (p. 44). See also Elizabeth Dipple, "'Unjust Justice' in the *Old Arcadia*," *SEL*, 10 (1970), 83–101; she claims that the trial shows that "there is no viable method of exercising justice purely" and that the main "theme" of the trial scene is "the imperfection of justice" (pp. 101, 85). I think it is a mistake to place Sidney's prime emphasis there; what Dipple focuses upon is one of the observations we might well come to in witnessing the trial, but Sidney's main emphasis lies in the direction of exhorting us to act as Euarchus does, whether or not the justice he seeks to administer is attainable in this world.

27 · That Euarchus's pursuit of justice, in the case of Gynecia particularly, is too absolute in its denial of equity is the objection raised by Lindheim, *The Structures of Sidney's "Arcadia*,*"* pp. 157–61, and by Hamilton, *Sir Philip Sidney*, pp. 55–56. Philanax does describe Euarchus as "one that hath always had his determinations bounded with equity" (*OA*, 361); but he (and Sidney) here and throughout the *Old Arcadia* would appear to have in mind the general meaning of equity as "fairness or even-handedness," rather than the technical and judicial (Aristotelian) meaning, which allows a judge to correct the law when it fails, because of its universality, to take into account the particular circumstances of the acts judged or the past history of the accused.

28 · This is the justification for the ending offered by Lanham, *The Old "Arcadia*,*"* pp. 316–17, 375, and by Dipple, "The 'Fore Conceit' of Sidney's Eclogues," p. 43.

29 · Ringler's objection, p. 379.

30 · It is Sidney's often ironic but generally understanding and sympathetic narrative voice which, more than anything else, finally renders Franco Marenco's reading of the *Old Arcadia* untenable because so overstated. In "Double Plot in Sidney's Old 'Arcadia,'" *MLR*, 64 (1969), Marenco calls the work a "gloomy, almost desperate book, mocking and not glorifying the worldly hero" (p. 250). And in *Arcadia puritana* (Bari, 1968), he argues that the *Old Arcadia* is an "anti-conventional" work, written specifically to undermine both heroic and pastoral ideals as handed down by the Humanistic literature of the Renaissance (pp. 10–11). In the place of those ideals, Marenco would have Sidney emphasizing a Cal-

vinist view of man as totally depraved. As the overall argument of my study no doubt makes clear, I am drawn to Marenco's discussion of the *Old Arcadia* as antipastoral in its ideals (see his pp. 200–208); but his insistence upon an adamantly Calvinist Sidney who wishes his characters and his readers simply to know "their degradation, their folly and the misery of their flesh" (p. 220) is untrue to the tone of the whole work. With his focus so firmly fixed on Calvin's thought (as mediated particularly through DuPlessis Mornay), Marenco would have Sidney's characters and readers simply recognize the extent of their fallen nature and their own worthlessness and then place all faith in God for any earthly accomplishment whatsoever. Marenco does not have Sidney suggesting any other course of action—for instance, adhering to Euarchus's active stance in order to stave off further manifestations of man's fall from grace. If Sidney were as firm and inflexible in his Calvinistic insistence upon the worthlessness of human achievement as Marenco would have him be in writing the *Old Arcadia,* we cannot even begin to explain what prompted Sidney to undertake his revision, a revision that among other things moves toward eliminating some of the princes' more serious faults and gives them more legitimately heroic action to perform. Marenco is left merely insisting that the *Old Arcadia* is Sidney's most important work (p. 10). Calvinism, or at least Protestantism, is indeed one of the intellectual influences on the *Old Arcadia,* but not in the inflexible and limiting form Marenco suggests. Much the same objection has, I think, to be lodged against Andrew Weiner's more recent study of the *Old Arcadia* as an expression of Sidney's presumed Calvinism in *Sir Philip Sidney and the Poetics of Protestantism* (Minneapolis, 1978).

Among recent critical views of Sidney, the gentlest and hence the one most opposed to Marenco's is that of Dorothy Connell, who sees the key element in Sidney's thought throughout his career as his ability to encompass and balance contradictions: "Sidney is clear about the limitations of fallen mankind, yet faith and a genial humor combine to make his vision of the world a positive one" (*Sir Philip Sidney: The Maker's Mind* [Oxford, 1977], p. 5). The true Sidney resides between Connell's benign, optimistic figure and Marenco's gloomy, totally pessimistic one.

CHAPTER III. SIDNEY'S *New Arcadia*

1 · Myrick, *Sidney as a Literary Craftsman,* especially Chaps. 4 and 5, pp. 110–93. The importance and influence of Myrick's study are reflected in the fact that it is one of the few critical books on Sidney to appear in a second edition—and a paperback at that (Lincoln, Nebr., 1965). Attributes of the *New Arcadia* that made it a heroic poem in Myrick's eyes were its equivalent to a classical epic's invocation (in Strephon's and Klaius's opening praise of Urania), its beginning *in mediis rebus* rather than *ab ovo* (as did the *Old Arcadia*), its presentation of past events by *dramatis personae* rather than by the poet in his own voice, its concern with warfare and great events (subjects which add dignity to the story), and its use of episodes

to present action outside the main fable (a practice adding epic magnificence and ornamentation).

2 · There have been a number of studies suggesting that the *Old Arcadia* too has cause to be considered a heroic poem; see, for instance, Alan D. Isler, "Heroic Poetry and Sidney's Two *Arcadias*," *PMLA*, 83 (1968), 368–79; Robert W. Parker, "Terentian Structure and Sidney's Original *Arcadia*," *ELR*, 2 (1972), 61–78; Lawry, *Sidney's Two "Arcadias,"* pp. 1–153; and P. Jeffrey Ford, "Philosophy, History, and Sidney's *Old Arcadia*," *Comparative Literature*, 26 (1974), 32–50. But the view that the final disposition of the princes is quite divergent in the two versions continues to be argued: Helgerson and Hamilton, in studies that appeared in 1976 and 1977, respectively, both envision the reader moving from "a divided response" toward the princes at the end of the *Old Arcadia* (Hamilton, *Sir Philip Sidney*, p. 56; Helgerson, *The Elizabethan Prodigals*, p. 138) to total admiration of the "unambiguously praiseworthy" princes at the point the *New Arcadia* breaks off (Helgerson, p. 149; Hamilton, p. 156).

3 · The critic who carries this line of reasoning on Sidney's Arcadian landscape to its fullest extent is perhaps Elizabeth Dipple, who, in arguing that "one of our primary realizations about the two *Arcadia*'s ought to be that they are different works with different directions and ideological bents," suggests that the shepherds of the eclogue sections of the *Old Arcadia* "present a view of Arcadia and pastoral possibilities which Sidney, when he rethinks his romance in order to make a new version, will adopt as central. Through their existence and world they teach a Neo-Platonic idea that will supplant that basic indictment which is the moral end of the *Old Arcadia*" ("The 'Fore Conceit' of Sidney's Eclogues," pp. 34, 14).

4 · The 1593 version of this scene is to be found on pp. 52–61 of Vol. II of Feuillerat's edition of Sidney's *Prose Works;* it replaces pp. 215–27 of that edition's Vol. IV (*The Old Arcadia*). The changes in the bedchamber scene itself begin on line 6 of p. 52 of Vol. II (and the calculation of lines in my discussion uses Feuillerat's edition). In Robertson's edition of the *Old Arcadia*, the replaced bedchamber passage occupies pp. 228–43, the changes beginning at line 9 of p. 228, and the 1593 variants are printed at the foot of the page in the Textual Apparatus. In citing 1593 passages attributable to Sidney, I shall provide references in my text both to Robertson's Textual Apparatus (for instance, *OA*, 228, Textual Apparatus) and to Feuillerat's edition (providing volume and page number; for instance, II.52). Because Feuillerat's text is not modernized, direct quotation of such passages will be from Robertson's Textual Apparatus.

5 · Ringler, pp. 375–78. For the text of Greville's letter to Sir Francis Walsingham containing Greville's reference to a "direction," see Ringler, p. 530.

6 · The excisions are from pp. 201–2 and 306 of *OA;* in Feuillerat's edition, they occur on pp. 190 and 286 of Vol. IV (*The Old Arcadia*), and the emended passages of the 1593 *Arcadia* appear on pp. 27 and 118 of Vol. II.

7 · See Robertson's Introduction, *OA*, lx–lxi; and my "Sidney's *Arcadia:* The

Endings of the Three Versions," *HLQ,* 34 (1971), 205–18. As I have already suggested, the changes involving Pyrocles and those treating Musidorus are closely related and can be presumed to have been conceived at the same time. The revision of the bedchamber scene and the account of Euarchus's journey to Arcadia are in turn closely related in that both refer to a second uprising of the Helots against the king and nobility of Laconia (their first revolt having taken place in Bk. I of the *New Arcadia* and having been settled to the Helots' satisfaction through the heroic efforts of Pyrocles). Reference to the Helots' second uprising, I should note, occurs not directly within the revised bedchamber scene but in a closely related passage some ten pages earlier (*OA,* 217, Textual Apparatus; II.41). In that passage we are told of Pyrocles' plan, once he convinces Philoclea to elope with him, to travel at least as far as what he could assume would be a friendly stronghold of the Helots, should he prove unable to meet up with the fleeing Musidorus (or succeed in getting all the way to his intended Macedonia). The details of his plan outlined in this passage are in full accord with his intentions as they are described in the revised bedchamber scene, and we are, I believe, fully warranted in considering it as written at the same time as, and in effect as an integral part of, the revised bedchamber scene itself.

8 · The *New Arcadia* would in fact appear to have been taking full shape in Sidney's mind only as he proceeded. Bk. III of the revision eventually takes the narrative off into territory unfamiliar to him, so unfamiliar that the new material there would, among other things, force him to make further changes yet in the scene in Philoclea's bedchamber which he had already revised. It is unlikely, for instance, that Philoclea would have to doubt that Pyrocles still cares for her, as she does in the 1593 bedchamber scene, after she has seen him earlier in Bk. III of the *New Arcadia* attempt suicide in despair arising from the belief that she herself has been killed.

9 · Quotations from the *New Arcadia* are based on Feuillerat's edition of Sidney's *Prose Works,* Vol. I, and citations in my text are to volume and page number of that edition. However, in the interest of consistency and in an effort to provide a more readable text, I have modernized and normalized the spelling and punctuation of Feuillerat's text, attempting as far as possible to follow the practice and model of Robertson in *OA.* As Robertson has done, I have tended to retain parentheses when they appear in the text, and I have retained intentionally archaic forms (e.g., *strake* instead of the modern *struck*); when there is disagreement in the various manuscripts and printed editions of the different versions of the *Arcadia,* I have adopted Robertson's spelling of characters' names (e.g., Klaius, Otanes, Euarchus).

10 · Except in the present instance, I use the term "episode" to refer to an interpolation which does not appreciably carry forward the main plot (taking place in the present). An episode thus provides material that could be moved or removed and not alter the progress of the main action, although such a change would affect our understanding of that action, since the interpolated accounts usually provide thematic amplification of material in the main plot; see Lindheim,

"Vision, Revision, and the 1593 Text of the *Arcadia*," pp. 136–38 (or her *The Structures of Sidney's "Arcadia,"* pp. 133–35), and her use of Gerald F. Else's *Aristotle's Poetics: The Argument* (Cambridge, Mass., 1957), pp. 325–26nn and 505n. According to this conception, the episodes of Bk. I are (1) the story, in Chaps. 5–7 (pp. 31–51), of the love of Argalus and Parthenia (excluding the account of Pyrocles' and Musidorus's heroism in the Helot War in the midst of that tale); (2) the story of Helen and Amphialus (Chap. 11, pp. 66–74); and (3) Phalantus's tournament (Chaps. 15–17, pp. 96–112). In Bk. II, the episodes include the account of the past adventures in Asia Minor of Pyrocles and Musidorus and of Plangus and Erona. What is commonly called "the Captivity Episode" of Bk. III (in which Pamela, Philoclea, and Pyrocles are imprisoned by Amphialus and Cecropia) is by this definition not a detachable episode at all, but part of the main plot; Bk. III does, however, contain material that I would term "episodic": a series of five individual jousts taking place during pauses in the main fighting (see below, n. 13).

11 · Even the heroic acts carried over from the *Old Arcadia* are made to conform to this pattern. At the end of Bk. II, Pyrocles, dressed as an Amazon, confronts and calms a mob of rebellious peasants, just as he did in the *Old Arcadia*. But whereas Pyrocles' valor there eliminated the threat to the state from the rebels, in the *New Arcadia* rebellion breaks out again in more serious and dangerous form immediately afterward. The account given by the *Old Arcadia*'s narrator of the origin of the rebellion—the duke's birthday celebration turned into a mutiny by the effects of wine—is in the *New Arcadia* put in the mouth of Cecropia's retainer, Clinias. And Clinias uses the account to conceal his own role in inciting the mob. Immediately after giving his false account, Clinias returns to Cecropia to stir up further trouble, and Pyrocles' heroic action in this incident, like his action on behalf of the Helots in Laconia, has no lasting effect.

12 · "As armies grew in size with the domination of the field by the infantry pikeman and as the technical services like pioneers and ordnance increased in importance, war ceased to be an exciting *chevauchée* led by high-spirited young men out for a lark. Now that small-arms had been invented, strength, courage, and skill on horseback were no longer any protection against sudden and ignominious death. War was no fun any more, and the tiltyard at Westminster Palace had to serve as a substitute for the fields of Crécy and Agincourt" (Lawrence Stone, *The Crisis of the Aristocracy, 1558–1641,* abridged ed. [London, 1967], p. 130; quoted in a different context and applied to Sidney himself, rather than his Amphialus, by Richard C. McCoy, *Sir Philip Sidney: Rebellion in Arcadia* [New Brunswick, N.J., 1979], p. 17).

13 · As already noted, there are five individual combats which take place during lulls in the main fighting and which have better claim to be considered mere jousts. They are preceded by formal challenges and extensive descriptions of the participants' armor and accoutrements, and all take place on an island between the two camps which provides an ideal tilting ground (see I.415). But taken together, even these five combats—between Phalantus and Amphialus (I.413–18), Argalus

and Amphialus (422–27), Clinias and Dametas (428–34), Parthenia and Amphialus (445–48), and the Forsaken Knight (Musidorus) and Amphialus (453–62), respectively—reveal a disturbing falling off from the ideal conditions of the early combat between Pyrocles and Musidorus. Even the fights not intended as mock-heroic encounters point to chivalry's limitations, the dangers of its excesses, and its vulnerability to subversion by men bound by no ethical system at all. For a detailed discussion of the five jousts, one which also sees them as stressing "the inapplicability of chivalry to war," see Arthur K. Amos, Jr., *Time, Space, and Value: The Narrative Structure of the "New Arcadia"* (Lewisburg, Pa., 1977), pp. 161–66.

14 · Edwin A. Greenlaw, "Sidney's *Arcadia* as an Example of Elizabethan Allegory," in *Kittredge Anniversary Papers* (Boston and London, 1913), pp. 327–37; Walter R. Davis, "Thematic Unity in the New *Arcadia*," *SP*, 57 (1960), 123–43, later incorporated into Chap. 5 of his *A Map of Arcadia*; Nancy Rothwax Lindheim, "Sidney's *Arcadia*, Book II: Retrospective Narrative," *SP*, 64 (1967), 159–86, incorporated into her *The Structures of Sidney's "Arcadia,"* pp. 87–108. As will be plain to anyone familiar with Lindheim's study, the discussion of Bk. II which follows here is greatly indebted to hers; it is, in fact, because of the thoroughness of her analysis that my own discussion can be much briefer than the complication of Bk. II's episodic material might otherwise warrant.

For an earlier expression of exasperation over the heroic material spread throughout the *New Arcadia* (one which would probably prove still typical of the reaction of many students encountering the work for the first time), see Samuel Lee Wolff's comment: "One who reads for pleasure simply cannot understand the 'Arcadia.' He gets a dim notion, after awhile, of the course of the Main Plot; but most of the Episodes, with their relation to each other, to the Main Plot, and to the Previous History of the Princes, remain in a fog" (*The Greek Romances in Elizabethan Prose Fiction* [New York, 1912], p. 352).

15 · Davis ("Thematic Unity," pp. 129–37, or *A Map of Arcadia*, pp. 119–26) also views the Erona-Plangus episode as the "thematic center" of the other tales and thus sees it as in effect epitomizing the whole narrative of past actions. The overall pattern he sees shared in all the tales, though, is simply one of "private passion causing public chaos." See also Lindheim, "Sidney's *Arcadia*, Book II," pp. 180–83. My focus here is on the Erona story alone, without reference to the story of Plangus's adventures.

16 · Cf. Elyot's *The Governor*, Bk. I, Chap. x, in which he both advises against too long a concentration upon grammatical rules and endorses an early reading of Aesop's fables, which are deemed to contain much moral and politic wisdom and which by proper choice may be made to encourage the growth of whatever virtue the tutor sees his young charge as already possessing.

17 · Davis (*A Map of Arcadia*, p. 121) and Lindheim ("Sidney's *Arcadia*, Book II," pp. 179–80) both discuss the change in narrative technique.

18 · See Lindheim, "Sidney's *Arcadia*, Book II," p. 169, on the difference be-

tween Musidorus's and Pyrocles' narratives: "The two sets of tales move, in a sense from the simple to the complex, from situations in which issues are clear and responses unequivocal to situations where both sides are often partially wrong and values must be ranked one above the other before response is possible." She notes further that the narrative complexity of Pyrocles' account is the formal equivalent to the moral atmosphere pervading Pyrocles' tales: the reader's sense of complication and confusion in proceeding through the interwoven tales corresponds to the difficulty Pyrocles and Musidorus experience in handling the episodes narrated (p. 180). To this observation we can add that even the geography, which is ordinarily expected to help travelers and readers alike to find their bearings and which Sidney took considerable care to present accurately everywhere else in the *New Arcadia,* goes awry in the midst of Pyrocles' narrative: Andromana's Asian province of Iberia (actually located in what is today's Georgia, between the Black and Caspian seas) is placed in Asia Minor, some eight hundred miles to the southwest of where it should be.

19 · Daiphantus was the name Zelmane (Plexirtus's daughter) had assumed when she became Pyrocles' page, in order to be near the man she loved; Palladius (Andromana's son) was the young man whose love Zelmane did not return but who died carrying out her wishes to free Pyrocles and Musidorus from Andromana's clutches. The names the princes choose suggest to us, if not necessarily to the princes themselves, the commitment to love that residence in Arcadia is likely to entail.

20 · Myrick, *Sidney as a Literary Craftsman,* pp. 134–36.

21 · Spenser, *The Faerie Queene,* I.vii.2–7.

22 · I have preferred the 1593 edition's version of the last sentence here to the 1590's less sensible reading; subsequent sixteenth- and seventeenth-century editions follow the 1593 reading. See Feuillerat's Textual Notes, I.532.

23 · Similarly, we would witness the Second Eclogues conscious that Clinias had just gone off to urge Cecropia to quick action lest Philanax's inquiry into the recent peasant revolt reveal her designs upon Basilius's kingdom (I.325). And it ought come as no surprise, to us at least, that at the beginning of Bk. III Cecropia's henchmen should be lying in wait to take Pamela, Philoclea, and the Amazonian Pyrocles captive when those three are seated in the woods awaiting the start of yet more pastoral entertainments (I.361–62).

24 · Ringler, pp. 376–78. The maps appeared independently at Cologne in 1578 and then were included in the 1584 Cologne edition of Ptolemy.

25 · Friedrich Brie (*Sidneys Arcadia* [Strassburg, 1918], pp. 209–17) argued for Sidney's extensive reliance upon Strabo as a source for the *New Arcadia;* Ringler (p. 376) acknowledges briefly that Sidney "may have consulted Strabo VIII.viii for the revised description of Arcadia," but in his desire to show Sidney's reliance on recent maps he does not pursue the possibility further.

26 · See Buxton's introductory remarks to his transcription of the letter, appearing in the March 24, 1972, issue of *TLS,* pp. 343–44. Once again, in the

interest of consistency, I have modernized spelling and punctuation when quoting the letter. The text of the letter is also to be found in James M. Osborn, *Young Philip Sidney, 1572–1577* (New Haven, 1972), pp. 537–40.

27 · The princes are initially shipwrecked, in the *New Arcadia,* on the coastal province of Phrygia in Asia Minor. Mercator's Map I of Asia clearly shows a "Phrygia Minor" on that coast, whereas Ortelius's Map 93 (entitled "Graecia" but also picturing the western half of Asia Minor) labels the relevant area only as "Troas"; the only Phrygia on Ortelius's map is the landlocked "Phrygia Maior" in the center of Asia Minor. In the *Old Arcadia* the princes were initially shipwrecked on the coast of Lydia (*OA,* 11, 68), a province which both the Mercator and Ortelius maps show to be landlocked (Strabo is inconsistent on this point, in one passage denying Lydia a coast [Bk. II, Chap. v] and in another giving it back again [Bk. VIII, Chap. vii]). It appears unlikely that Sidney would change the landing place from Lydia to Phrygia unless the map he had before him pictured a Phrygia with access to the sea.

For a detailed discussion of the geographical accuracy of both versions of the *Arcadia,* see my "The Geography of Sidney's *Arcadia,*" *PQ,* 63 (1984), 524–31. Cf., though, Connell, *Sir Philip Sidney,* pp. 131–35; she prefers Ortelius's claim to be a source for Sidney and then argues, quite incorrectly, I believe, that Sidney sought geographical accuracy more assiduously in the *Old Arcadia* than in the *New.*

28 · It must be admitted that the increased geographical detail and higher incidence of place-names in the *New Arcadia* also involved Sidney in what might appear to be some new errors in geography. See, for instance, his placement (recorded above in n. 18) of the Asian province of Iberia in Asia Minor rather than between the Black and Caspian seas, where it rightly belongs. But it is significant that such a mistake or liberty should occur only in the geography of Asia Minor. In the case of Arcadia, Sidney is arguing with a prior literary tradition and seeking to redefine that province as an actual, historical place; he has no such argument or aim in treating Asia Minor. That area of the world simply constitutes the heroic training ground for the princes, both for their future ruling and for their entry into Arcadia, and it does not matter very much precisely where individual events in that training take place. Greater liberties could thus be taken or allowed with the geography of Asia Minor than with Greece and the Arcadia Sidney wished to redefine.

29 · "Omnis intentio ad Aeneae pertinet gloriam. Nam et ex eo quod hosti cogitat parcere, pius ostenditur: et ex eo quod eum interemit, pietatis gestat insigne. Nam Euandri intuitu Pallantis vlciscitur mortem" (Servius, note on lines 940–41 of Bk. XII, in Virgil's *Opera* [Venice, 1555], p. 526^r). Servius's commentary, along with those of other ancient and Renaissance writers, was included in numerous Renaissance editions of Virgil. For the modern interpretations of Aeneas as subject to violence and irrationality in killing Turnus, see Michael C. J. Putnam, *The Poetry of the Aeneid* (Cambridge, Mass., 1966), pp. 192–93; and Kenneth Quinn, *Virgil's Aeneid: A Critical Description* (London, 1968), pp. 275–76. Brooks

Otis, *Virgil: A Study in Civilized Poetry* (Oxford, 1963), pp. 380–81, presents an opposing view, arguing that it is too late for Turnus to receive mercy; as Pallas's destined avenger, Aeneas has an obligation that overshadows any *humanitas* he might wish to display toward his beaten foe, and Aeneas stands out at the end, more than ever before, as one hero who has subjected his own desires to a social purpose. Otis observes that the end of the *Aeneid* is thus "certainly not Christian."

30 · John F. Danby, *Poets on Fortune's Hill* (1952; rpt. London, 1964, as *Elizabethan and Jacobean Poets*), p. 70.

31 · For this particular formulation of the differences between the *Old* and the *New Arcadias*, and of the narrative difficulties Bk. III was getting Sidney into, see Elizabeth Dipple, "The Captivity Episode and the *New Arcadia*," *JEGP*, 70 (1971), 418–31 and especially 430–31. I agree with Dipple's suggestion that the difference between Bk. III of the *New Arcadia* and even the material preceding it in the *New Arcadia* makes the argument for willful truncation of the work by Sidney a likely one. I do not, however, share her view that the introduction of Amphialus and his fall into sexual sin frees Pyrocles and Musidorus from such fault (p. 430), a view recently echoed by Helgerson, *The Elizabethan Prodigals,* pp. 149–50. The existence of Amphialus in Bk. III does perhaps make Pyrocles and Musidorus look relatively uncomplicated and more noble by comparison, but, as I have been arguing, there are signs up to the point where the *New Arcadia* breaks off that Sidney continued to view the princes as sharply divided beings.

32 · See, for instance, Joseph Anthony Mazzeo, *Renaissance and Revolution* (1965; rpt. New York, 1967), p. 134; and Wayne A. Rebhorn, "Ottaviano's Interruption: Book IV and the Problem of Unity in *Il libro del Cortegiano*," *MLN*, 87 (1972), 51.

33 · Citations in parenthesis are to book and the standard section numbers as found in Bruno Maier's edition of Baldesar Castiglione, *Il libro del cortegiano,* 2nd ed. (Turin, 1964). Subsequent Italian quotation will be from that edition, and direct translations are my own.

34 · In seeing as much coherence as I suggest here in Castiglione's Fourth Book (often accused of having little unity), and particularly in the connection between Ottaviano's discourse and Bembo's subsequent description of the ladder of love and the contemplative life, I am indebted to the studies of Lawrence V. Ryan, "Book Four of Castiglione's *Courtier:* Climax or Afterthought?" *Studies in the Renaissance,* 19 (1972), 156–79; and Dain A. Trafton, "Structure and Meaning in *The Courtier*," *ELR,* 2 (1972), 283–97.

CHAPTER IV. SHAKESPEARE'S "GOLDEN WORLDS"

1 · Northrop Frye, "The Argument of Comedy," in *English Institute Essays: 1948,* ed. D. A. Robertson, Jr. (New York, 1949), pp. 67–68.

2 · Walter R. Davis, *Idea and Act in Elizabethan Fiction* (Princeton, 1969), p. 60;

see also Davis's more extended discussion on the development of the pastoral romance form in Chap. 1 of *A Map of Arcadia*, pp. 7–44.

3 · Shakespeare's use of this green-world comic structure extends from *Two Gentlemen*, perhaps his earliest comedy, to *The Tempest*, his last, and is to be found also in varying degrees of articulation in *A Midsummer Night's Dream*, *The Merchant of Venice*, *As You Like It*, *The Merry Wives of Windsor*, *Cymbeline*, and *The Winter's Tale*. It is reflected as well in *King Lear*'s movement from the court to the heath and back to court.

4 · Northrop Frye, *A Natural Perspective* (New York, 1965), pp. 142–43. Pp. 132–59 of this later book present an extended elaboration upon Frye's brief comments on the green-world structure in "The Argument of Comedy," and particularly upon the connection he sees between the green world and the Golden Age or Eden. Davis asserts the connection even more categorically: "The inner pastoral circle inherited from classical pastoral represented concretely a realization of more than the usual possibilities in life, or a life of conscious artifice. It always suggests the paradisiacal, whether explicitly—as when it is called 'a second *Elisium*' or 'Nature's Eden'—or implicitly, when it is described, like the godhead, by negatives asserting a peculiar state of stasis without cold or heat, without either direct sunlight or complete shade, a place of eternal becoming. It is always presented as the place where the natural and the supernatural join, where heaven meets earth (often, concretely, as a place habitually visited by the pagan gods)" (*Idea and Act*, p. 57).

5 · Quotations from *The Two Gentlemen of Verona* are from the Arden edition, ed. Clifford Leech (London, 1969).

6 · For a fuller discussion of this education and a consideration of the play's virtues (and there are some), see my "Education in *The Two Gentlemen of Verona*," *SEL*, 15 (1975), 229–44.

7 · R. P. Draper ("Shakespeare's Pastoral Comedy," *Études Anglaises*, 11 [1958], 1–17) and David P. Young (in his chapter on the play in *The Heart's Forest: A Study of Shakespeare's Pastoral Plays* [New Haven, 1972]) have written most extensively on the ways in which *As You Like It* is "a consideration . . . of pastoral itself" (Young, p. 70). Draper notes that Shakespeare used pastoral as "a means of exploring instead of escaping from life" (p. 17), and Young sees Shakespeare as writing *As You Like It* "out of a sympathetic interest in pastoral, which he undertook to explore more fully than Lodge had done," and definitely not as "bent on demolishing or ridiculing his source" (p. 39). My own view is closer to that of Albert R. Cirillo, in "*As You Like It*: Pastoralism Gone Awry," *ELH*, 38 (1971), 19–39: "by consistently undercutting the pastoral convention *as a convention*, he [Shakespeare] also suggests that the ideal of the pastoral is not an end in itself" (p. 39).

8 · See Harold Jenkins, "*As You Like It*," in *Shakespeare Survey 8*, ed. Allardyce Nicoll (Cambridge, 1955), 40–51; Helen Gardner, "*As You Like It*," in *More Talking of Shakespeare*, ed. John Garrett (London, 1959), pp. 17–32; and Anne

Barton, "*As You Like It* and *Twelfth Night:* Shakespeare's Sense of an Ending," in *Shakespearian Comedy,* ed. Malcolm Bradbury and David Palmer, Stratford-upon-Avon Studies 14 (London, 1972), pp. 160–80. This dramaturgical casualness by no means in itself denotes faulty craftmanship. But there is evidence of inattention to matters of basic dramatic technique, such as the handling of characters' exits and entrances. Characters enter, say their pieces, and then are often inelegantly hustled off stage again; see, for instance, the exits of Touchstone and Corin in III.ii and that of Silvius in IV.iii. What such evidence points to is that the mere unfolding of plot was not Shakespeare's primary concern in constructing the play; its main thrust or organizing principle is what we would probably call thematic.

9 · It is not necessary to assert this observation as forcefully as it might have been in the past, thanks to Cirillo's article "*As You Like It:* Pastoralism Gone Awry" and to Francis Berry, "No Exit from Arden," *MLR,* 66 (1971), 11–20, later incorporated into his *Shakespeare's Comedies* (Princeton, 1972). In their opposition to the older view of Arden as an idealized Golden Age or Edenic landscape, both Berry and Jan Kott before him ("Shakespeare's Bitter Arcadia," in *Shakespeare Our Contemporary,* trans. Boleslaw Taborski [Garden City, N.Y., 1966], pp. 314–42) overstress the amount of bitterness and struggle within the play's forest world and hence upset the play's balance in a new direction.

Several more recent studies of *As You Like It* have also darkened the play, by emphasizing the conservative, patriarchal social structure that underlies its action and both inhibits the play's spirit of festivity and limits our sense of Rosalind's dominance of its world. See especially Peter Erickson's chapter "Sexual Politics and Social Structure in *As You Like It,*" in his *Patriarchal Structures in Shakespeare's Drama* (Berkeley, 1985), pp. 15–38. Erickson offers a modification upon C. L. Barber's seminal study of the play in the latter's *Shakespeare's Festive Comedy* (Princeton, 1959). While Erickson's approach is helpful in pointing out how socially conservative Shakespeare may have been, he betrays a measure of anger at the playwright for not being as liberated as he himself is. Louis Adrian Montrose, in "'The Place of a Brother' in *As You Like It:* Social Process and Comic Form," *SQ,* 32 (1981) 28–54, strikes a slightly better balance with the statement that "if *As You Like It* is a vehicle for Rosalind's exuberance, it is also a structure for her containment" (p. 52). At risk of being accused (by Montrose) as being among those generations of critics who are quite infatuated with Rosalind, I still find the issue of patriarchal authority only an undercurrent in what is, after all, one of Shakespeare's most festive plays, the guiding central intelligence or sensibility of which is Rosalind's.

10 · Quotations from *As You Like It* are from the Arden edition, ed. Agnes Latham (London, 1975).

11 · See Draper, "Shakespeare's Pastoral Comedy," p. 9: "Although the Duke has been banished to the Forest of Arden, he brings with him his old cultivated, polite, chivalric life and makes that a part of his environment."

12 · Thomas Lodge, *Rosalynde*, in *Narrative and Dramatic Sources of Shakespeare*, Vol. II, *The Comedies, 1597–1603*, ed. Geoffrey Bullough (London, 1958), pp. 188–89.

13 · Lodge does occasionally betray a city or court inhabitant's condescension toward country people: the Coridon who has been accepted earlier as an eloquent and intelligent proponent of country life appears at the marriage of Alinda and Saladyne overdressed in a holiday suit which is an incongruous mixture of elegant and extremely rustic articles of clothing and which makes its wearer look slightly ridiculous (*Rosalynde*, p. 247; for comment on the suit, see Roy Lamson and Hallett Smith, eds., *The Golden Hind* [New York, 1942], pp. 665–66n). Similarly, a moment later Coridon offers a mazer of cider to the exiled Duke Gerismond "with such a clownish salute, that he began to smile" (p. 248). But such instances of recognition of the gap between court and country, occurring primarily near the end of the work, stand primarily as lapses in tone and inconsistencies in the fictive assumptions of the work as a whole; there is little in the rest of the action to point to a realistic view of either court or country figures.

14 · See Lanham's comments on *"homo rhetoricus"* and the rhetorical view of life, in the first chapter of his *The Motives of Eloquence* (New Haven, 1976), pp. 1–35.

15 · James Smith, "As You Like It," *Scrutiny*, 9 (1940), 13–16.

16 · *The Miscellaneous Works of Sir Thomas Overbury*, ed. Edward F. Rimbault (London, 1890), p. 74; cited by Agnes Latham, p. xlvii, in her Introduction to the Arden *As You Like It*.

17 · See Alice Lotvin Birney, *Satiric Catharsis in Shakespeare* (Berkeley, 1973), pp. 87, 97; Enid Welsford, *The Fool* (1935; rpt. London, 1968), pp. 141, 218–19; and Robert Hillis Goldsmith, *Wise Fools in Shakespeare* (East Lansing, Mich., 1955), pp. 68–93.

18 · Peter G. Phialas, *Shakespeare's Romantic Comedies* (Chapel Hill, N.C., 1966), p. 235. Rosalie L. Colie (*Shakespeare's Living Art* [Princeton, 1974], p. 256) similarly refers to Jaques as "the superpastoralist of the play."

19 · For a similar but brief treatment of Rosalind's and Orlando's attitude toward time, see Jay L. Halio, "'No Clock in the Forest': Time in *As You Like It*," *SEL*, 2 (1962), 203–7.

20 · These stanzas as rendered here and in modern editions of the play follow the stanzaic arrangement of the song as it appeared in Thomas Morley's *First Book of Ayres* (1600), rather than what is most likely the garbled version of the First Folio. In the Folio, the song's first stanza is followed immediately (and without a stanzaic break) by the final (fourth) stanza, with the second and third stanzas following thereafter. If one accepts the Folio's stanzaic order, the "therefore" of "Therefore take the present time" is deprived of its meaning, since that line would not follow upon "How that a life was but a flower," and the song might thus well merit Touchstone's judgment upon it as foolish and a waste of time to hear. See Latham's note to V.iii.15.

21 · Quotations are from the Arden edition of *The Winter's Tale,* ed. J. H. P. Pafford (London, 1963).

22 · For view of the play as reenacting the Christian drama of redemption, see S. L. Bethell, *"The Winter's Tale": A Study* (London, 1947), pp. 71–104 et passim; J. A. Bryant, Jr., *Hippolyta's View: Some Christian Aspects of Shakespeare's Plays* (Lexington, Ky., 1961), pp. 207–25; and S. R. Maveety, "What Shakespeare Did with *Pandosto:* An Interpretation of *The Winter's Tale,*" in *Pacific Coast Studies in Shakespeare,* ed. Waldo F. McNeir and Thelma N. Greenfield (Eugene, Oreg., 1966), pp. 263–79. And for emphasis on parallels between the play and fertility myths, see F. C. Tinkler, "*The Winter's Tale,*" *Scrutiny,* 5 (1937), 344–64, especially 357–59; E. M. W. Tillyard, *Shakespeare's Last Plays* (1938; rpt. London, 1958), p. 46; F. David Hoeniger, "The Meaning of *The Winter's Tale,*" *UTQ,* 20 (1950), 11–26; and E. A. J. Honigmann, "Secondary Sources of *The Winter's Tale,*" *PQ,* 34 (1955), 27–38. G. Wilson Knight (*The Crown of Life* [1947; rpt. London, 1965], pp. 76–128) seems to combine the Christian and fertility myth readings. He states that "Nature rules our play" (p. 88) and while himself viewing it as "scarcely orthodox," sees the play as expressing a "pantheism of such majesty that orthodox apologists may well be tempted to call it Christian" (p. 97).

23 · Pafford understands the phrase "the imposition clear'd / Hereditary ours" to mean that the boys would be able to plead themselves guiltless of all personally committed sin, that is, of all sin except original sin (note to I.ii.74–75). He thus takes "clear'd" to mean "excepted." This does not seem to be the easiest or most reasonable reading of "clear'd" or of the phrase as a whole. It is much more likely that "clear'd" takes on its more common meaning of "removed," a meaning the word has in legal contests ("to be cleared of the charges against one"); such a meaning is more consonant with the word's context here, which has Polixenes referring to filing a plea of "not guilty" before a judge, albeit an eternal one. Admittedly, my interpretation, which has the boys pleading "not guilty" to original sin, makes less immediate sense than Pafford's (since it is impossible to make such a plea), but it is, I believe, precisely because of the theological error in Polixenes' remark that Shakespeare has Hermione catch him up and query him further.

24 · Despite the attempts of J. Dover Wilson (in his notes to the New Cambridge edition of the play) and Nevill Coghill ("Six Points of Stage-Craft in *The Winter's Tale,*" in *Shakespeare Survey 11,* ed. Allardyce Nicoll [Cambridge, 1958], pp. 31–33) to explain away what critics before them saw as a flaw in the play's dramaturgy—the lack of psychological preparation for Leontes' initial outburst of sexual jealousy—it is difficult to find concrete evidence of Leontes' jealousy before the exchange between Hermione and Polixenes. Leontes has been rather unexpansive since his initial entrance, but the first possible indication of anything troubling him comes in his answer to Hermione's desire to be made as fat as a tame thing and be told when she first spoke to the purpose. In this speech Leontes, using his first notable or striking metaphor in the play, describes his own courtship of Hermione as taking "three crabbed months" which "sour'd them-

selves to death" (I.ii.102). And this rather discordant metaphor may only be his unsuccessful attempt to express a lover's impatience with waiting. Indeed, there may be an advantage in having Leontes' jealous outburst come upon us with dramatic suddenness at the "Too hot, too hot" of line 108, since the very suddenness of that outburst would help to emphasize and convey the violence and force of the insanity that has seized his mind.

25 · Derek Traversi, *Shakespeare: The Last Phase* (New York, 1955), p. 108.

26 · Ibid., p. 145. For further comment on the parallels between the two halves of the play, see Ernest Schanzer, "The Structural Pattern of *The Winter's Tale*," *REL*, 5, no. 2 (1964), 72–82. Tayler (*Nature and Art*, p. 133) notes that the two pastoral moments in the play balance each other structurally, the first preceding disruption and the second preceding integration.

27 · For the view of Perdita as unable to keep up with Polixenes' reasoning, see Pafford, p. lxxviii of the Arden ed., and his note to IV.iv.88–97.

28 · See, for instance, Pafford in his note to IV.iii.37. My own interpretation of these lines is in agreement with and indebted to the reading of William O. Scott, "Seasons and Flowers in *The Winter's Tale*," *SQ*, 14 (1963), 412–13.

29 · The Folio does not give any stage direction for lines 103–8. Pafford, in his note to line 103, assumes that the men of middle age are not Polixenes and Camillo, but rather some other guests. But since Camillo has the next speech and since no other guests speak up at this point, it is most reasonable to assume that Perdita has given the flowers of midsummer to Camillo and Polixenes.

30 · Knight, *The Crown of Life*, p. 120; Hoeniger, "The Meaning of *The Winter's Tale*," p. 12. It ought perhaps be noted that Florizel's lines here are apparently indebted to a slightly mocking passage in the *Arcadia* in which Sidney cites Pyrocles' passion for Philoclea as evidence of the strange ways in which love enchains the lover's judgment; the passage is to be found in *OA*, 230, and in Feuillerat's edition of the 1593 text, II.53–54.

31. · See, for instance, Frank Kermode's comments on Prospero's "apparently unnecessary perturbation" in the Introduction to the Arden edition of *The Tempest*, 6th ed. (Cambridge, Mass., 1958), pp. lxxii–lxxv, and his note to the stage direction at IV.i.138. Quotations from *The Tempest* will be from this edition.

32 · Given any textual warrant, I would prefer to follow Dryden and Theobald and assign Miranda's speech of I.ii.353–64, which tells of pains taken to teach Caliban to speak, to Prospero rather than to his daughter. The harsh tone of the speech is much more clearly in accord with Prospero's other lines in the play and quite out of character for Miranda. In any case, Caliban in the next, answering speech uses the plural form of "you" in cursing those who have taught him (I.ii.365–67). Despite the Folio's assignment of I.ii.353–64 to Miranda, then, Prospero clearly has had a role in educating Caliban, and undoubtedly (as Prospero's speech of IV.i.188–93 suggests) the major role.

For the observation that the true foil to Caliban in the play is Miranda rather than Ariel, see Stephen Kitay Orgel, "New Uses of Adversity: Tragic Experience in *The Tempest*," in *In Defense of Reading*, ed. Reuben A. Brower and Richard

Poirier (New York, 1962), pp. 121–22. I am greatly indebted as well to Orgel's comments on the betrothal masque.

33 · Leo Marx, *The Machine in the Garden: Technology and the Pastoral Ideal in America* (New York, 1964), pp. 52–57.

34 · I disagree, then, with Kermode, who views Prospero's stay on the island as contemplative preparation for a return to the active life and who thus considers the active and contemplative lives to be thoroughly complementary in the play; see his Arden edition Introduction, p. li.

CHAPTER V. MILTON'S PARADISE

1 · Quotations from Milton's works, unless explicitly stated otherwise, are from the text of *Complete Poems and Major Prose,* ed. Merritt Y. Hughes (New York, 1957).

2 · Isabel Gamble MacCaffrey, *"Paradise Lost" as "Myth"* (Cambridge, Mass., 1959), p. 30.

3 · *The Divine Weeks and Works of Guillaume de Saluste, Sieur du Bartas,* trans. Josuah Sylvester, ed. Susan Snyder (Oxford, 1979), Second Week, First Day, Part I ("Eden"), lines 281–88; quoted in MacCaffrey, *"Paradise Lost" as "Myth,"* p. 35. To the list MacCaffrey provides of those who shared Du Bartas's belief concerning Adam's prelapsarian mode of perceiving we can add Agricola Carpenter, who in *Pseuchographia Anthropomagica; or, A Magicall Description of the Soul* (London, 1652) claimed that Adam's knowledge before the fall was intuitive, "little beholden to this torturing reason which after obscured those clearer apprehensions of his intellect" (p. 17); Carpenter is cited by Christopher Hill, *Milton and the English Revolution* (New York, 1977), p. 378.

4 · Barbara Kiefer Lewalski has provided what amounts to a demonstration of Adam and Eve's use of their discursive reason, in her examination of our first parents' prelapsarian education through trial and error: "Innocence and Experience in Milton's Eden," in *New Essays on "Paradise Lost,"* ed. Thomas Kranidas (Berkeley, 1969), pp. 86–117, especially pp. 100–117.

5 · See Arnold Stein, *Answerable Style: Essays on "Paradise Lost"* (Minneapolis, 1953), pp. 66–67; Anne Davidson Ferry, *Milton's Epic Voice: The Narrator in "Paradise Lost"* (Cambridge, Mass., 1963), pp. 111–15; and especially Christopher Ricks, *Milton's Grand Style* (Oxford, 1963), pp. 109–17; and Stanley Eugene Fish, *Surprised by Sin: The Reader in "Paradise Lost"* (New York, 1967), pp. 107–57.

6 · Ricks, *Milton's Grand Style,* p. 110; see also Fish, *Surprised by Sin,* pp. 135–36.

7 · J. M. Evans has observed that the difference between unfallen and fallen man is a "difference of degree, not of kind" (*"Paradise Lost" and The Genesis Tradition* [Oxford, 1968], p. 271).

8 · Herein lies my main disagreement with Stanley Fish, who in *Surprised by Sin* insists upon the reader's fallen qualities as of primary importance at every point in the poem. Fish postulates a reader who up to the fall of Adam in Bk. IX

is constantly reacting in an incorrect manner to the verse in front of him and is having his reactions corrected by God or the narrator of the poem; this reader is thus consistently forced by Milton to realize that he does not have the full moral equipment to deal with the poem's subject properly and that it is specifically his fallen nature which makes him unable to react correctly to the poetry before him. Most critics and readers today would agree that Milton is using a method such as this in Bks. I and II: Satan's apparent heroism is a trap for the reader, who at first probably admires Satan but is eventually brought to recognize that he only *sounds* heroic. But even in Bks. I and II, not all of the confusion the reader experiences (for instance, he never does learn from lines 292–94 of Bk. I exactly how tall Satan's spear is) can be attributed to the reader's *fallen* nature; Milton might just as easily be telling the reader that simply because he is human, he cannot conceive of the dimensions of the fallen angels, who are beings totally foreign to normal human experience.

9 · Basil Willey, *The Seventeenth Century Background* (London, 1934), p. 255; A. J. A. Waldock, *"Paradise Lost" and Its Critics* (Cambridge, 1947), p. 61; E. M. W. Tillyard, *Studies in Milton* (London, 1951), pp. 8–13.

10 · Millicent Bell, "The Fallacy of the Fall in *Paradise Lost*," *PMLA*, 68 (1953), 863–83.

11 · For further comment on the mistake of imputing "absoluteness of perfection" to the unfallen Adam and Eve and on the flaws in Tillyard's and Bell's logic arising from that assumption, see H. S. V. Ogden, "The Crisis of *Paradise Lost* Reconsidered," *PQ*, 36 (1957), 1–19. One of the reasons why critics of *Paradise Lost*, myself included, have found it continually necessary to beat back Bell's reading of the poem is that her interpretation is not, after all, so very far from an acceptable one. Once one dispenses with Bell's preconception of what Paradise ought to be like and the conclusion she draws from that preconception (that there is no fall in the poem), her study has a good deal to offer. She is certainly right, for instance, in suggesting that "Milton's cast of mind was the reverse of the nostalgic" and that "his interests would be directed, not towards an irrecoverable past, but towards the present condition of humankind" ("The Fallacy of the Fall," p. 865).

12 · See Ruth Mohl, "Milton and the Idea of Perfection," in Mohl, *Studies in Spenser, Milton, and the Theory of Monarchy* (1949; rpt. New York, 1962), pp. 94–132; Ogden, "The Crisis of *Paradise Lost* Reconsidered," pp. 1–19; Joseph H. Summers, *The Muse's Method: An Introduction to "Paradise Lost"* (London, 1962), p. 149; Fish, *Surprised by Sin*, pp. 226–27; Evans, *"Paradise Lost" and the Genesis Tradition*, pp. 242–71; Lewalski, "Innocence and Experience in Milton's Eden," pp. 86–117; John S. Diekhoff, "Eve's Dream and the Paradox of Fallible Perfection," *Milton Quarterly*, 4 (1970), 5–7; and Thomas H. Blackburn, "'Uncloister'd Virtue': Adam and Eve in Milton's Paradise," *Milton Studies*, 3 (1971), 119–37. That there is still, despite all these critics, a different view of Milton's Eden to be argued with can be seen from John R. Knott, Jr., *Milton's Pastoral Vision: An Approach to "Paradise Lost"* (Chicago and London, 1971). Knott recognizes that

Milton's Paradise is "never static" (p. 36) but still looks upon Adam and Eve's life there as "both safe and without cares, if it had not been for the intrusion of Satan and for Eve's desire for knowledge beyond that gained from her life in the Garden" (p. 43). In trying to show that Milton's Eden is modeled after his picture of the life of the angels in their celestial paradise, Knott drastically misapprehends the conditions of Adam and Eve's unfallen life; he claims, for instance, that "Milton's Eden is much more Arcadian . . . than that of other works dealing with the fall of man" (p. xii) and that there is "no imperative to action" for Adam and Eve before the fall (p. 5).

13 · Bacon, *The Advancement of Learning*, pp. 137–38.

14 · My quotation here is from Gerald Friedlander's modern translation of the *Pirķê de Rabbi Eliezer* (London, 1916), p. 85. The *PRE* was probably compiled in the early ninth century, but it is made up of material extending much farther back in time. The same interpretation of Gen. 2:15 is to be found, among other places, in the *Aboth de Rabbi Nathan*, Version B (Chap. 21); the Pseudo-Jonathan Targum; and the apocryphal *Book of the Secrets of Enoch* (Chap. 31, verse 1); and hence it dates from the very beginning of the Christian era, if not earlier.

15 · Ambrose, *De Paradiso*, Chap. iv, par. 25, in *Patrologia Latina*, ed. J. P. Migne, Vol. XIV, col. 301. Philo considered the man of Gen. 2:15 to be "pure mind" which God did not suffer to go outside of himself, setting it rather "among the virtues that have roots and put forth shoots, that he might till and guard them." The tilling and guarding here, then, is of man's virtues, not a physical garden. See *Legum Allegoria*, Bk. I, sec. xxviii, in *Philo*, trans. F. H. Colson and G. H. Whitaker (New York, 1929), I, 205–7.

16 · Augustine, *De Genesi ad Litteram*, Bk. VIII, Chaps. viii–x, in *Patrologia Latina*, Vol. XXXIV, cols. 379–81. Augustine also added another possible reading of Gen. 2:15, one not generally accepted as admissible by subsequent commentators (although it was repeated with approval by Aquinas), namely, that the verse meant that *God* tilled and guarded man in Paradise (see Chap. x, par. 23, cols. 381–82; see also Aquinas, *Summa Theologica*, I, q. 102, a. 3). Such a reading renders Adam's physical labors even more insubstantial.

17 · Arnold Williams, *The Common Expositor: An Account of the Commentaries on Genesis, 1527–1633* (Chapel Hill, N.C., 1948), p. 20. See, for instance, John Salkeld's expression of the bias against allegorical readings: since interpretations denying that Paradise was a real or corporeal place seemed rather "dottages and dreames . . . then expositions of learned Doctors," they should therefore "in no wise be mentioned or uttered" (*A Treatise of Paradise* [London, 1617], p. 10). In practice, of course, Renaissance exegetes did not necessarily hold firm to their theoretical statements and themselves indulged in allegorical readings; see George L. Scheper, "Reformation Attitudes towards Allegory and the Song of Songs," *PMLA*, 89 (1974), especially 551–55.

18 · See Hughes's note to lines 146–51 of Bk. II.

19 · Hughes, in the *Complete Poems and Major Prose*, p. 733; emphasis is mine. There is a danger, of course, in having a mind that can wander beyond all limit

and satiety, but Milton is in this passage clearly grateful that man has a mind that can do so.

20 · See Waldock, *"Paradise Lost" and Its Critics,* pp. 78–80; John Peter, *A Critique of "Paradise Lost"* (New York, 1960), pp. 43–44; and R. J. Werblowsky, *Lucifer and Prometheus: A Study in Milton's Satan* (London, 1952), p. 9.

21 · Fish, *Surprised by Sin,* pp. 15–17. Fish's argument here is that Belial's speech marks one of those points in the poem at which the reader is brought to confront his own incapacity for reading the poem correctly. Even though forewarned of Belial's formidable rhetorical power, the reader is intended (by Milton) to fall victim to the speech's rhetorical appeal and then be caught up short by the summary comment that tells him that he has in fact not read the speech carefully enough. The reader is thus prompted to go back and reread the speech to see how he was misled and to determine to do better the next time a fallen angel (or Milton) sets a rhetorical trap for him.

22 · See Hughes's note to I.490–505 and p. 183 of his Introduction to *Paradise Lost.* The name "Belial" was firmly associated, in the Puritan mind especially, with lewdness, loose living, and specifically sexual vices.

23 · It can be argued that Milton has been unfair to the active stand in the debate as well. Howard Schultz, in *Milton and Forbidden Knowledge* (New York, 1955), quoted Robert Chamberlain's 1638 *Nocturnal Lucubrations:* "'As contemplation altogether without action is idleness, so constant action without contemplation is bestial'"; Schultz added, "Milton once substituted Belial and Moloch, and elaborated" (pp. 72–73). Moloch can be said to be arguing for activity when he actually wants annihilation. But Milton does not appear to have thought Moloch's appeal as insidiously dangerous as Belial's. Belial's speech is the one Milton made the more artful and rhetorically impressive and the one he considered deceptive enough to need warnings before and after delivery. It is the misleading presentation of the argument for contemplation that seems to have been Milton's particular interest and concern in placing the two speeches side by side.

24 · Evans, *"Paradise Lost" and the Genesis Tradition,* p. 249. Even with the adjustments I offer upon Evans's argument and findings, I do not wish to understate my debt to his whole book and particularly to his chapter on life in Milton's Eden, "Native Innocence," pp. 242–71.

25 · See, for instance, Du Bartas's description of that prelapsarian "plesant exercise" in Sylvester's translation of *The Divine Weeks and Works,* Second Week, First Day, Part I ("Eden"), lines 299–330; or John Calvin's comment on Gen. 2:15: "men were created to employ themselves in some work, and not to lie down in inactivity and idleness. This labour, truly, was pleasant and full of delight, entirely exempt from all trouble and weariness" (*Commentaries on the First Book of Moses Called Genesis,* trans. John King [Edinburgh, 1847], I, 125).

26 · For comments on Adam's "calling" in Eden, see Nicholas Bownde, *The Doctrine of the Sabbath* (London, 1595), p. 5; William Perkins, *An Exposition of . . . the Creed,* in Perkins, *Works* (London, 1612–13), I, 152; George Herbert, *The Country Parson,* in Herbert, *Works,* ed. F. E. Hutchinson (Oxford, 1941), p. 274;

and John Dod and [Robert] Cleaver, *A Plaine and Familiar Exposition of the Ten Commandments* (London, 1614), p. 128. And for the subject of Adam's work providing a pretext for an admonition against postlapsarian idleness, see Du Bartas, *The Divine Weeks and Works,* Second Week, First Day, Part I ("Eden"), lines 299–308; Perkins, *An Exposition of . . . the Creed,* p. 152; Gervase Babington, *Certaine Plaine, Briefe, and Comfortable Notes upon Everie Chapter of Genesis* (London, 1592), fol. 10ʳ; and Salkeld, *A Treatise of Paradise,* pp. 143–44. Thomas Adams, in his *Meditations upon Some Part of the Creed,* finishes his comments on Adam's work in Eden and on the fact that even the state of innocence did not exempt man from diligence with the catchy aphorism, "Christianitie is a vocation, not a vacation" (in Adams, *Workes* [London, 1629], p. 1130).

27 · Evans, *"Paradise Lost" and the Genesis Tradition,* p. 248.

28 · Dod and Cleaver, *Exposition of the Ten Commandements,* p. 128. For a discussion of the connection between Puritan Sabbatarian arguments and Milton's emphasis on Edenic work, see Boyd M. Berry, *Process of Speech: Puritan Religious Writing and "Paradise Lost"* (Baltimore, 1976), pp. 73–79 and 245.

29 · It would be convenient for my overall argument if we could say that Protestants invariably emphasized the value of physical labor, even in Paradise, in opposition to (let us say) the more Catholic ideal of contemplative withdrawal from life in this world. It *is* generally true that Protestants were the ones who tended to note that Adam had a calling in Paradise. Luther jumped from discussion of Gen. 2:15 to one of his attacks on the idle life of monks and nuns (*Works,* ed. Jaroslav Pelikan [St. Louis, 1958], I, 103). And Donne used Adam's work as an argument in favor of the active as opposed to the contemplative life: "man is not placed in this world onely for speculation; He is not sent into this world to live out of it, but to live in it; *Adam* was not put into Paradise, onely in that Paradise to contemplate the future Paradise, but to dresse and keep the present" (*Sermons,* ed. Evelyn M. Simpson and George R. Potter [Berkeley, 1954], VII, 104). But, unfortunately, there remains an occasional Protestant anomaly: John Weemes, for instance, in *The Pourtraiture of the Image of God in Man* (London, 1627), p. 303, expresses the view that "Man's life before the fall was more contemplative than practicke." For a helpful discussion of Protestant and Catholic attitudes toward work, see Chap. 3 of Charles H. George and Katherine George, *The Protestant Mind of the English Reformation, 1570–1640* (Princeton, 1961), pp. 117–43.

30 · For Tillyard's analysis of Eve's motives, see *Studies in Milton,* pp. 17–20. "Proud self-presumption" was the motive Augustine ascribed to Eve when she took the apple, and the phrase is used by Evans to describe Eve's motives in making the suggestion to work apart (*"Paradise Lost" and the Genesis Tradition,* pp. 274–75).

31 · Giamatti has noted that this is "one of the great commonplaces of Milton criticism" (*The Earthly Paradise and the Renaissance Epic,* p. 299). Since Giamatti's 1966 remark, the parallels between the garden and the gardeners have been examined again, most extensively by Evans, *"Paradise Lost" and the Genesis Tradition,* pp. 250–57, and more recently by M. W. R. Symes, "'A Paradise within Thee':

The Relationship between the Garden and Man in *Paradise Lost*," *Yearbook of English Studies*, 3 (1973), 94–107.

32 · See, for instance, the Babylonian Talmud, *Sanhedrin,* 38b: "in the eighth [hour], they ascended to bed as two and descended as four" (*Sanhedrin,* trans. Jacob Shachter and H. Freeman [London, 1935], I, 242). The *Pirkê de Rabbi Eliezer* uses the same formula to refer to the intercourse of Adam and Eve but has that sexual union occur in the ninth hour of their first day. Most, but not all, Jewish sources assumed that there was sexual consummation before the fall: the *Midrash Rabbah,* the great compilation of rabbinic exegesis through the fifth century, has several passages revealing such an assumption (*Bereshith Rabbah,* Chap. 18, par. 6; Chap. 19, par. 3); and the eleventh-century commentator Rashi, whose work Milton was probably familiar with either directly or through the Hebrew lexicons of his day, argues that the tense of the verb—perfect having the force of pluperfect—in Gen. 4:1 ("And the man *knew* his wife . . .") shows that the conception of Cain took place before the expulsion from Eden narrated at the end of Chap. 3 (see *Pentateuch with . . . Rashi's Commentary,* trans. M. Rosenbaum and A. M. Silberman [New York, 1934], I, 17). The *Zohar,* however, suggests that Adam did not beget any offspring until he had sinned (60b–61a), and the *Aboth De Rabbi Nathan* (Version A), while presenting a timetable of man's first day similar to that provided in the *Sanhedrin* and *PRE,* gives no specific indication of there being any intercourse before the fall (17b).

33 · For a summary of the passages of Cats's *Trou-ringh* ("The Marriage Ring") relevant to *Paradise Lost* and a discussion of the possible connections between the two poets, see Geoffrey Bullough, "Milton and Cats," in *Essays in English Literature . . . Presented to A. S. P. Woodhouse,* ed. Millar MacLure and F. W. Watt (Toronto, 1964), pp. 103–24.

34 · For English translations of Grotius's Latin play and Vondel's Dutch adaptation, see Watson Kirkconnell, *The Celestial Cycle* (Toronto, 1952), pp. 96–220 and 434–79. Also worthy of notice in this context is Babington's comment on Gen. 4:1 in his *Notes upon Everie Chapter of Genesis,* fols. 21^v–22^r. The strongly Protestant Babington was anxious to prove that godly marriage was in every way holy and hence that its physical consummation was proper and fitting for Adam and Eve even in Paradise. He thus opposes those "wicked spirites" who have "snatched at" the observation that the first mention of intercourse between Adam and Eve occurs only after the account of the expulsion from Eden "and thereby sought to blemish godly marriage, saying it was then used, when paradise was lost and not before." Babington points out, using an example from 1 Samuel as evidence, that it was quite common for the Holy Spirit "to speake of that last that was done first, and of that before that was done after." And "so it may be heere very well, that Adam knew her before, although now spoken of, and not before, and so the Act of Mariage nothing impeached by this order of wordes." Babington would plainly have liked to be able to assert that there was sexual intercourse before the fall, and he came close to taking such a stand, but unfortunately his

own (as it happens, mistaken) translation of Gen. 4:1 as "*Afterward* Adam knew his Wife" (emphasis added) would not allow him to do so.

35 · Andrew Willet, *Hexapla in Genesin* (Cambridge, 1605), pp. 59, 54.

36 · Milton may well have read some or even all of the imaginative works and commentaries which granted Adam and Eve sexual union before the fall, but none of them is likely to have been directly responsible for his taking the stand he did in *Paradise Lost*. Of them, only Cats's *Trou-ringh* gives anything like the emphasis Milton does to the first marriage and its physical consummation. If we wish to find the "source" for Milton's belief in and insistence upon prelapsarian sexual love, we are probably safest in looking no farther afield than the Puritan bias of Milton's own mind. For his stand on the very existence of prelapsarian sexual love can be seen as an extension of the general definition of marriage that he put forward in his divorce tracts in the 1640s. In discussing Gen. 2:18 in *The Doctrine and Discipline of Divorce,* Milton stated that "in Gods intention a meet and happy conversation is the chiefest and noblest end of mariage"; and later, in the *Tetrachordon,* he defined marriage as "*a divine institution joyning man and woman in a love fitly dispos'd to the helps and comforts of domestic life,"* there identifying the "final causes" of wedlock as "help and society in Religious, Civil and Domestic conversation, which includes as an inferior end the fulfilling of natural desire, and specifical increase" (*Complete Prose Works,* ed. Don M. Wolfe et al., 8 vols. [New Haven, 1953–82], II, 246, 612, 608). The Church of England's *Book of Common Prayer* listed the three causes for which marriage was ordained as (1) the procreation of children, (2) a remedy against sin and to avoid fornication, and (3) the mutual society, help, and comfort that one ought to have of the other; among Anglican writers and preachers of the sixteenth and seventeenth centuries (as among their Roman Catholic predecessors), and among many of the more radical English Protestants as well, the chief or most important of these ends was understood to be the first, procreation. By relegating "increase" to the status of an "inferior end" and elevating the status of "conversation" (meaning companionship or society), Milton was, as John Halkett has pointed out, in effect making the marriage relationship itself the chief end or purpose of marriage and refusing to subordinate it to any further end or result, such as the procreation and rearing of children (see Halkett's *Milton and the Idea of Matrimony: A Study of the Divorce Tracts and "Paradise Lost"* [New Haven, 1970], p. 13). By not concerning himself, in *Paradise Lost,* with the question how or when Cain was conceived, Milton was once again viewing the marriage relationship (and its sexual union, which, in *Paradise Lost* if not in the *Tetrachordon,* epitomizes it) as a good or end in itself, capable of being discussed and considered in its own right without subordination to the further end of procreation.

The degree of Milton's originality or debt to his Puritan contemporaries in his definition of marriage and its ends has been the subject of a good deal of scholarly discussion. Chilton Powell (*English Domestic Relations, 1487–1653* [New York, 1917], pp. 93–97) and William Haller and Malleville Haller ("The Puritan Art of

Love," *HLQ*, 5 [1942], 235-72) argued that Milton's view of matrimony as instituted primarily for the mutual benefit of husband and wife (instead of for the procreation of children) was merely a reflection or slight extension of contemporary Puritan preachers' statements on marriage. Halkett has objected to this analysis, claiming that no writer before Milton, Puritan or Anglican, "ever states flatly that mutual help is the primary end of marriage" (*Milton and the Idea of Matrimony*, p. 5). But Thomas Adams contended that the reasons for which woman was created were "first, For mutuall society and comfort. . . . Secondly, For the propagation of the world. . . . Thirdly, To encrease the Church of God. . . . Fourthly, That from her might come that *Promised Seed*, which alone doth save us all" (*Meditations upon Some Part of the Creed*, p. 1134); and it seems a relatively short step from Thomas Gataker's statement that "children are the gift of God; but the Wife is a more speciall gift of God: shee commeth in the first place, they in the second" (*A Good Wife Gods Gift* [London, 1623], p. 12), to Milton's more explicit assertion that it is mutual help and society and not procreation which is marriage's chief end. James Turner Johnson's comprehensive study of Puritan marriage doctrine, *A Society Ordained by God: English Puritan Marriage Doctrine in the First Half of the Seventeenth Century* (Nashville, 1970), reaffirms the view of the Hallers.

37 · Gregory of Nyssa, "On the Making of Man," in *A Select Library of Nicene and Post-Nicene Fathers*, ed. Philip Schaff and Henry Wace, 2nd ser. (Grand Rapids, Mich., n.d.), V, 407. How far removed Milton is from Gregory's view can be easily seen from the fact that Milton, like no writer before him, attributes to angels loving embraces markedly similar to human sexual embraces. When at the end of Bk. VIII Raphael describes how spirits embrace, he is talking about angelic love and not about angelic procreation, but the particular expression of love described there ("Total they mix, Union of Pure with Pure," etc. [626ff.]) certainly reflects the human physical union that Gregory was so anxious to assert would not have been necessary for unfallen man. On Milton's originality in attributing embraces of affection to angels, see Robert H. West, *Milton and the Angels* (Athens, Ga., 1955), p. 170.

38 · Augustine, *The City of God*, trans. Marcus Dods (New York, 1950), Bk. XIV, Chap. xxiii, p. 470. Augustine himself did not name Gregory of Nyssa explicitly in Chap. xxiii. Rather, it is from Aquinas and later commentators that we learn that Augustine's quarrel was specifically with Gregory (see *Summa Theologica*, I, q. 98, a. 2).

39 · Augustine, *De Genesi ad Litteram*, Bk. IX, Chaps. iii-v, cols. 395-96; Aquinas, *Summa Theologica*, I, q. 98, a. 2. In the view of St. Paul, of early Christian theologians generally, and of Milton, because Adam was created first and explicitly in God's own image, he (like all men after him) was closer to God and hence a more perfect being than Eve (like all women after her), created "occasionally" by God for man. While most Christian exegetes may not have gone as far as Milton in saying that Eve was created in Adam's image as opposed to God's, they still held to the belief that woman was inferior to man. Were it not for the need for

procreation, the more perfect being would necessarily have been a more effective helper for Adam.

40 · Augustine, *The City of God*, Bk. XIV, Chap. xxvi, p. 475.

41 · Augustine, *De Genesi ad Litteram*, Bk. IX, Chap. iv, cols. 395–96; *The City of God*, Bk. XIV, Chap. xxvi, p. 475.

42 · Aquinas, *Summa Theologica*, I, q. 98, a. 1–2; Lombard, *Sententiarum Libri Quatuor*, Bk. II. Chap. xx, in *Patrologia Latina*, CXCII, col. 692; Comestor, *Historia Scholastica: Genesis*, Chaps. x, xxv, in ibid., CXCVIII, cols. 1064, 1076; Pererius, *Commentariorum et Disputationum in Genesin* (Cologne, 1601), pp. 203, 227.

43 · Luther, *Works*, I, 220, 237, 241; Salkeld, *A Treatise of Paradise*, pp. 178–81.

44 · Thomas N. Tentler, in *Sin and Confession on the Eve of the Reformation* (Princeton, 1977), pp. 162–232, documents the softening of the rigorist stand against marital intercourse that can be seen in many Catholic summas and manuals for confessors written from the thirteenth century on, after the influence of the great Aristotelian Scholastics had made itself felt. But even the moral theologians of the pre-Reformation era who could view the conjugal act as mandatory and even meritorious did not develop, as Tentler notes, a "consistent laxist doctrine" (p. 231). The confessional literature Tentler studies, written as it was by a celibate clergy, could not free itself completely either from the shadow of St. Augustine or from the fear of sexual pleasure; this celibate clergy was at best always "searching for ways to *excuse* the exercise and pleasure of conjugal intercourse" (p. 232).

45 · Luther, *Works*, I, 135; Calvin, *Commentaries on Genesis*, I, 128–34.

46 · William Perkins, *Christian Oeconomie*, trans. Thomas Pickering (London, 1609), p. 11.

47 · Du Bartas, *The Divine Weeks and Works*, Second Week, First Day, Part I ("Eden"), lines 657–60; the epithalamium for Adam and Eve's marriage appears at First Week, Sixth Day, lines 1051–78.

48 · Ibid., Second Week, First Day, Part I ("Eden"), lines 636–37, 626.

49 · Ibid., lines 375–78.

50 · For another, less overt reflection of the debate, see Adam's speech in Bk. X, when he lashes out at Eve with an attack which both recalls Augustine's argument that but for the purpose of procreation a male companion would have been better for Adam and expresses the wish that Gregory of Nyssa's conception of an angelic prelapsarian Adam and Eve had been correct after all:

> O why did God,
> Creator wise, that peopl'd highest Heav'n
> With Spirits Masculine, create at last
> This novelty on Earth, this fair defect
> Of Nature, and not fill the World at once
> With Men as Angels without Feminine,
> Or find some other way to generate
> Mankind?
> [X.888–95]

51 · Sister Mary Irma Corcoran (*Milton's Paradise with Reference to the Hexameral Background* [Washington, D.C., 1945], p. 74) and Williams (*The Common Expositor,* p. 88) both point out that it is not uncommon for expositors of Genesis to use Adam and Eve's marriage in Paradise as an occasion to launch into extended praise of marriage and into an attack on all lustful and illicit relationships. But the fact that this digression here in *Paradise Lost* has precedents in no way softens the impression the outburst has upon us as we read through the poem.

52 · Again, that Milton should reduce the dramatic impact of this scene does not mean that Adam has already fallen, that he is "fallen before the fall"; for it is precisely the mistake of looking upon his decision as already made, of *refusing* to engage himself fully in his decision, that is the failure of will which constitutes Adam's fall.

53 · Waldock, *"Paradise Lost" and Its Critics,* pp. 43–44. Waldock was assuming, however, that Raphael was "obviously Milton's spokesman" (p. 42) in his answer to and rebuke of Adam. Halkett (*Milton and the Idea of Matrimony,* p. 111) observes that Raphael throughout *Paradise Lost* tends to espouse the view that Eve was created expressly to bear children, a view characteristic of those who looked upon marriage primarily as a physical bond. And among these, Milton argued in the divorce tracts, were even the Reformers before him who would allow divorce only for adultery (a physical violation of the matrimonial bond) and not for any spiritual or emotional incompatibility. In the tracts Milton insisted that Eve's particular fitness for Adam was spiritual and emotional as opposed to merely physical. Raphael, with his almost exclusive focus in this debate in Bk. VIII on Eve's physical presence (and the dangers arising therefrom) can be seen, then, as expressing a view of the marriage relationship which Milton sharply opposed earlier in his life; Adam, on the other hand, with his emphasis on Eve's "greatness of mind and nobleness" and, a few lines later, her "sweet compliance," "graceful acts," and thousand daily "decencies" (VIII.600–603), would be standing closer to Milton's own earlier conception of true matrimonial "conversation."

54. · This second meaning of "virtue-proof," that Eve is proof against the Angelic Virtue (Raphael), is also recorded by Alastair Fowler in the note to V.384 of his Longman edition of *Paradise Lost* (London, 1971).

55 · Waldock, *"Paradise Lost" and Its Critics,* pp. 21, 25, 49–51.

56 · Empson, *Some Versions of Pastoral,* p. 23 et passim. Even while using Empson's definition of pastoral here, I would myself still hold out for Milton's Eden as a version of anti-pastoral. For, again, built into Milton's act of portraying a difficult Eden is his implicit argument with all those earlier versions of Eden which are expressions of dissatisfaction with the present and which look longingly toward a time when man's life was considerably easier and less complicated.

57. · Ibid., p. 178.

CHAPTER VI. ENGLISH ANTI-PASTORALISM

1 · Miguel de Cervantes, *Six Exemplary Novels,* trans. Harriet de Onís (Great Neck, N.Y., 1961), p. 10.

2 · Miguel de Cervantes, *The History of Don Quixote of the Mancha,* trans. Thomas Shelton [1612, 1620], ed. James Fitzmaurice-Kelly, Tudor Translations (London, 1896), Bk. IV, Chap. 24; Vol. II, p. 272.

3 · A number of recent critics—Stephen Greenblatt, Richard McCoy, and, most thoroughly, Louis Adrian Montrose—have been examining the ways in which the writing of pastoral in Elizabethan England was deeply rooted in the conditions of Elizabethan court life. Elizabeth's courtiers, this group has it, were under the "color of otiation" (the phrase is Puttenham's) using pastoral to advance their own claims for political power or to express their political frustrations. My own very different approach, looking at pastoral more as a literary convention than as a social form, has been to focus upon the more general ethical and ideological biases of English Renaissance pastoral writers, as differentiated from whatever more immediate political motives the authors might have had for writing. What I see Montrose's and my own studies as sharing, however, is a recognition of how serious were the social uses to which pastoral could be put in Renaissance England. See, particularly, Montrose's "Of Gentlemen and Shepherds: The Politics of Elizabethan Pastoral Form," *ELH,* 50 (1983), 415–59; and the earlier comments describing Montrose's general approach in Jonathan Goldberg's "The Politics of Renaissance Literature: A Review Essay," *ELH,* 49 (1982), 525–29.

4 · For a fuller study of Googe's antagonism toward pastoral writing before him, see Paul E. Parnell, "Barnabe Googe: A Puritan in Arcadia," *JEGP,* 60 (1961), 273–81.

5 · Tasso, *Gerusalemme liberata,* VII.12; Edmund Spenser, *The Faerie Queene,* VI.ix.24. Quotations from Spenser will be from *The Faerie Queene,* ed. J. C. Smith (Oxford, 1909).

6 · See Cheney, *Spenser's Image of Nature,* pp. 219–20.

7 · See ibid., p. 221: "The reader is left with the impression that shepherd and knight, for all their courteous discourse, have never made themselves fully understood by one another." Judith H. Anderson (*The Growth of a Personal Voice: "Piers Plowman" and "The Faerie Queene"* [New Haven, 1976], pp. 177–84) and James Nohrnberg (*The Analogy of The Faerie Queen* [Princeton, 1976], pp. 717–19) have both noted a similarity between Meliboe's description of pastoral life and the offer of ease in Despair's appeal to Red Cross in Canto ix of Bk. I. Anderson suggests that Meliboe's picture of his own life reveals that he, like Despair, is spiritually dead. This may be so, but I would argue that Spenser has little interest in attacking the old shepherd for any personal failing; what he wishes to render suspect is, rather, Meliboe's appeal (even when properly understood) as representative of pastoralism to a figure who rightly belongs in the active, heroic world.

8 · To the list of examples of English moralizing upon foreign pastoral material we can add also Shakespeare's handling of his pastoral source in *The Two Gentlemen of Verona.* Shakespeare took the material for the Julia-Proteus-Silvia triangle, including Proteus's unfaithfulness to Julia and virtually all of Julia's actions in the play, ultimately from the tale of Felix and Felismena in Montemayor's

Diana, perhaps through an intermediary lost English play. While most of this particular tale in the *Diana* is a court adventure merely told to shepherdesses by Felismena, its basic assumptions and attitudes are thoroughly representative of the rest of the *Diana* and of Continental pastoral romance generally. Felismena's story is a sentimental account of initially unfortunate and then successfully achieved love, in which romantic love and even Felix's unfaithfulness are treated sympathetically and uncritically. In writing his play Shakespeare combined this love story with another tale (the moral fable of Titus and Gisippus, probably as found in Elyot's *The Governor,* Bk. II, Chap. xii), taken from the friendship literature of the Renaissance. He thereby added an example of ideal male conduct to contrast with Felix's (or Proteus's) unfaithfulness. The effect of this union of sources is to emphasize Proteus's villainy and need for improvement; and by combining the two sources, Shakespeare takes Felismena's story out of the world of Montemayor's idyllic and sentimental pastoral romance and places it in the more moral realm of Sidney's *Arcadia.*

9 · Spenser, *The Faerie Queene,* I.iv.18–20; Perkins's position on monasticism appears in his "Treatise of the Vocations, or Callings of Men," in his *Works,* I, 755–56; Gough's comment is in *A Godly Boke Wherein Is Contayned Certayne Fruitefull Godlye, and Necessarye Rules, To Bee Exercised . . . by All Christes Souldiers* (London, 1561), sig. A3ʳ [Prologue] (the Prologue is reprinted, along with comment on Gough's Puritanism, in *Elizabethan Puritanism,* ed. Leonard J. Trinterud [New York, 1971], pp. 25–39).

10 · Andrew Willet, *Synopsis Papismi* (London, 1592), p. 236. Willet's point was that it is impossible for any human being now to perform even the law and commandments of God, much less more than is commanded; for a similar statement on man's inability to achieve perfection in this world, see Willet's correction of Popish Error No. 63, in *A Catholicon* (Cambridge, 1602), p. 163. For Milton's attack on, among others, "Embryos, and Idiots, Eremites and Friars," see *Paradise Lost,* III. 444–96.

11 · Hans Baron, "Cicero and the Roman Civic Spirit in the Middle Ages and the Early Renaissance," *Bulletin of the John Rylands Library,* 22 (1938), 72–97, and *The Crisis of the Early Italian Renaissance,* 2nd ed. (Princeton, 1966), pp. 121–29 et passim. The "characteristically Italian" treatment of pastoral I referred to earlier was the product of despotically ruled (and elitist) courts and principalities (and in the case of Sannazaro's Naples, a kingdom) whose political conditions differed markedly from those of the Florentine Republic of 1402–34. The major literary works of the Civic Humanist period in Florence do not seem to have been poems, much less pastoral poems. Rather, it was a period of dialogues and history writing, political tracts and orations. Pastoral poetry does not appear to have become a favored form in quattrocento Florence until after the Medici had firmly established themselves, after 1434. It was during the Medici hegemony also, and particularly under Lorenzo il Magnificio (himself the author of some pastoral poetry), that Neoplatonism became in effect the accepted ideology of Florence, replacing the Ciceronian activism of the earlier part of the century.

12 · For this observation, see Gene A. Brucker, *Renaissance Florence* (New York, 1969), pp. 234–37. Probably Baron's severest critic has been Jerrold E. Seigel, who has objected that Baron's Civic Humanists were not as unequivocally devoted to participation in civic life as Baron claims: their devotion was to rhetoric or eloquence itself rather than to the service of the state to which such art might be put. And in any case, whatever interest in rhetoric and/or participation in civic life Baron's Humanists expressed was by no means new to early quattrocento Florence; it was merely a continuation of a strong medieval Italian emphasis on rhetoric as opposed to scholastic philosophy, which latter discipline never took a strong hold in Italy's centers of learning. See Seigel's " 'Civic Humanism' or Ciceronian Rhetoric?" *Past and Present,* No. 34 (July 1966), 3–48, and Chaps. 7 and 8 of his *Rhetoric and Philosophy in Renaissance Humanism* (Princeton, 1968), pp. 200–254.

Whether or not Baron's Civic Humanism actually took the form he claims in early fifteenth-century Florence (and I find Baron's argument persuasive even after Seigel's attack), something resembling the ideals and movement Baron describes does seem to have been behind the educational reforms of the English Humanists of the sixteenth century: see Fritz Caspari, *Humanism and the Social Order in Tudor England* (Chicago, 1954), especially Chap. 1; Arthur B. Ferguson, *The Articulate Citizen and the English Renaissance* (Durham, N.C., 1965), especially Chap. 7; and for the application of those educational ideals (and of Baron's ideas) to Sidney's particular case, Levy, "Philip Sidney Reconsidered."

13 · What happened to the young men who were educated to give the finest political advice in the most eloquent possible language to a monarch not very interested in hearing their opinions has been well described by G. K. Hunter in the opening chapter of his *John Lyly: The Humanist as Courtier* (London, 1962), pp. 1–35. See also L. C. Knights, *Drama and Society in the Age of Jonson* (London, 1937), pp. 315–32.

14 · The account book in which Sidney's servant, Thomas Marshall, recorded the purchase of this catechism in February 1565/6 is reprinted as an appendix in Malcolm William Wallace's *The Life of Sir Philip Sidney* (Cambridge, 1915); see p. 410. Ashton's strong antipapal feelings and extreme Protestant tendencies were evidently well known; see Wallace, *Life of Sir Philip Sidney,* p. 43; and George W. Fisher, *Annals of Shrewsbury School* (London, 1899), pp. 429–30.

15 · This is the view of Michael Walzer, who in *The Revolution of the Saints: A Study in the Origins of Radical Politics* (Cambridge, Mass., 1965), pp. 199–231, 300–310, et passim, presents a helpful corrective to Max Weber's view of Calvinistic work as important mainly for the signs it might provide of one's election. Weber considered Calvinism, with its distancing of God from man and its doctrine of predestination, an anxiety-inducing theology; successful work could then serve to calm the spiritual anxieties to which a believer might be subject (see *The Protestant Ethic and the Spirit of Capitalism,* trans. Talcott Parsons [New York, 1958], especially pp. 109ff.). Walzer's argument is that Calvinism probably did not itself induce anxiety; rather, it provided first an explanation (God's estrangement from

the world of fallen men) for the social and political change sixteenth- and seventeenth-century men found so distressing and then guidelines for proceeding through a disordered world. As Walzer notes, the emphasis of the Puritan preachers was most often on the social and moral effects of hard work, not (as Weber suggests) on its spiritual significance.

16 · William Haller, *The Rise of Puritanism* (1938; rpt. New York, 1957), especially pp. 128–72.

17 · Gough, *A Godly Boke,* sig. A1r [numbered separately from the Prologue]. Erasmus's rendering of Job 7:1, which opens the *Enchiridion,* is based on the Vulgate version of that text; the King James version is less explicitly military: "Is there not an appointed time to man upon earth? are not his days also like the days of a hireling?"

INDEX

Abel, 3, 36
Aboth de Rabbi Nathan: Version B, 217 (n. 14); Version A, 220 (n. 32)
Active life: and anti-pastoral sentiment, 1, 185–89; vs. contemplative life, 36–38, 109–10, 134–35, 149, 185; vs. idle life, 38, 149; endorsed by Sidney, 43, 87, 89–90; endorsed by Shakespeare, 134. *See also* Contemplative life
Adams, Thomas, 219 (n. 26)
Aeneas, 53, 81
Alpers, Paul J., 192 (nn. 8, 10)
Ambrose, Saint, 143–44
Anderson, Judith H., 225 (n. 7)
Anti-pastoral sentiment: defined, ix, 1, 17–18, 21, 90, 185–90, 191 (n. 3). *See also* Active life
Aquinas, Saint Thomas, 139, 149, 154, 159, 160
Arcadia: implications of, 1, 2; as defined by Sannazaro, 7–10; merging with myths of Golden Age and Eden, 12–17, 21, 35, 37, 92, 113, 193–94 (n. 20); described by Sidney, 24–25, 73–74; as defined by Sidney, 34–52, 73, 77–79; as envisioned by Valentine (*Two Gentlemen*), 93; as envisioned by Duke Senior (*As You Like It*), 97–98; as defined by Lodge, 99. *See also* Eden; Golden Age
Ashton, Thomas, 188, 227 (n. 14)
Augustine, Saint, 149, 219 (n. 30); on work in Paradise, 144, 151, 217 (n. 16); on sexual union, 159–61, 162, 223 (n. 50)

Babington, Gervase, 219 (n. 26), 220 (n. 34)
Bacon, Sir Francis, 3, 36, 143, 144
Barber, C. L., 211 (n. 9)
Baron, Hans, 187, 227 (n. 12)
Bell, Millicent, 141, 216 (n. 11)
Berry, Francis, 211 (n. 9)
Bloom, Harold, x
Boas, George, 12, 195 (n. 28)
Book of Common Prayer, 221 (n. 36)
Book of the Secrets of Enoch, 217 (n. 14)
Brie, Friedrich, 207 (n. 25)
Bruni, Leonardo, 149
Bush, Douglas, 15
Buxton, John, 78

Cain, 3, 158, 167
Calvin, John: on marriage, 161, 164; on monasticism, 186; on life as perpetual warfare, 189; on work, 218 (n. 25)
Carpenter, Agricola, 215 (n. 3)
Castiglione, Baldassare, 87–90, 134
Cats, Jacob, 158, 162, 221 (n. 36)
Cervantes, Miguel de, 181
Chamberlain, Robert, 218 (n. 23)
Chrysostom, Saint John, 159
Cicero, 187, 189
Cirillo, Albert R., 210 (n. 7), 211 (n. 9)
Civic Humanism, 187–89, 226 (n. 11), 227 (n. 12)

Cleaver, Robert, 154, 219 (n. 6)
Colet, John, 187
Colie, Rosalie, 212 (n. 18)
Comestor, Peter, 160
Congleton, J. E., 194 (n. 20)
Connell, Dorothy, 202 (n. 30), 208 (n. 27)
Contemplative life: associated with pastoral, 3, 36, 41, 185; praised by Castiglione, 88–89; treated unfairly by Sidney, Shakespeare, Milton, 109, 148–49, 185; associated with Edenic life, 143–44; Protestant opposition to, 186. *See also* Active life
Conti, Natale, 15
Corcoran, Sister Mary Irma, 224 (n. 51)
Cullen, Patrick, 191 (n. 3), 193 (n. 13), 196 (n. 33)
Curtius, Ernst Robert, 39, 200 (n. 20)

Damascene, Saint John, 159, 161
Danby, John F., 83
Dante, 79, 200 (n. 21)
Davis, Walter R., 91–92, 198 (n. 17), 200 (n. 21), 206 (nn. 14, 15, 17), 210 (n. 4)
Denny, Edward, 78
Dipple, Elizabeth, 197 (n. 7), 201 (nn. 26, 28), 203 (n. 3), 209 (n. 31)
Dod, John, 154, 219 (n. 26)
Donatus, Aelius, 13–14, 16, 194 (n. 25)
Donne, John, 219 (n. 29)
Draper, R. P., 210 (n. 7), 211 (n. 11)
Drayton, Michael, 180
Du Bartas, Guillaume Saluste, 137, 139, 161–62, 218 (n. 25), 219 (n. 26)
Du Plessis Mornay, Philippe, 15, 202 (n. 30)

Eden: confused with pastoral Arcadia, 12, 16–17; joined with Myth of Golden Age, 14–16, 194–95 (n. 28). *See also* Arcadia
Elyot, Sir Thomas, 64, 206 (n. 16), 226 (n. 8)
Empson, William, ix, 27, 178, 197 (n. 10), 224 (n. 56)
Erasmus, Desiderius, 187, 189
Erickson, Peter, 211 (n. 9)
Evans, J. M., 150, 154, 215 (n. 7), 216 (n. 12), 218 (n. 24), 219 (nn. 30, 31)

Fish, Stanley Eugene, 147, 148, 215 (nn. 5, 8), 216 (n. 12)
Frye, Northrop, 91–92, 210 (n. 4)

Gataker, Thomas, 222 (n. 36)
Geneva Bible, 153
Giamatti, A. Bartlett, 195 (n. 28), 219 (n. 31)
Golden Age: conditions of, 12–13; confused with pastoral Arcadia, 12–14, 193–94 (n. 20); in Sannazaro and Tasso, 13; associated with Eden, 14–16, 194–95 (n. 28). *See also* Arcadia
Golding, Arthur, 15–16
Googe, Barnabe, 182, 184
Gough, John, 186, 189
Greenblatt, Stephen J., 197 (n. 10), 225 (n. 3)
Green-world comedy, 91–93, 210 (n. 4)
Greg, Walter W., 192 (n. 10)
Gregory of Nyssa, Saint, 159, 160, 161, 164, 223 (n. 50)
Greville, Fulke, 55
Grotius, Hugo, 158

Halkett, John, 221–22 (n. 36), 224 (n. 53)
Haller, William, 188–89; and Malleville Haller, 221–22 (n. 36)
Hamilton, A. C., 196 (n. 5), 201 (n. 27), 203 (n. 2)
Helgerson, Richard, 196 (nn. 2, 5), 203 (n. 2), 209 (n. 31)
Heliodorus: *Aethiopica,* 53
Hoeniger, F. David, 124, 213 (n. 22)
Hughes, Merritt Y., 175
Humanism. *See* Civic Humanism; Sidney, Sir Philip: Humanist training of
Hunter, G. K., 227 (n. 13)

Kalstone, David, 9, 193 (nn. 17, 18), 197 (n. 11)
Kermode, Frank, 128, 214 (n. 31), 215 (n. 34)
Knight, G. Wilson, 124, 213 (n. 22)
Knott, John R., Jr., 216–17 (n. 12)

Languet, Hubert, 40, 187, 199–200 (n. 19)
Lanham, Richard A., 102, 200 (n. 24), 201 (n. 28)

Lawry, Jon S., 201 (n. 26), 203 (n. 2)
Lewalski, Barbara Kiefer, 215 (n. 4), 216 (n. 12)
Lindheim, Nancy R., 62–63, 200 (n. 21), 201 (n. 27), 204–5 (n. 10), 206 (nn. 14, 15, 17), 206–7 (n. 18)
Locus amoenus: defined, 37–38, 39, 200 (n. 20); examples of, in Sidney's *Arcadias*, 37, 42, 73, 74, 75, 76
Lodge, Thomas: *Rosalynde,* 96, 99–101, 110, 180, 212 (n. 13)
Lombard, Peter, 160
Lovejoy, Arthur O., 12
Luther, Martin: on marriage, 160, 161, 164; on monasticism, 186, 219 (n. 29)

MacCaffrey, Isabel Gamble, 137, 141
McCoy, Richard C., 205 (n. 12), 225 (n. 3)
Mantuan (Baptista Spagnuoli), 182, 184, 191 (n. 3)
Manual labor: Protestant attitude toward, 153–54, 219 (n. 29); Catholic attitude toward, 154. *See also* Work
Marenco, Franco, 201–2 (n. 30)
Marriage: Protestant attitude toward, 161, 188, 221–22 (n. 36); Catholic attitude toward, 162, 188, 223 (n. 44); *Book of Common Prayer* on, 221 (n. 36); Milton's definition of, 221 (n. 36)
Marvell, Andrew, 19, 180, 189, 195–96 (n. 33)
Marx, Leo, 133
Mercator, Gerhard, 77–78, 207 (n. 24), 208 (n. 27)
Midrash Rabbah: Bereshith Rabbah, 220 (n. 32)
Milton, John, 19, 20, 21, 190, 195 (n. 32)
—*Paradise Lost:* anti-pastoral dimension of, 18, 142–43, 149, 188, 224 (n. 56); and myth, 136–38, 141; prelapsarian understanding in, 137–38; similarity between pre- and postlapsarian life in, 138–39, 140–41, 178–79; difference between men and angels in, 138–39, 176, 179; "paradisal language" in, 139–40, 153, 178; implied reader of, 140, 176–77, 215–16 (n. 8); Eden as version of pastoral, 140, 178; difficult Edenic existence in, 141–42, 156, 177–79, 185, 188; and the hexameral tradition, 142, 143–44, 150–51, 159–62; Belial as false contemplative, 145–49, 218 (n. 23); narrator in, 146–47, 163, 164–69; contemplation deemphasized in, 149–50; Protestant emphases in, 150, 154, 161–62, 188; Edenic work in, 151–57, 177; garden described, 152–53, 155–56; double perspective in, 156, 174, 178–79; garden as reflection of Adam and Eve, 156–57; Adam's superiority to Eve in, 157, 222–23 (n. 39); prelapsarian sexual love in, 158–59, 162–77, 221 (n. 36); Adam's fall in, 169–70, 224 (n. 52); dialogue between Raphael and Adam in, 170–76, 178; Raphael as teacher in, 172–77, 224 (n. 53); angelic lovemaking in, 175–76, 222 (n. 37); man defined in, 179; Paradise of Fools in, 186; and the divorce tracts, 221 (n. 36), 224 (n. 53)
—*Areopagitica,* 146
—"Lycidas," 165
—*Comus,* 174
—*Eikonoklastes,* 195 (n. 32)
—*Commonplace Book,* 195 (n. 32)
—*Divorce tracts,* 221 (n. 36)
Minturno, Antonio, 53, 72
Mohl, Ruth, 142
Monasticism: English criticism of, 185–86; Protestant objections to, 186, 219 (n. 29)
Montemayor, Jorge de: *Diana,* 16–17, 96, 181; and Sidney's *Arcadia,* 30–31, 33–34, 184, 198 (n. 15); and Shakespeare's *Two Gentlemen,* 95, 225–26 (n. 8)
Montrose, Louis Adrian, 221 (n. 9), 225 (n. 3)
Myrick, Kenneth Orne, 53, 72, 201 (n. 26), 202 (n. 1)

Neoplatonism: and contemplation, 7, 40, 89, 149, 186, 220 (n. 21); and pastoral writing, 7, 192 (n. 11), 226 (n. 11)
Nohrnberg, James, 225 (n. 7)

Ortelius, Abraham: *Theatrum Orbis Terrarum,* 78, 208 (n. 27)
Otis, Brooks, 208–9 (n. 29)
Otium, 4, 6, 16, 74, 99, 101, 191 (n. 3), 193 (n. 17). *See also* Pastoral

Overbury, Thomas, 103
Ovid: *Metamorphoses,* 8, 15–16, 75

Pafford, J. H. P., 213 (n. 23), 214 (nn. 27, 28, 29)
Panofsky, Erwin, 11, 93
Pastoral: definition of, ix, 21, 191 (n. 3); pastoral ideal defined, ix, 6–7; English misrepresentation of, x, 3, 7, 32, 109; Poggioli on, 6; grounds for opposing, 7, 16–18; Italianate, 88, 226 (n. 11); conventions criticized in England, 180, 185; conventions criticized on Continent, 181; English moralization upon, 182, 184, 225–26 (n. 8). *See also* Anti-pastoral sentiment; Arcadia; Contemplative life
Pastoral romance form, 7, 31, 52, 91–92, 95–96, 127, 198 (n. 17)
Paul, Saint, 161, 164, 166
Pererius, Benedictus, 160
Perkins, William, 161, 186, 218–19 (n. 26)
Peter, John, 146
Petrarch, Francesco, 10, 143, 193, (n. 18)
Phaer, Thomas, 14, 194 (n. 25)
Phialas, Peter, 104
Philo, 144, 217 (n. 5)
Pirķê de Rabbi Eliezer, 217 (n. 14), 220 (n. 32)
Poggioli, Renato, 6–7, 193–94 (n. 20)
Polybius: *History,* 24–25
Powell, Chilton, 221–22 (n. 36)
Primitivism, 12, 144, 194 (n. 21)
Protestantism: Sidney's, 19, 187–88; Milton's, 19, 188; *See also under* Manual labor; Marriage; Milton: *Paradise Lost;* Work
Pseudo-Jonathan Targum, 217 (n. 14)
Ptolemy: *Geography,* 77
Puttenham, George, 14

Rashi, 220 (n. 32)
Reynolds, Henry, 15
Ricks, Christopher, 139, 215 (n. 5)
Ringler, William A., Jr., 23, 27, 41, 55, 77, 201 (n. 29)
Rosenmeyer, Thomas, 2, 5, 192 (nn. 7, 10), 193 (n. 17)

Rudenstine, Neil L., 197–98 (n. 11), 199–200 (n. 19), 201 (n. 26)

Salkeld, John, 161, 217 (n. 17), 219 (n. 26)
Salutati, Coluccio, 149
Sannazaro, Jacopo, 13, 16, 96, 181, 226 (n. 11); *Arcadia,* 7–12, 88, 91, 93, 182, 191 (n. 3), 193 (nn. 12, 13, 18); and Sidney's *Arcadia,* 24, 25, 30–33, 77, 78, 184
Scaliger, Julius Caesar, 14
Schultz, Howard, 218 (n. 23)
Seigel, Jerrold E., 227 (n. 12)
Servius, 30, 81
Shakespeare, William, 20, 145, 189–90; anti-pastoral argument of, 17–18, 21, 95–96, 110, 113, 135, 136, 185
—*As You Like It:* 14, 17, 92, 95, 96–110, 113, 127, 136, 184, 185; criticism of conventional pastoralism in, 96, 98–102; Rosalind as controlling sensibility in, 96, 105–8; Arden differentiated from Eden, 96–97; Duke Senior's version of pastoral, 97–98; Corin's function in, 99–100; Touchstone in, 101–2, 103–4; Jaques's role in, 102–5, 109–10; Jaques's version of pastoral, 104, 113; time in, 105–9; Jaques as contemplative, 109, 135, 185; active life endorsed in, 109–10
—*King Lear:* 18, 68
—*Troilus and Cressida:* 62
—*The Two Gentlemen of Verona,* 91, 92–95, 225–26 (n. 8); and green-world comic structure, 92–93; forest scenes in, 93–95; education in, 94–95
—*Henry VI, Part 3:* 92
—*The Winter's Tale:* 95, 111–27, 136; time in, 111–12, 122–23, 125–27; use of pastoral romance form, 112–13, 119; relation to *As You Like It,* 113; Polixenes' version of pastoral, 113–15; Polixenes' and Leontes' fear of sexuality, 116–17, 118; Bohemia as harsh Arcadia, 119; Perdita's version of pastoral, 120–23, 127; nature and-art debate, 121; sheepshearing feast, 121–25
—*The Tempest:* 127–35, 136; relation to Shakespeare's earlier pastoral plays, 127–28, 135; Edenic landscapes in, 128–29,

132–33; betrothal masque in, 128–30; Caliban as reminder of the fall, 130–31, 133; time's importance in, 132, 133; appeal of contemplative life in, 132–33; active life endorsed in, 134–35
—*Henry VIII:* 135
Sidney, Mary (Countess of Pembroke), 23, 49, 197 (n. 6)
Sidney, Sir Philip, 3, 14, 17–21, 91, 109, 148–49, 190, 214 (n. 30), 226 (n. 8); antipastoral argument of, 17–18, 52, 90, 95, 185; Humanist training of, 19, 23, 39–40, 187–88, 199 (n. 18); Protestantism of, 19, 187–88, 201–2 (n. 30); social views of, 26–27, 197 (n. 10), 198 (n. 13); letter to Robert Sidney, 35, 199 (n. 18); correspondence with Languet, 40, 187, 199–200 (n. 19); letter to Edward Denny, 78
—*Old Arcadia:* genre of, 2, 53, 203, (n. 2); as source of *New Arcadia,* 22–24, 83; prefatory letter of, 23, 197 (n. 6); manuscript revisions of, 23–24, 198 (n. 13); in relation to pastoral tradition, 24–26, 30–34, 51–52, 96, 185, 199–200 (n. 19); and Sannazaro's *Arcadia,* 25, 30–33; social decorum in, 25–26, 29, 198 (n. 13); debate between Lalus and Musidorus in, 26–29; foreign-born shepherds in, 29–30, 198 (n. 13); Strephon and Klaius in, 30–34; and Montemayor's *Diana,* 33–34, 198 (n. 15); debate between Philanax and Basilius in, 34–35; debate between Pyrocles and Musidorus in, 35–41, 72, 149, 199–200 (n. 19); Platonism in, 40; trial scene in, 43–47, 48–49; Euarchus's role in, 43–48, 201 (n. 26); justice in, 45, 201 (n. 27); Christian patience in, 48; ending of, 48, 52; humor in, 49; implied audience of, 49–50; narrator's role in, 49–50, 72; revised into the *New Arcadia,* 53–57
—*New Arcadia:* genre of, 2, 53, 202–3 (n. 1); relation to *Old Arcadia,* 54, 56, 85; opening of, 57–58; Strephon and Klaius in, 57–58; heroic episodes in, 57–69, 204–5 (n. 10), 205–6 (n. 13); man defined in, 58, 71, 82–84, 86–87; Argalus and Parthenia episode in, 58–59; Helot War in, 58–60, 60–61, 63, 64, 67; moral complexity in, 60, 62, 65–66, 70, 79–80; Amphialus in, 61–62; Erona episode in, 63–64; Euarchus as Sidney's ideal prince in, 64–65, 66, 84–85, 89–90; narratives of Musidorus and Pyrocles compared, 65–66, 206–7 (n. 18); active life endorsed in, 68, 83–87, 89–90; debate between Pyrocles and Musidorus in, 69, 70, 72–73; narrative technique of, 71–73, 76, 205 (n. 11); humor in, 73, 80; *loci amoeni* in, 74–76; geographical accuracy in, 77–79, 207 (n. 18), 208 (nn. 27, 28); love in, 79–82; and the chivalric code, 80–82; Pamela's role in, 83–84, 89; Christian patience in, 83–87; oracle in, 84, 86–87; Milton's judgment upon, 195 (n. 32)
—*1593 Arcadia:* emendations by Sidney himself, 23, 24, 54–56, 196 (n. 4), 203 (n. 4), 203–4 (n. 7); bedchamber scene in, 54–55, 82; Musidorus's conduct in, 55–56, 82; Euarchus's journey to Arcadia, 60, 89
—*Defence of Poetry:* 53, 54, 81
Sidney, Sir Robert, 35, 199 (n. 18)
Smith, Hallett, 2, 192 (n. 10)
Smith, James, 102
Snell, Bruno, 6, 192 (n. 10)
Sorel, Charles: *Le Berger extravagant,* 181
Spenser, Edmund: *The Faerie Queene,* 1, 19, 22, 75, 109, 129, 182–84, 186; *The Shepheardes Calendar,* 19, 20
Stone, Lawrence, 62
Strabo, 77–78, 208 (n. 27)

Talmud (Babylonian): *Sanhedrin,* 220 (n. 32)
Tasso, Torquato: *Gerusalemme liberata,* 1, 182–83, 184; *Aminta,* 13
Tayler, Edward William, 194 (n. 20), 195 (n. 28), 196 (n. 33), 214 (n. 26)
Tentler, Thomas N., 223 (n. 44)
Theocritus, 3, 5, 12, 21, 98, 192 (n. 7), 193 (n. 17)
Tillyard, E. M. W., 141, 156, 213 (n. 22)
Traversi, Derek, 117, 118

Virgil, 2, 10, 13–14, 194 (n. 25); *Eclogues*, 11, 12, 21, 77, 78; First Eclogue, 3–6, 9, 30, 98; Fourth Eclogue, 12–13; Tenth Eclogue, 193 (n. 17); *Aeneid*, 81
Vondel, Joost van den, 158

Waldock, A. J. A., 141, 146, 169, 172, 177, 224 (n. 53)
Walzer, Michael, 227–28 (n. 15)
Weber, Max, 227 (n. 15)
Weemes, John, 219 (n. 29)
Werblowski, R. J., 146–47
Willett, Andrew, 158, 186, 226 (n. 10)
Willey, Basil, 141
Williams, Arnold, 217 (n. 17), 224 (n. 51)

Wolff, Samuel Lee, 206 (n. 14)
Work: in Eden, allegorical interpretation of, 143–44; in Milton's Paradise, 151–57; Calvinist and Puritan enthusiasm for, 188, 227–28 (n. 15). *See also* Manual labor

Xenophon: *Cyropaedia*, 62, 63

Yeats, William Butler, 190
Young, David P., 210 (n. 7)

Zandvoort, R. W., 22, 198 (n. 15)
Zohar, 220 (n. 32)

FEL